Izzy and the Tumble Thunder

11/9/23

Izzy and the Tumble Thunder
ISBN: 978-1-7391726-0-2

First published in Great Britain
in 2022 by Whalebone Publishing.

Whalebone Publishing is a trade name of The Book Writers' Resource Ltd

Produced in the UK by The Book Writers' Resource Ltd
www.tbwr.co.uk

All artwork created by Tom Willet.

Acknowledgments

For my mam and dad, for making me who I am.

For my kids for being the driving force of my life.

For My Lady, for giving me the courage to chase the dream.

And for you, new reader. Your Tumble Thunder lies within.

Izzy & The Tumble Thunder

Stuart Rowson

Chapter 1

The filthy black clouds roll over themselves like charcoal mashed potato. There is dread in the air.

Izzy strains her neck upwards as they grow bigger. Grumbling and rumbling. They seem to pause, mid heave. Lightning flashes horizontally across the dark sky.

Opening her mouth to count – a trick her dad taught her to measure the distance from the storm – she barely mouths the O of "one" before thunder shakes the sky. It bounces off the faceless, shiny buildings surrounding her.

Then the rain begins. A single drop falls next to her feet. Within seconds it's a deluge of angry, black bees stinging her skin.

She wipes dirty rain from her forehead. Her reflection catches her eye in the building next to her. In the mirror, she is dry. Her pyjamas are still crumpled from where she keeps them wrapped in a ball under her pillow. She feels the rain. She can taste its grimy oiliness. In her reflection, she is not wet at all.

"Weird," she says. But the mouth of dry Izzy staring back doesn't move. Despite it all, she feels calm. Like she belongs.

A man emerges from around a corner, running through the storm as fast as he can. It takes her a second to recognise him. It is three years since she last saw his face.

"Dad...?" the shout leaves her throat but there is no noise. "It's me!"

His chest is heaving as he draws nearer. After three years of not knowing whether he was alive or dead, he is here.

"Dad!" Tears erupt and her voice breaks. She lifts her arms to embrace him, but he sprints past.

She whizzes around, trying to follow but her legs are locked in place and her dad is leaving.

Running away. An enormous sob wracks her body.

"DAD!" one last effort, anger replacing excitement, fury closing in. She closes her eyes and she is alongside him, matching his every step. Their strides in perfect unison. Running together, just a few metres apart.

They splash through huge puddles and run closer to the buildings to shelter from the rain. He is so close she can almost touch him.

They stop and suck in air. Izzy's chest hurts from the effort. Her dad's steely blue eyes shine in the middle of his wet face despite the gloom. She reaches out but her palm is met by an invisible barrier.

The glass is smooth and cold as the rain runs down on the other side.

Her dad leans on it, tantalisingly close. His fingers are splayed in his tell-tale way; three fingers tucked in at the knuckle, his index finger pointing out, like a gun.

But on this side, her sodden clothes are replaced by dry, crinkled pyjamas. Her face is damp from tears, but not rain.

Her dad is soaked. The rain running down his face and dripping down his nose.

'I am inside the building. It makes no sense.'

She screams - silently - and anger takes over. A fuzziness is building inside her chest. It feels cold and warm, like hot hands on cold snow. It lingers and everything feels like it is suddenly in slow motion.

Holding the cold warmth in her chest, she reaches out to him with every inch of her being.

Daddy.

With that, he turns, and looks straight at her. He smiles, in his 'hey kid' kind of way, like he knew she was there all along. Like he's never been away.

Her heart jumps so hard her feet almost leave the floor. It feels like it might break her.

He lingers, as he studies her face. In his right hand is what looks like a gold medallion. It sparkles briefly as lightning fills the square. Switching it quickly to his left, he raises his now free hand and begins to write with his index finger. The letters, black from the grimy rain, appear right to left.

Finished, he looks directly at her again, pausing for a few seconds. Meeting her gaze, he smiles and winks. Wiping the rain from his face he turns and sprints away toward the centre of the square.

A blinding lightning flash illuminates a huge black pyramid, silhouetted against the storm.

Another flash, brighter than the last. She shields her eyes.

But when her arm drops from her face. He is gone.

Her eyes are drawn back to the words on the glass.

'Find me.'

Chapter 2

"Dad!"

She awoke shouting as a nearby dustbin truck sent wheelie bins full of glass crashing into its innards.

Her long hair was stuck to her face from a mixture of tears and dream drool. In fact, she was wet with sweat and could almost taste the storm. She could still see her dad's face. The sky-blue steel of his stare. But the dream was gone and so was he.

She was alone in her attic bedroom above the clock shop. Everything was normal. The sun blazed through her solitary, open window. The noise rising from the narrow street below. Soon, the central London traffic would wake and snarl up the roads all around.

Izzy swung her legs out of bed, knocking aside her favourite teddy. Her smelly trainers hit the floor. She always slept in them, much to the annoyance of her mum. It was her dad's fault.

"You should always be ready," he'd told her. So, she made sure she was.

That was before.

It had been three years now. At Stonehenge, just after sunrise on midsummer's day during the trip they made every year, he had left their breakfast picnic spot and headed into the crowds to buy coffee. He never came back.

At first, they weren't really concerned. Then Izzy's worry gave way to panic. After about an hour that was pushed aside by raw fear.

Nan asked all the people she knew in the crowds. Mum asked everyone she could find.

No-one had seen him. It was as if he had vanished in the middle of thousands of people.

The police hadn't been interested. They just said he was a grown-up who had decided to leave. They eventually visited Nan's cottage and asked a few questions. But nobody had ever really given Izzy an answer she liked or understood about why her dad disappeared. Not even Mum.

For months she had woken in tears. Her mum hated to talk about it. It was like she couldn't explain it properly. She never really had. No-one did. Not the professor. Not even her nan.

Days had become weeks. Weeks turned into months. The pain had never gone away. She just learned to live with it.

In the end, it became how it was. Dad had gone. They tried to get on with life, and Mum and Nan hardly ever talked about him.

Yet Izzy refused to consider that he was gone forever, whatever people told her. They acted like he was dead. As if it made it easier for them. But Izzy didn't believe it.

She felt he was still alive. Sometimes it was like she knew it. Even if it didn't make sense.

Dreaming of him was nothing new. At first, it was as if her favourite childhood memories were zooming down a helter-skelter towards her every time she slept.

But lately, that had changed. There were no childhood memories, only visions of him in places she had never seen but somehow felt she knew. It was like he was showing her things she was meant to see.

Recalling the shape of the buildings and the black, sludgy rain she headed to her desk. It was a child's dressing table but she'd long since dispensed with playing princesses. She rifled through a pile of used notebooks. She pushed aside old schools, Nan and London until she found what she was looking for: *Dad Dreams.*

Over the next five minutes she wrote down every detail of her dream. She even included the look on dry Izzy's face and what her dad was wearing and described the huge pyramid she saw in the lightning.

But mainly her brain focused on his back-to-front window message: 'Find Me.'

He had never spoken to her like that before in a dream.

The more she thought about the words, the more she was convinced she could hear her dad saying them. He was still out there.

It felt more real than ever.

Writing everything down was one of the best things Izzy had ever started doing. If she didn't, she knew her dreams and ideas would be gone forever. Most of the time, she was rubbish at remembering details.

It wasn't that she had an untidy brain. It just felt like she'd spent her entire life having a thousand ideas a minute and not having a clue which one she should do next.

So, she made lists. It helped her see how things should be ordered.

She made lists of everything. Dreams, ideas, facts. Whenever things occurred to her that she thought would be important, she wrote them down. She didn't always use them, but at least she had them. She called them her *Scramblings*. Every time she started a new list, or scribbled in a new book, she thought of her old friend, Hattie, who had given her the idea in the first place. She pushed the memory away. Thinking of Hattie, the friend she'd lost several schools ago, made her feel sad.

Closing *Dad Dreams*, the words slapped Izzy again.

'Find me.'

It felt clear as day. It was a message from him to her. Stronger than that, it was an instruction.

Two weeks before, she'd had a similar dream, but without her dad. That time she'd been walking, alone, towards the buildings. The black pyramid in the distance. She could see the dark, threatening clouds hanging over them. It was nowhere she recognised or remembered seeing. But it felt like she knew it. Like it was out there waiting for her to visit.

Weird.

Before Dad left, she would often get that feeling. Like a vague premonition. Her dad had called it her *Seeing*. But when he left, it seemed to leave too. She hadn't felt it for ages. Instead, her biggest problem now was her temper. Her calm *Seeings* had been replaced with a furious temper she couldn't control. It would sometimes just rush from within like an angry bull in a cloud of mist.

She'd named it the *fuzziness*, because that's just how it felt. In his absence it had grown stronger. It rumbled around in her chest and sometimes wanted to jump right out.

Since her recent dreams it felt like her *Seeing* and the *fuzziness* wanted to make friends and over-run her thoughts. Like split sides of her personality were finally ready to make amends.

Stashing her favourite trainers in her schoolbag she changed into her uniform. She hated her black school shoes and smuggled her trainers out of the house every day. She tidied her bedroom and headed down to the kitchen. The spiral staircase was at the back of the building. She took the wooden steps two at a time.

"Morning!" her mum said without turning as Izzy entered. The kitchen was on the second floor above a clock shop owned by an old man called Professor Wigglesworth. He lived in a flat on the first floor, but they shared the kitchen. It was like they were in the same house, except no-one was allowed in his apartment. They'd lived there for as long as she could remember. He was like an old, eccentric uncle who was always nice to her. Her mum ran the shop for him most days, meaning they paid hardly any rent.

"Your juice and toast are ready. We'll start in a couple of minutes. Make time to make time," said her mum, sweeping hair from her eyes as she set about tidying the rest of the small kitchen.

It had started out as something Dad had said. But Mum had made it Izzy's mantra for life. She believed that if a person cared enough about doing something, they would make sure they made time for it.

It was written on a sign above the counter

where Izzy's breakfast lay waiting. Mum said it at least three times a day, as if to remind her. 'Make time to make time'.

But that wasn't the half of it. Next to her toast was this morning's first test before school - five pieces of an old pocket watch that needed assembling before she could leave the house. Sometimes it would be just a piece of the innards that needed fixing. Sometimes it would be a simple test of assembling five small cogs in the right order. This morning, it was straightforward: restoring the hour, minute and second hands and clicking them into place, with a tiny pair of tweezers, as fast and as delicately as she could.

Pushing her plate away, she slid the pieces of pocket watch over in front of her. They were laid out on a red square of velvet no bigger than a plate. The hands lay in perfect order on the cloth. Taking a deep breath, she picked up the tiny pair of tweezers and hastily assembled the watch. It was brass, and unlike any she had seen before. She was comfortable enough with the design and style to finish it quickly. It was intricate work, but she loved it. Completing each piece brought her a sense of deep calm. It was as if the *fuzziness* in her chest hummed. It always made her feel closer to her dad, who'd started what had become a twice-weekly tradition when she was around six.

Her mum looked on, her hand on one hip, unblinkingly focused on Izzy's work. She did the same every morning. Without fail.

"You've got your dad's quick hands," she said. "But I think you're better than him."

"If he was still here, he could show me." Izzy said without looking up. Her mum didn't reply. She never did. It seemed mentioning him was fine. But talking about him wasn't allowed.

"I dreamed about him again last night," Izzy said. Looking up from her work she studied her mum's face. "We were running through a storm."

Nothing.

"He told me to find him."

Her mum gave a sympathetic smile and went slightly pale. Her lips thinned and she put her hand on Izzy's shoulder.

"We were in a huge, black square with enormous buildings, and a pyramid," Izzy added, looking into her mum's face. Searching.

She was sure Mum's eyes had widened at the mention of the pyramid. Ever so slightly. After a pause, Izzy turned back to her work.

The watch face stared blankly back. Izzy wished Mum would talk about it. She wondered if her mum was angry at him for leaving them.

Maybe she didn't want to find him. She washed the thought away with a long gulp of orange juice and finished her work.

"That was the easiest one for ages. Surely, we must've worked our way through all the different types of clocks and watches by now?" she asked.

"Not by a mile," said her mum. Her colour had returned. "They're getting easier because you know what you're doing. The professor and I are actually choosing harder pieces. You'll have completed them all soon. It must have taken your dad years to learn what you already know about clocks and watches. He was the real expert. He could make anything. At this rate, the professor will have you running the shop before you're 13."

Izzy laughed. "As if he'd let anyone else be in charge. He's been here forever. Besides, he'll have to pay more than he does now to do that. Twenty pounds a day is almost child slavery. I should tell the government."

"Good luck with that. What about school today? Settling in yet?" Her mum played with her hair as she asked, her wedding ring glinting in the sunlight that streamed through the kitchen window.

Izzy didn't stay at schools long. She either ended up leaving after a few months, sometimes weeks, or her mum was asked to move her. Izzy could never quite understand it. Sometimes things happened and she got blamed when she couldn't actually remember anything. It was like the *fuzziness* took over and her mind went blank. It was like that when her best friend Hattie had been hurt.

That seemed like a long time ago.

At the next school, she promised herself she would never make a friend again.

Moving schools had become a recurring theme. One thing she did know, was that the *fuzziness* always came when people made her really, really angry. It was like a bad feeling that boiled deep within her. It would either slow things down or make the rest of the world stop dead still. She could never really remember what happened after.

She'd been at her latest school, St Mary's, for less than two weeks. At the school before that, the form teacher, Mr Gilbert, had taken an instant dislike to her. He'd picked on her all day. Izzy had got angrier and angrier. Her first - and last - day had ended with him being calmed down by the school nurse while two other teachers argued with the headmistress about who should take responsibility. All Izzy could remember was the *fuzziness*, the arguments and the inevitable school meeting where her mum was told she couldn't go there ever again. After a fairly normal time in a single primary school, she was gradually working her way around most of the secondary schools in London. It had started after her dad had disappeared. At least, that's how it felt.

He had once told her she could stay calm by watching the second hand of a clock and counting the seconds. That she could literally use time to her advantage if she really tried. It never seemed to work well enough. But she kept trying.

"It's not too bad, Mum," said Izzy, snapping back to the present. "I just about know my way around now. Everyone seems really nice. There are even more Phoneys at this one than the last school. See you later."

Her mum rolled her eyes. She'd long since stopped asking Izzy not to call other children 'Phoneys'.

"Don't get into trouble," her mum's voice sounded expectant rather than concerned. Izzy smiled and headed out of the kitchen and down the stairs. She passed Professor Wigglesworth's flat, and headed into the shop.

"Try and make some friends?" The shout rattled down the stairs in hope rather than expectation. Izzy wouldn't do that. She couldn't allow herself to make another friend. Not after Hattie. Besides, most of the other children just bored her. Especially the small gangs of girls whose lives seemed to revolve around having their heads stuck in their mobile phones and taking selfies. They were always trying desperately to be popular, usually by being nasty to others. Izzy called them Phoneys and couldn't bear to be around them.

Neither Izzy, nor her mum, had a mobile phone. They didn't want one, not even for emergencies. Her dad had always said that you should focus on the world around you. She would dodge through crowds of people on the way to school every day with their heads stuck in their phones. Dad said it was dangerous.

Izzy knew the other kids thought she was weird. But she didn't care. Most of the time she liked being weird. Weird was good. It meant you got left alone. Weird was armour.

Pulling her black rucksack onto her shoulders she headed through the old clock shop. It opened at 8am every weekday and was deserted. She looked briefly for the professor behind the glass-topped counter but couldn't see him. It wasn't unusual. Sometimes he didn't seem to be around for days. This morning she had a feeling he was probably still upstairs.

The writing above the window of the clock shop proclaiming "Wigglesworth and Son" was faded. The words "clocks and repairs since 1825" looked apologetically small. She could never quite work out how the professor managed to afford a shop in the middle of west London. It seemed totally out of place with its faded sign and flaking window frames. The designer shops on either side seemed to hide it in plain sight. The thousands of tourists who passed down Foubert's Place every day, to cut through to the famous Carnaby Street, were seemingly oblivious to it, too. It was normally empty.

It took her 45 minutes to get to school. The Tube was faster but the claustrophobic darkness outside of the carriages made her nervous. She'd never been a fan of tunnels or enclosed spaces. The warm sunshine and the open air as she stepped into Foubert's Place made her feel alive. She loved the hustle and bustle of London. It was like she could disappear into the crowds.

She dropped around the corner and hopped into a doorway behind the old Liberty department store, where the rather grandly named Kingly Street met the narrow alley of Little Marlborough Street. Glancing around to check for her mum, she quickly swapped her pristine school shoes for her favourite comfy trainers. She had hidden them in her bag, below her lunch and PE kit.

In an archway across the narrow street, an old homeless man, with a sign proclaiming: "Good day to you", looked up from a steaming coffee and smiled a toothy grin. She smiled back. Every day, on the way to school, she gave him the cake her mum added to her pack-up.

"Hi George! See you later!" said Izzy, above the heads of the few tourists who were already milling about.

With hands covered in green, fingerless gloves, he deftly caught the small iced-bun she tossed in his direction. He grinned at the street of early risers and tipped his tatty, old felt hat at Izzy: "Have a good day, young miss."

She would. But not for long.

As she wove between the crowds and headed for school, a huge red bus blared its horn as she absent-mindedly made to cross the road. The rush of the wind as it passed momentarily reminded her of the storm in her dream. It snapped her back to her senses and her breakfast chat with Mum.

She knew Dad was alive. Somewhere. But now there was something else. She was convinced her Mum knew it too. Izzy suspected she always had.

Chapter 3

She was bored ten minutes into science, the first lesson of the day. The familiar nerves of her new school hadn't lasted long. She had pretty much managed to avoid most people at morning form. It was just how she liked it. She'd also worked out that eagerly answering one of the first questions of every lesson meant she could zone out for the rest of it.

After so many different schools, each day had become a draining challenge of trying to get to home time without losing her temper. Avoiding attention helped keep the *fuzziness* at bay.

Besides, she needed to focus her energies on finding her dad.

Her teacher, Mrs Mainwaring, was writing on the whiteboard but Izzy was watching the Phoneys in the corner.

One of them, a popular girl with pigtails, was the ringleader. Izzy knew that much already. Her name was Ellie Smith. Every school had one: pretty, clever and downright nasty with it. She was encouraging her two friends to throw rubbers at the back of the head of the biggest boy in the class.

Ellie's two friends, Harriet and Georgia, were almost carbon copies of one another. They were always ready to impress their self-appointed leader. Their pristine pigtails sat perfectly on their shoulders, swinging around like weapons when they turned to check for Ellie's approval. Breaking off the rubber from the end of her pencil, Harriet took aim. Ellie conducted proceedings from the next desk back with encouraging smiles and nods.

The boy brushed off the first rubber to hit the back of his head. But when the second bumped off his shoulder and ricocheted against his cheeks he turned around, red faced and stared at Ellie. She smiled innocently and stuck her tongue out.

"STOP IT!" he bellowed, just as a third rubber hit him squarely on the nose. Georgia flexed an elastic band proudly.

"Porter Horace! What on earth is going on? Ellie Smith what are you doing?" Mrs Mainwaring had been shaken from her script by Porter's outburst. Her face had gone from red to purple.

"It's them, Miss, throwing rubbers," said Porter. "Ellie, bloody, Smith, as usual."

"Me, Miss? I didn't do anything," said Ellie with a smile.

"Porter, that's enough of that language," said Mrs Mainwaring. "Or you'll end up in the..."

"Please Miss, I think I know what the formula is," Izzy interrupted to change the subject. She'd seen the whole thing unfold with the three Phoneys.

The teacher spun around with her arms outstretched like an expectant ballet dancer. Her eyes settled on Izzy, who had stood to try to gain full attention. Porter frowned.

"Ah, someone was listening," said the teacher excitedly, her arms falling to her side. "Izzy, you're already putting the class to shame and you've only been here two minutes. What do you think it means?"

It was exactly the sort of attention she'd been trying to avoid. Ellie stared at her with spiteful eyes.

Guessing she'd been marked out for some Porter-esque stationery themed assault in the not-too-distant future, she held Ellie's stare across the room. There was something in those eyes that made Izzy slightly nervous. In her chest, the *fuzziness* fluttered.

She turned back to the teacher and purposefully got it wrong in an 'I'm-positive-I'm-right' kind of way. As she finished, Porter slowly raised an eyebrow. Mrs Mainwaring was wearing a broad, yet weary, smile.

"Excellent try, Izzy. Thank you so much, but not quite right I'm afraid," she said, with a sigh.

She began another speech about physics, oblivious to the attention Ellie and her gang were now giving Izzy. A rubber bombardment seemed inevitable for Porter, but it was no business of Izzy's. Her mum would be none-too-pleased if she ended up leaving another school.

Despite her best hopes three rubbers bounced off her head before the lesson was out. She tried to ignore them and stay calm, but she could feel the *fuzziness* rising up.

It was like trying to hold a snowball with warm hands. Something was going to give.

She focused on the second hand of her watch. Counting as it swept around, she slowed her breathing. The *fuzziness* shrank back a little and hovered in her chest just as the bell sounded for the end of the lesson.

It startled the class into action and they filed towards the door for the morning break. All except Porter. He made a beeline for Ellie.

"I don't know who you think you are!" his voice was deep and loud. "You and your friends better leave me alone this week or you'll be sorry!"

Porter was a foot taller than Ellie. He had to look down into her face to shout. Suddenly the spiteful ringleader of earlier was replaced with a seemingly terrified victim. She expertly turned on the waterworks and began blubbing.

"It wasn't me. It was them," Ellie sobbed. "Why don't you leave us alone, Tree Trunk? Miss, he's scaring me," the hurtful acid in her voice was at odds with the tears and her bowed head. Izzy had seen Phoneys do this before. Provoke the big kid, make trouble, then act all innocent and get away with it. She didn't think a teacher in the land had ever attempted to punish a crying girl. Who'd want to explain that at parents' evening?

She couldn't stop herself getting involved.

"Stop it, Porter," Izzy said, stepping closer to the action and looking up at him. "You're all as bad as each other. It was Harriet and Georgia, if you must know, Miss."

A hefty shove from behind sent her sprawling into Porter who responded with a muffled "geddoff" as he stumbled backwards. They clattered to the floor in a clumsy embrace. Porter crashing into two chairs and Izzy's rucksack flinging up and stinging the back of her head.

"Porter and Izzy, that's it! The unit at once with the pair of you!" shouted a despairing Mrs Mainwaring.

"But..."

Their protests made little impression. Izzy barely had time to get angry. The *fuzziness* bubbled but didn't erupt. The commotion receded as the children were ushered out of the classroom in a wave of whispers and chuntering. Izzy and Porter were at the head of the queue, accompanied by a now furious teacher. Ellie, Harriet and Georgia were giving them both snide smiles, with Harriet motioning a fake push in the air as a gleeful admission of guilt.

Having found the Behaviour Unit empty of a teacher, Mrs Mainwaring had instead sent them to the next door down. The dressing down from the headmaster, Mr Tompkins, had been short and sharp.

Sitting outside his office Izzy had felt the *fuzziness* building at being summoned - yet again - to a headmaster's office when she had believed she had done nothing wrong. She fought to control it and wondered how long it would be before she was thrown out of this school too.

She had zoned out while he talked, focusing on a large grandfather clock in the corner as she took slow breaths and tried to stay in control.

"Isabella, are you listening?" his stern tone snapped her back to the present.

Her head flicked from the clock to the headmaster: "Yes, sir."

"I said I'm going to confiscate your mobile phones until the end of the week. Hand them over."

Porter had fumbled for his own mobile phone and handed it over. Izzy noticed the screen was cracked and chipped and it looked barely usable. Mr Tompkins took it between his thumb and forefinger like a dead mouse. It landed with a crunch in his desk, and Porter winced.

Mr Tompkins held his hand out to Izzy, expectantly.

"Sir, I don't own a mobile phone. I've never wanted one. I don't see the point."

"What?" he was befuddled. Mobile phone restrictions had become his stock punishment even though many of his staff thought phones shouldn't be allowed in school at all. "Of course, you have a phone. You all do."

"No sir. Those are for Phoneys. That's not me."

Mr Tompkins raised an eyebrow and considered her for a moment: "How very strange. In that case, don't do it again. Porter, you can have yours back at the end of the week."

Porter didn't protest, but just nodded.

"You're dismissed. I don't want to see you here again."

* * *

By the end of the next week at St Mary's, the only two children that seemed to care that Izzy existed were Porter and Ellie - and it was getting harder and harder to avoid them both.

Porter seemed to have taken to following her, from a distance, and would pop up nearby at various times of the day.

"Err, hello," he'd said as they passed in the corridor two days after their telling off by Mr

Tompkins, before lowering his head and walking on as Izzy frowned.

"Hello. Y'alright?" took another three days, this time as they entered geography. Izzy ignored him.

"Hiya," was the next day. Without thinking, she answered with a polite hello, and walked on, cursing herself for forgetting to ignore him.

The following week, Porter sidled up beside her in the corridor, leaning against the wall in the lunch queue eating crisps.

"Err, hello. Y'alright? Look, I just wanted to say, well, you know, sorry and that. I didn't mean to get you into trouble with old Tompkins," his face flushed red.

He blocked the light from the corridor so much that he was almost in silhouette. Izzy had to crane her neck to talk to him. The Phoneys called him 'tree trunk'. She'd never seen anyone give him any real trouble. Looking up at him, she was slightly scared herself.

"It's okay," she said, warmly. "I thought it was quite funny in the end. I thought Mrs Mainwaring was going to pop."

With a laugh that seemed to shake most of his body, he momentarily relaxed, and then looked awkwardly at his feet. Izzy guessed he didn't have any friends either.

"Can't stand that Ellie Smith. She's a pain in the arse," said Izzy, glancing down the corridor.

"I know."

"They're all as bad as each other, walking around with their heads in their phones or taking selfies. All the Phoneys are. In every school I've ever been," she said.

"Phoneys?" he chuckled and gave her a friendly punch on the arm.

"Oww," she said, pulling back. "Don't do that again."

"Sorry. Again. What do you mean 'every school'?"

She laughed it off as the lunch bell went.

"Fancy sitting together?" she said, pointing her thumb in the way of the dining hall and ignoring the school question.

It wasn't the grandest gesture she'd ever made, but Porter's face lit up like she'd just invited him on a free holiday.

They sat in the corner, her with a wholemeal sandwich, apple and a glass of water, and Porter with a cheese and ham roll, cake, crisps, flapjack, mars bar and a can of coke.

"You going to eat all that?" she asked. "That's a lot."

"Yeah," he said, taking a huge mouthful of sandwich as the Phoneys strolled in. "I've got a fast metabolism, or something."

Harriet and Georgia were right behind Ellie. They carried her bags like a Hollywood entourage. To them, Ellie was a rockstar. Being her friend made them almost celebrities.

Ellie's hair was pulled back on her head so tight it looked like moving her face would be painful. She never smiled much anyway. Her shirt and trousers were perfectly ironed and her tie was ramrod straight.

"Ooooh, are you two going out?" shouted Ellie as soon as she spotted Izzy and Porter. "You look like you're in love. What do you see in Tree Trunk?"

Izzy stared. Porter went bright red, again, and took a huge bite from his sandwich.

"Do one Ellie. Go flush your head down the bog," said Izzy, picking at her own lunch.

"I can't," sniggered Ellie. "Looks like you got there first."

"Get. Stuffed," said Izzy, through gritted teeth.

"Ooh, did I hit a nerve? Don't go breaking my arm like you did your best friend at your old school." Encouraged by the blood draining from Izzy's face, Ellie carried on. "Yeah, that's right, I heard about you. My mum is a governor and apparently all the teachers have been told to watch themselves around you. They say you need special attention because you might lose your big, fat, temper. Something to do with your daddy running away. Boohoo."

That was all it took. Izzy's *fuzziness* came rushing out of her chest like an Olympic sprinter bursting from the blocks. Hot hands on cold ice. She made two fists and hit the table so hard that both her lunch, and Porter's feast, jumped into the air. She was nose to nose with Ellie in front of the apple crumble before anyone even noticed that she had stood up.

She barely had time to register Ellie's wide eyes before the shrieking started.

Harriet and Georgia were standing next to her, open-mouthed, and shocked. Vanilla custard dripped down their pristine hair and onto their faces. A gloopy string of congealed pudding was trailing down Georgia's left cheek.

Izzy's hand was sticky and warm. In it was a ladle from the counter, and Ellie's eyes had widened at the prospect of a vanilla-flavoured drenching. She took a step back at the sight of the improvised weapon.

A second later Porter lifted Izzy by the elbows. She dropped the ladle as she was carried out of the dining hall and down the corridor, away from the pudding-themed carnage and outraged girls.

After the initial shock, the dining room had erupted in laughter, but Ellie had started shouting for anyone that would listen. "I told you! My mum was right, she's mental. Mental! NUTCASE!"

Her insults faded behind them as Porter put Izzy down, and then dragged her by her hand further down the corridor.

Alone at the bottom of the stairs to the drama block, Izzy felt like she was in a daze. It took her a couple of minutes to come around properly, as the *fuzziness* faded. Porter just sat next to her, waiting.

"Thank you," she said, finally, wiping custard from her hand. "But what happened?"

"I dunno but it's alright. For a second there I thought you were going to punch her lights out. And you made me leave my lunch. I'm starving now. How did you get over to them so fast?"

She looked at him, puzzled.

"What?" she asked.

"One minute you were next to me, hitting the table and then, whoomph, you were in front of her ready to smash her lights in with a custard spoon. How Harriet and Georgia got it all over them I'll never know. It was like I blinked, and it had all happened. You looked like a crazy zombie or something. I grabbed our bags and got you out before you whacked her one."

"Oh... I don't remember..." was all Izzy could say. She didn't remember anything between hitting the table and the fear in Ellie's eyes.

"And I left my lunch," Porter repeated, in case she hadn't heard first time round. "I'm starving now."

"Soz," she said, half-heartedly. The *fuzziness* had settled, but still felt agitated.

It stayed that way the whole afternoon as she waited to get collared by a teacher and sent to the Unit.

Not being able to remember what happened had scared her. Finding her dad seemed more important than ever, but she just didn't know where to start.

The *fuzziness* was getting stronger and she felt powerless to control it. Like it could take charge of her whenever it wanted.

Chapter 4

Turning into Kingly Street after her long walk home, she noticed George had moved since the morning. He often did. Though he was always cheery and polite, he'd often tell her that to stay in one place too long would make him a nuisance. He always stayed close to the clock shop though, and she almost always saw him somewhere. He'd been down these streets every day for as long as she could remember.

Despite the May sun, he still wore his green woolly gloves. His hat was pushed back on his head.

"Hi Izzy. Good day?" he said cheerily. Izzy could never quite place his accent.

His 'Good Day to you' sign was on a low ledge in front of him. An empty coffee cup balanced next to it held a few coins spared by passers-by.

"It was okay, George. I think I like it better than my last school. How was your day?" said Izzy.

"The usual Izzy, thank you so much for asking. The usual. I smiled at a few people. I wished them, 'have a good day.' I got brought a couple of coffees - I'd much rather tea ¬- and some other delightful people gave me a few coins."

"George?" she said, without pausing for an answer. "Don't you ever get lonely?"

The old man pushed his hat further back on his greying head, put his hands on his stomach, and looked at her.

"Lonely, miss?" he laughed and rubbed his thick black and grey beard. His heavy overcoat shook as he opened his arms at the people in the street. "I've got the whole of London for company. So much time, and so many people. You get off. I'll see you tomorrow."

She laughed too. George had a huge toothy grin that lit up his face, but Izzy was sure he was lonely. Sadder than he ever let on to anybody. Sometimes, she felt lonely too, just thinking of him. It was like he was waiting for something, but she had no idea what.

George waved to her and hollered, "good day to you," as another group of tourists passed by. One of them glanced at his coffee cup of coins, but she didn't put anything in. Instead, they all smiled nervously and walked on. The homeless man with the old-fashioned English accent was used to it.

It was almost five o'clock as she turned into Foubert's Place. The narrow road was fit to bursting with a mixture of tourists and people rushing home from work. She pushed her way through, passing the designer clothes shops to the front door of Wigglesworth and Son. Parts of the faded, gold leaf shop name above the window glinted in the evening sun. Even the front door and the lock was ancient and made of cast iron. It seemed as old as the shop itself and her key often got stuck. She'd lost count of the times she had to jiggle it in the lock to make it turn. Izzy had once asked the professor why he didn't replace it.

"Everything has a time and a place, Izzy," he'd said, slightly mysteriously.

Snapping back into the present, she clunked the handle. For a change, the shop wasn't empty.

"Al give y'all a hundred bucks for it," said an American tourist. His drawl was like something out of a Hollywood movie. His shades hid most of his face and his wife, wearing similarly oversized sunglasses, egged him on.

"That's right, Tom. A hundred bucks. Y'all go for that mister? It's the best price you're gonna get today." His wife's accent was identical, and she looked encouragingly at her husband.

Professor Wigglesworth looked more tanned than the last time Izzy had seen him, a few days earlier. He was leaning forward with both hands flat on the counter. His face showed little emotion. His perfectly trimmed, white moustache quivered. Izzy knew he oiled it every morning. He looked down at the clock, held it up in the dusty sunshine that was filtering through the glass frontage of the shop, and back at the tourists. He pointed at a barely visible marking on the back.

"You see this here," he lifted it higher to ensure he had their full attention, moving it from one hand to the other. Their eyes followed. He reminded Izzy of an actor in the theatre ensuring everyone was listening in the back row.

"It's the mark of one of the most famous clockmakers in the whole of Europe. Edwin Van Seizminger. He was a Swiss clockmaker around the turn of the 1800s and this mark is his. It's one of only 27 remaining time pieces like it in the world." Mr and Mrs American Tourist looked at him sceptically. Undaunted, he carried on.

"Once when he was travelling around Egypt, he found a sundial near one of the pyramids, in the shadow of the sphinx itself. He was so taken with the power and the majesty of how the sun aligned itself with the sphinx at the height of the day, that he made 100 of these time pieces in its honour."

He pointed to another, smaller piece of decorative carving at the base, and pushed it towards the faces of the couple.

"You see that at the bottom. That's his depiction of a sphinx and the hands are made from gold he brought back from Egypt. He made 100 before he ran out of the metal. The clockwork inside is pure, Swiss genius. The windings are as good today as they were when Seizminger first put it together. It is a tribute to the great Egyptian goddesses themselves."

Mr and Mrs American Tourist looked on, now paying full attention.

Don't overdo it, thought Izzy. She leaned against the pillar in the corner of the shop, enjoying the performance.

Seizing the moment, Professor Wigglesworth went for broke.

He turned his attention to the American woman. He took the drama in his voice up another notch: "It is said that the owner of these time pieces should not only be as beautiful as the goddesses themselves. They would have bestowed upon them the ability to stay young for so long as they cared for the time piece as if it were one's own child."

"Cooool." Her eyes were wide and believing. Her husband raised one eyebrow, and glanced over at Izzy, seemingly not convinced. The professor noticed but ignored him.

"So, you see," said the professor, enjoying himself a little too much, "this is more than just a time piece. It is a true relic of a bygone age when clockmaking was a fine art. It is a tribute to the horologists of ancient Egypt."

His eyebrow still raised, Mr American Tourist cut to the chase: "How much?"

"It is a rare piece in my collection. I cannot let it go for less than one thousand pounds," he finished with a flourish, and presented the clock on the counter as if he'd just carried out the world's finest magical feat.

"Amaaaaazzing! Tom, honey, I wann'it." She chewed gum excitedly.

The professor twitched his perfect moustache, looked over his glasses at Mr American Tourist and smiled: "We take Visa or Mastercard and you're welcome."

Moments later they breezed toward the door. As she carried her neatly wrapped antique she excitedly babbled about eternal beauty as her husband mumbled about a "crazy British guy's baloney." Izzy smiled at Professor Wigglesworth. He smiled back, with a sly wink.

As he passed Izzy, Mr American Tourist looked at a picture on the wall. Pausing for a second, he looked closer and turned to the professor.

"That Churchill? Winston Churchill? Here?"

Professor Wigglesworth settled into a wide, proud smile, and gestured to the weathered picture that showed Prime Minister Winston Churchill outside the shop in 1940.

"Yes. Actually, it is." Said the professor, standing up a little straighter. "He paid a visit during the

Second World War with his private entourage just before he took office and bought one of our finest pieces. We were so proud we took a picture and it's been on that wall ever since."

"Coooooool," said Mrs American Tourist lamely. She gave it a cursory glance before looking down at her horde of designer shopping bags and pulling her husband out into the London afternoon.

As the door closed with a ring of the shop bell, the professor ushered Izzy behind the counter. He lifted the curtain to the back storage area without a word. Peeking in, she saw a stack of boxes. On top of the sixth box, she saw an exact replica of the limited-edition, Egyptian-inspired, Swiss clock he'd just sold. There were only 27 in the world, but Professor Wigglesworth seemed to have around a hundred.

"Just arrived this morning from my contact in China. Twenty-five pounds apiece. Not a bad day's work, eh?" he chuckled, twisting his moustache.

"Professor, I don't know how you get away with it. I wouldn't dare do that. What if they complain?"

"Ah Izzy, my dear girl, there's an art to it you know. Tourists who look tired at the end of the day are ripe. They've walked most of London, and just want to head to their hotel. If they have just the right amount of weariness at our weather, you know they're ready for the plane home. They can't bring it back from Chicago, now, can they? And if we can help them find a new home for their tourist pounds, then we can all keep a roof over our heads."

Izzy raised one eyebrow and smiled: "I suppose. It doesn't feel very honest though. Is there even a sundial near the Sphinx in Egypt?"

"Well, not that I can remember. Maybe I just stretched the truth a little more than normal."

Unsure whether to be impressed or dismayed, Izzy headed upstairs. Her mum was out. She usually was straight after school, usually running some errands for the professor. Though the shop tended to have very few actual customers, Izzy's mum was always busy either making deliveries or collections for something or other. The professor was often away for days at a time.

Izzy closed her bedroom door behind her, only for it to annoyingly spring back. It had needed fixing years ago, and Dad hadn't done it properly. Dropping her rucksack against it to hold it closed had become a necessary habit. It was the only way she could get any privacy.

Sitting at her desk she stared at her *Scramblings*. It was less than six months since she'd started filling notebooks.

It was already like a mini library of her innermost thoughts. Thinking of her dad and her dreams, she wondered if there were any clues in the notebooks she'd filled. There must be something.

She thought about hiding them away. But the truth was that there was no-one to hide them from. Her mum never came in her room and she had no brothers or sisters to appear unannounced.

But you can't have friends, she thought to herself. *Not after last time. It's not safe.*

Her *Scramblings* seemed to be the only thing that made sense. It had been Hattie's idea and that made it even more precious to her.

It had never been easy to explain why her head was always full of different things. Most of the time she didn't understand it herself. To her, it was normal. Her brain felt like it was permanently in overdrive.

When she had tried to explain it, a few schools ago, it hadn't ended well.

She had been thoroughly bored in the middle of an English lesson. Mrs Partridge, who had a horrible, hairy top lip, asked why she could never sit still or do a simple task without causing a fuss.

"Well, Miss, it's kind of hard to explain," said Izzy slowly, glancing around.

"Go on, child. Try me," the teacher had said, pushing her heavily rimmed glasses up her big nose. The rest of the class went silent.

"Well, Miss, imagine you've got a plate of scrambled eggs and you throw it up in the air."

The rest of the class sniggered. A group of school Phoneys were looking at each other and rolling their eyes in the corner. Izzy took a deep breath.

"Well, imagine all that scrambled egg going up into the air. Big bits, little bits, everything. As it's still going up you have to decide the order of how you're going to eat it before it lands on your plate. Or before it goes all over the floor. That's what it's like in my head."

"Flying scrambled egg? That about sums you up child."

The Phoneys had fallen about in fits of giggles. Mrs Partridge had muttered something about her being an attention seeker. Izzy had never felt so embarrassed.

The blood rushed to her face as she hid her eyes with her hand. Tears began to well up and the *fuzziness* demanded to be set free.

She reached out for her best friend's arm and glanced up. Hattie would know. She'd help everyone understand.

But Hattie wasn't there.

Her best friend was laughing along with everyone else. Worse, she had joined in with the Phoneys near the door and was giggling with them. Giggling at Izzy. She could almost taste the betrayal.

Everything disappeared into a dangerous, hazy fuzz after that.

The laughter turned to screaming as Hattie lay on the cold floor with blood running from her forehead.

The headmaster had dashed in from his office next door. He had almost fallen over Hattie's chair, which had somehow ended up on the opposite side of the room.

The only thing Izzy could remember was Hattie's accusatory glare as the paramedics wheeled her away with a huge bandage on her head, and what looked like a broken arm from the fall. The look in Hattie's eyes made Izzy's heart sink. They had been sad. It was crushing.

It was the first and only time she'd tried explaining what it was like to have so many thoughts at the same time, all the time, every single day.

It was also the last time she had allowed herself to make a friend. She had never seen Hattie again. She missed her. It was why there was no way she could be friends with Porter.

It was too dangerous. For both of them.

Chapter 5

She spent most of the next two days desperately trying to avoid Porter between lessons. When she blanked him, his eyes had been wide, almost longing for a conversation. It made her feel rotten. He was only trying to be nice.

But at home time the following day, her wannabe-friend-avoidance strategy failed miserably.

Just before she took a sharp left behind a group of year sevens at the school gate, her cover was blown.

"Hey! Izzy! Over here!" the hopeful smile on his face was just too persuasive.

"Hi," she said. "Sorry. I didn't see you at first." Lying made her feel worse.

They crossed the open courtyard in front of the main entrance, and out onto the busy road without another word. Even at this time, the traffic was noisy. It was a welcome distraction.

The longer the silence went on, the more awkward she felt.

Turning right toward her house, Porter followed. Izzy stopped in her tracks.

"Do you live near me?" she said in an almost accusatory tone. "I thought I saw you the other day when I went past the Palladium."

"Yeah, I've seen you walk home a few times," he replied, his eyes darting away. "I go past there on my way home. Takes me at least an hour to get home. I like walking through the crowds. It's good to be with people. Anyway, can I ask you something?"

"I suppose." She had little appetite for the inevitable conversation. She thought of Hattie and kept her guard up. She was a dangerous friend to have.

"Why do you get things wrong on purpose in class?" he asked.

"I don't."

"You do. I've seen you do it a few times now. First, that day when we got sent to Mr Tompkins and about four times since. You do that funny thing with your lips. Then you get it wrong."

There wasn't an answer she could share. It had become a habit since the Hattie incident. She had found it so easy. She got all the questions right, all of the time. But it made her stand out and people didn't like it; neither did she. So, she played dumb.

Porter was the first person ever to have noticed. She felt ashamed.

At the disappearance of her smile, Porter changed the subject.

"So why did they kick you out of your old school? Did you really break your friend's arm?"

Izzy fought back tears, wiping her cheek with the butt of her hand.

"That wasn't at my old school. It was a few schools ago. I didn't do it. At least I didn't mean to. It just kind of happened. You shouldn't be friends with me. Leave me alone."

She jogged slightly ahead, but Porter caught up.

"Hey," he said, offering a crumpled, seemingly damp tissue. "I was only trying to be nice."

They walked in silence for the next 10 minutes. He didn't know what to say. She was glad.

After crossing Regent Street, Izzy and Porter paused to let a man and his daughter pass.

The youngster was holding her dad's hand tightly and clutching her new, prized possession. It was a teddy bear from Hamley's, the famous toy shop around the corner.

Izzy remembered when she'd done the same on her sixth birthday. It had been a special treat, just her and her dad. They'd gone to see the Lion King at the Palladium and then for cake before he'd taken her to the old toy shop. It was her favourite place back then. She'd felt like a princess. She still slept with the teddy every night and took it with her whenever she went to Nan's.

The memory of the teddy was a constant reminder that Izzy had a job to do, and friends were just a distraction. Worse. They could get hurt.

She couldn't explain it, but she just knew her dad was out there, she just knew.

Even the *fuzziness* felt connected somehow. Like something inside her was waking up. The feeling was getting stronger, egged on by her increasingly vivid dreams. It felt like she'd been writing down all the details for months.

"That's it," she said out loud to herself. "The *Scramblings*. There must be something in them."

"The what-now?" said a puzzled Porter through a mouthful of crisps. "Sorry, starving."

Distracted by the girl and her teddy and the racing thoughts of how she could find her dad, she didn't spot her headteacher just ahead of them.

"Look. It's Mr Tompkins," said Porter, nudging her out of a daze.

Twenty metres ahead of them, a familiar face headed down Kingly Street in the direction of the clock shop.

Izzy picked up her pace and Porter fell in behind, dodging through crowds. She crossed the road and passed through the old Liberty archway, just as Mr Tompkins disappeared around a corner.

"Hi George," she said as she passed the old man in the doorway. "Can't stop. Sorry."

George didn't seem to mind. He was deep in conversation with a grey-haired old lady who seemed to have a thousand plastic carrier bags.

Porter followed Izzy and they paused at the corner, peering round just as Mr Tompkins went inside the old clock shop. The bell on the top of the door clanged loudly.

A home visit from the headmaster last thing on a Friday wasn't exactly what Izzy had hoped for. The hairs on her neck stood up and she shivered.

They crept up to the side of the shop.

"Wow. What is this place?" Porter asked, staring up at Wigglesworth and Son as he backed into the middle of the narrow street to get a better view at the ancient shop. Izzy shushed him and pulled him back.

"I thought you followed me." she whispered. "It's where I live."

"I didn't follow you all the way," he said, with a hurt look on his face. "I'm not a stalker."

Through the dusty glass of the old window, she could see Mr Tompkins in his bright red waistcoat. His jacket was over his arm and he was in deep conversation with the professor.

They were hunched together over the counter and Mr Tompkins kept glancing around, waving his arms to help make his point. In the light from the old window, he looked more full of life than Izzy had ever seen him at school. He kept taking in deep breaths, puffing his chest out as he did so, as if he was inhaling pure oxygen.

Izzy and Porter stayed put.

I'm going to get expelled again, she thought.

But as Izzy began to get neck strain and Porter started to sweat in the late afternoon sun, the professor passed something to the teacher and the conversation ended. Izzy couldn't see what it was. She turned to Porter and jumped.

"Izzy! What are you doing?" it was her mum, loaded down with two bags of shopping. "Are you spying on the professor? He won't like that you know. And who's this strapping young man?" said her mum, ignoring Izzy's protest.

"What? Oh, Porter?" said Izzy, momentarily off guard.

"You never told me you'd made a friend at your new school. Pleased to meet you. I'm Jane, Izzy's mum," she said, switching a shopping bag and thrusting out her hand energetically in the boy's direction.

Porter's face flushed. His tatty blazer seemed to shrink as he offered a nervous hand. He pulled the sleeves down consciously.

"Hullo. I'm Porter." His lips wrestled the words from his mouth and he added clumsily: "I go to Izzy's school. We go to school together."

Izzy rolled her eyes. Her mum smiled broadly.

"Well, I hope she's told you it's her birthday tomorrow and her Nan is coming to visit. We're having a birthday tea and you should come along.

About four o'clock. We'd love to have you there."

Porter nodded, fumbling over his words.

"You will? Wonderful."

"Mum!" Izzy protested again at the one-way conversation.

Her mum looked Porter up and down and talked out of the side of her mouth to him, leaning in, as if revealing a great secret: "You look like just the sort of friend Izzy should make. She's a bit of a lone wolf, you see."

"I'm standing right here."

"You know," her mum carried on, ignoring her daughter's glare. "Someone to keep her out of trouble. Izzy doesn't bring many friends home. None in fact. Not since..."

The sentence hung in the air and she looked down the street.

"Tomorrow at four? Okay." Porter looked at Izzy, who forced a thin smile.

She had started the week trying to avoid Porter for his own good, and hers. Now, at teatime on Friday, he was being invited round for her birthday and she knew her desperate attempts to avoid making a friend had been in vain.

The week hadn't gone how she'd planned, even if she did think Porter was, at best, all right.

"Great," said Izzy flatly as the shop bell rang and Mr Tompkins emerged.

"Hello Izzy. Hello Porter. Fancy seeing you two here. Hello Mrs Latimer," his surprise at seeing the children was quickly replaced with a warmth at seeing Izzy's mum.

"Richard! How are you?" said Jane in such a familiar way it made Izzy curious.

As far as she knew, her mum had only met Mr Tompkins once. That was at the meeting with the local education authority, when he'd openly accepted an appeal for Izzy to be allowed a place at St Mary's, despite her history of getting expelled. That news had surprised Izzy more than anyone. Headmasters normally argued against her coming to their school. It seemed she had a reputation. Mr Tompkins had actually wanted her to join his school.

Now here he was outside of her home and being all matey with her mum.

He pointed at the clock shop behind: "Love these old places. Buried right in the heart of all of these fancy shops. So glad you took the time to tell me about it, Jane."

Jane!

Izzy's mum smiled broadly at him. She saw Izzy looking at her and stopped immediately: "You're welcome. It's great to see you again. I hope you got what you came for."

Looking around at the hustly-bustly crowds and back toward the shop, he switched his jacket to his other hand, and revealed a small, brown parcel in his inside pocket.

"I did indeed. Anyway, lovely to see you. Must

dash. See you Monday, you two," he said, beaming, and marched off with a spring in his step.

"That was weird," said Izzy. "Mum, why are you being weird with Mr Tompkins?"

"What?" said Jane, before Porter interrupted.

"I've got to get going too. Bye Izzy. Nice to meet you Mrs... Latimer?" said Porter, who towered over Izzy's mum, despite his age.

"Call me Jane. And see you tomorrow. Just after lunch?" she said, as Porter disappeared into the crowd of tourists. He nodded a 'yes' over his shoulder as he slipped into the river of people.

Izzy tilted her head and put her hands on her hips.

"Really, Mum?" said Izzy. "Really?"

Chapter 6

The shop bell didn't so much ring, as clang when Nan pushed it open with a shove. The door banged loudly on the wall.

"Hello. Where's the birthday girl?" her shout echoed through the shop and up the stairs.

Two floors up, Izzy pushed aside the sixth, and last, of Professor Wigglseworth's not-so-rare Egyptian clocks that were mass produced in China, and quickly cleared her desk.

Even though it was her birthday, her mum had insisted she made time to do at least part of her Saturday job for the clock shop. It turned out that quite a few of the professor's Chinese antiques had been broken. Three had hands that actually went backwards. She'd managed to sort most of them in less than two hours. It was fiddly work, but she loved it. There was something about fixing a clock or a watch that made her feel accomplished. Like she had achieved something more.

"Up here, Nan. Down in a sec," she shouted back, folding away the small instruments of her horology kit. It had been almost six years since her dad had explained that horology was the study of clocks and time.

Izzy reached the kitchen before her nan, who wheezily clumped up the two sets of stairs from the back of the shop. Izzy's nan was a heavily set woman. Her adoration of her granddaughter was only matched by her fondness for a nice Victoria sponge.

"There she is. Happy Birthday, Isabella," said her half-deaf nan, more loudly than was needed. She threw her arms around Izzy, almost squashing the air out of her lungs. She followed up with a hefty kiss on the cheek.

"Thanks, Nan. It's good to see you, too."

"You are looking more beautiful by the day," said her Nan. "Look how long your hair is getting. When did you start getting so tall? You're becoming a proper, young lady. How is school?"

"One question at a time, Betty," laughed Izzy's mum, who knew she would have to wait while the familiar routine played out.

Without taking her eyes off Izzy, Nan mumbled,

"hello," in the direction of her daughter-in-law, and cupped her granddaughter's face in her hands.

"Your dad would be so proud of the young lady you've become. I bet he's missed you so much," she said, as Izzy looked into her nan's crystal blue eyes. They were just like her dad's. Nan's short hair was curled and framed her face. She didn't wear make-up apart from the faintest hint of old-fashioned blusher and red lipstick.

"Betty, you must be tired out. Come and have a cup of tea. I've made cake," said Izzy's mum, keen to change the subject from her absent husband.

Nan didn't need a second invitation. Dropping her bags where she stood, she plonked herself down at the kitchen table and immediately began recalling almost every step of her journey on the train. It was a one-way conversation with very few pauses for breath. Not a detail was missed, with the occasional sigh and a sip of tea to wash down cake. She even included how a 'rude, American tourist' had stolen her taxi outside of Paddington station. Like Izzy, she hated the Tube. She considered it 'too full of sweaty people hanging around'. Unlike Izzy, she had zero interest in actually looking at London.

"...And as usual I could feel the city up my nose before I even got off the train. Dirty place. I don't know why you like living here so much. If being here and near Izzy didn't reinvigorate me so much, I wouldn't bother coming," she finished, and took a final, almost triumphant, gulp of tea.

"I know what you mean," said Jane. "Sometimes I feel like that too. It's worse on a hot day like this. When there's no wind, the smog is horrible. Some days I wonder if it can get any worse."

"We both know it can dear. It could smell worse too. We've both heard those stories about before they built the sewers. Eeew. Now, where is your card?" said Nan, turning to Izzy as if her granddaughter should know the answer. "Ah yes, it's here. There you go. The delivery men will be along with your present before too long."

"Delivery men?" asked Izzy, as she opened the envelope. "Thanks, Nan."

"Yes dear. Delivery men. Should be here by now really. And where is that professor? I didn't see him conning any tourists, and he certainly didn't rush out to help me with my bags. Is he off at one of those clearance auctions, buying more rubbish he thinks he can sell on?"

"I haven't actually seen him since he closed the shop yesterday," said Jane, looking at her watch. "I opened up this morning. He must still be in his flat."

The sound of the shop bell made Izzy's mum jump up and head downstairs.

Izzy turned to her nan and leaned in from her own seat.

"I keep dreaming about him, Dad, I mean," she said, in little more than a whisper. "But it's different than before. Nan, I think he's alive."

Nan looked at her with worried eyes and took Izzy's face in her hands again.

"Izzy, dear," said Nan. "You need to be careful. You need to take time to understand."

"Understand what?" Izzy asked, momentarily thrown off guard. "You're being weird. I think he's alive, Nan. I think he wants me to find him."

Her dad was Nan's only son. Izzy couldn't remember ever having a grandad. As far as Izzy was aware, her dad had been the only man in all of their lives, apart from the professor. But he didn't really count in that way.

Her Nan smiled and looked toward the door.

"What I know, what I'm sure about, is that he loved you more than anything. More than any of us ever could. You're special, see. I'm sure he had to do what he did. And he'll always be with you. In here," Nan tapped her chest and smiled.

"But in my dreams, he's alive. And he told me to find him. It felt real." She blurted it out and looked straight at Nan, waiting.

Nan's face slowly dropped. The warm concern was gone, replaced with a thin-lipped look of what Izzy thought might be worry - maybe even fear. She fiddled with her over-sized ear lobe and looked around, making sure they were alone.

"It might be just a dream," she said, in a strangely hushed tone, looking toward the door again to check for Jane. "But it might be more than that. You're turning 13. It'll be time soon."

"Time for what?" Izzy pulled back in her chair. "Nan, you're still being weird." She didn't get it. They locked eyes for a second. Izzy thought Nan wanted to say more.

"Izzy! It's for you," her mum broke the moment. Nan looked around and sat back in her chair, pushing out a big breath, relieved at the escape.

"About time too," she said in the direction of the open door. Then she turned to her granddaughter. The conspiratorial look had returned. "Things will happen to you Izzy, and you'll need to conquer it. Believe what you feel is true."

She paused again and looked in the direction of the footsteps on the stairs.

"I'm sorry," she said quickly. "I've said too much. It's important you work it out for yourself. Don't tell your Mum I said anything. It needs to be our secret. She's, well, she's not like your dad. He was special. It's all about you. You're more special than any of us."

She gave Izzy a kiss on the cheek and then was up and clomping her heavy frame downstairs shouting instructions at the delivery men.

"You know," Izzy whispered to herself, watching her nan. "You know, but you can't say. This is bonkers."

* * *

It took about 10 minutes for the gigantic parcel to be shoved, pushed and pulled up the three flights of stairs to Izzy's bedroom. Nan had insisted the delivery men took it straight upstairs, despite their protests about the weight and the other deliveries they still had to make.

Porter had arrived at the same time and after some nervous hellos, followed the delegation to the second and then third floor.

At one stage, on the fourth step of the spiral staircase leading up to the attic, they'd nearly all gone backwards in a heap and fallen onto Nan. She loudly co-ordinated their movements in a less-than-helpful way. Thankfully, the larger of the two men had regained his balance at the last second, helped by a panicked push from Porter right behind.

The near-death experience didn't deter Nan from bossing them around any less. She didn't leave them alone until they left, with nothing but her signature, and a, "took you long enough," ringing in their ears.

In the attic, Izzy walked around the now unwrapped parcel with a quizzical, if slightly unimpressed, look.

"Nan," she said, as politely as she could, as the old woman appeared, out of breath. "It's a desk. A beautiful desk," she added quickly, failing to disguise her lack of enthusiasm. Porter just looked puzzled.

"This is handmade from solid, English oak, from the New Forest. It belongs in this room. Trust me, it does," said Nan matter of factly. "It's got loads of room for those notebooks you told me about. There's plenty of room for you to fix your clocks and whatnots, too."

"It really is beautiful," chimed Jane, seemingly trying to convince her daughter. "Look at the carvings. Must be worth a fortune, Izzy."

"You've got room for a massive telly on that," said Porter unconvincingly and then, from the side of his mouth and just to Izzy: "And loads of drawers for crisps and sweets."

As Izzy's mum headed back downstairs, Nan put her head back around the door.

"Your dad said you should have that desk when you were 13." Then, after a pause. "Remember what I said earlier."

She disappeared, and Izzy looked at Porter.

"Porter," she said, as she heard Nan make it to the kitchen downstairs. "I really need to talk to you."

"Is it about biscuits and cake? Because I am totally up for that right now."

"No," she said, rolling her eyes.

"Chips?"

"No," she giggled.

"Cool. Pizza?" and he giggled back.

For no reason at all, Porter's giggle was quickly replaced by a rolling belly laugh that made most of his body shake and his white T-shirt ride up his stomach. As Porter went full-on guffaw, Izzy's own giggle gave way to a chuckle. Seconds later the chuckle grabbed her by the funny bones and refused to let go.

They stayed that way, giggling and guffawing, until Izzy felt dizzy and stars appeared around the edges of her world. When her cheeks started to tingle, she had to take deep breaths and force her universe to right itself. Her sides actually hurt. It was the most she'd laughed since her dad had left.

As Porter tried to slow his breathing, he wiped a couple of escapee tears from his cheeks.

"So, what did you want to talk about?" he asked.

"Izzy!" her mum shouted from the floor below. "Come down for cake."

Izzy looked at Porter, who had smoothed down his t-shirt.

"It'll have to wait. Come on."

As the old steps creaked under their feet on the landing, Porter paused, and pointed toward some other stairs that ran down the back wall, almost separate to the rest of the building.

"That looks spooky," he said, pointing into the dinginess.

"If you follow them down, they lead to the old cellar," said Izzy. "Go up, and they lead up to my bedroom. There's a tiny door but it's painted shut. The professor says the cellar flooded once, years ago, and he's never had the money to get it properly fixed. The door at the bottom is locked. We're not allowed down there. The professor says it's unsafe.

I crept down once, when no-one was around, but the lock is jammed."

"Yes, it is, and you're never to go down there," said a voice behind them. Before adding with a chuckle, "it's where I keep my dragons!"

"Hi, Professor," said Izzy, turning to greet him, unimpressed by the drama. "Where have you been? Nan's been asking after you as usual."

"Ha! Has she now? Happy Birthday. Sorry I'm late. Been chasing up a bit of business and had to go south of the river to see a man about a dog."

"Are you getting a dog?" Porter jumped in. Izzy and the professor looked at him, and then at each other.

"Professor, this is Porter. He's a..." she paused. "He's a friend from school."

Porter's face lit up at the title. He virtually bounced into the kitchen. If he'd been happy at being called a friend, he was positively ecstatic at the sight of a table full of birthday buffet.

Professor Wigglesworth walked with a slight limp and paused to rub his hip just short of the doorway. Izzy had always considered the professor to be wary of her nan who, likewise, always seemed to be a little cross with him. It was like they were constantly play-fighting for no reason at all.

"Where on earth have you been?" it was more a demand than a question from Nan as he limped in, tweaking the end of his moustache and smoothing his hair back on his head.

"Betty, it's lovely to see you too," he replied with a coy smile. "There's no need to shout, you know. You're the deaf one, not me. How was your journey? Terrible, noisy, and one of the worst ever, I presume. How were the people? Smelly and rude? I don't know how you manage to stay positive through it all."

"Don't you start Professor Wigglesworthless. I'm not in the mood for you today."

Nan sounded stern, but her eyes gave her away. They traded fake insults for the next couple of minutes. Izzy's mum rolled her eyes at the double act. Nan and the professor had known each other for years and seemed like two really good friends who pretended they couldn't stand the sight of one another.

It had been like this on her birthday for as long as Izzy could remember, even before Dad disappeared.

The rest of the afternoon was lost in cake and more volumes from Nan's World Travels. Porter listened attentively as he attempted to eat his own weight in vanilla sponge.

Even though it was her birthday, Izzy may as well have been somewhere else. Her head wasn't in the room.

While everyone buzzed around, and Porter just ate and listened, Izzy's head was spinning. She had so many thoughts to unravel and wanted to escape to her *Scramblings*.

The dreams of Dad, the way the *fuzziness* was getting stronger, and now Nan telling her something was going to change after bringing her a desk, of all things.

None of it added up. It all made her feel a little sick. And scared. Like there was something big she was going to have to do to find him.

The sound of the shop bell downstairs shook her from a slight daze.

“Izzy!” her mum was almost shouting from across the kitchen. “Porter had to go. Said he had to get home. I’ve invited him round tomorrow.”

“Oh,” said Izzy. She felt tired. Drained.

Porter’s departure also stirred her nan into action.

She never stayed overnight when she visited. It was a good two-hour trip to get home to her little cottage between Salisbury and Stonehenge. Her dogs would be missing her, and she couldn’t bear to be in London longer than she had to, even if being with Izzy in the clock shop seemed to restore her zest for life.

“I’ll share a taxi with you to the station, Betty,” said Professor Wigglesworth, as they made their way down the stairs and into the shop. “I’ve got to pop out and see a man near Paddington anyway. He might have a few pieces for me.”

“Only if you’re paying, Wigglesworthless,” said Nan, pulling on her coat. “I don’t want to stay in the city any longer than I have to. Ladies, I’ll see you in a couple of weeks. I've got a feeling it's going to feel extra special this year."

Nan loved the summer solstice - the longest day of the year - and would insist every June that Jane and Izzy came to visit. For Nan, midsummer's day was a festival to be thankful for everything they had. She loved walking the three miles from her cottage to Stonehenge before dawn to see the sun rise. There were always thousands of people there and all of Nan's friends always treated Izzy and her mum like royalty when they turned up.

Nan pulled Izzy close again and whispered in her ear so no-one else could see: "Remember what I said. You're special, Izzy."

She looked so deep into Izzy's eyes it was like she was trying to communicate with her soul. With a smile she stepped out into Foubert's Place. She glanced left and right, and then headed for Kingly Street, the professor in tow. He had insisted they go and flag down a black cab around the corner, despite carrying both of her heavy bags.

With Mum tidying away the modest party, Izzy headed upstairs to the attic. She flung her rucksack behind the door to keep it closed, dropped her cards onto her new desk and collapsed into her bed. The cake was heavy in her stomach and she could feel sleep sneaking in.

After a minute or two of staring at the ceiling and chewing it all over, she looked at her desk. What did Nan mean about her dad wanting her to have it on her birthday? Why would her dad want her to have a boring, old desk?

She had to admit, though, it was beautiful. Long stems with small, beaded flowers carved into the legs.

It was lavender, Nan's favourite. She had it everywhere at her cottage. The carving seemed to wrap itself from the top of the left-hand leg, down through the front of the three drawers.

But something wasn't right.

She sat up and switched from her bed to her desk chair.

The third drawer down was slightly narrower than the top two. It wouldn't be obvious to anyone unless they really looked.

There was a scratched panel no more than five centimetres wide and as long as the drawer, where the bottom drawer itself didn't match the others.

It slid out easily enough, but the hole it left only matched what was in her hands, not the whole width of those above it. Rolling it back again, she reached underneath, intrigued. Her fingers found a hole, no bigger than a pound coin. She paused before pushing her finger inside. It met a small piece of wood that sprung back on her like the top of a pen. Izzy pressed it.

There was a small clunking, like small levers being activated by tired springs. The five-centimetre panel of wood that had fitted perfectly to the desk, slowly opened.

There in the secret compartment, was a small parcel wrapped in brown paper. On top of it, was a piece of old paper, a note!

Chapter 7

Izzy was puzzled and slightly afraid.

Her heart was pounding in her chest as she picked up the small parcel and the note.

"Weird," she said.

The paper was thick and light brown in colour. It crumbled slightly in her fingers, as if it had been there for years.

Carefully thumbing it open, she held it up to the light from her attic window.

> 'Dear Isabella.
> This is a Tumble Thunder,
> It is for you, and you are for it.
> Yours to complete,

To complete you.
Three times you must go.
For there is only you left.
It ends where two worlds meet.
Beware the Time Shadow
Find me.'

She read it again, and then a third time. Then a fourth.

The two words sprung out at her like a slap in the face: 'Find me.'

Like in her dream. Her *Seeing*. It was Dad. It was from him. She knew it.

This was proof that he was alive. That maybe she hadn't dreamed it at all. Dad was alive and wanted her to find him.

Her thoughts danced with confused excitement until she remembered what Nan had said.

"It's all about you."

This was more than a feeling. It was a thing. A note. Proof.

But she couldn't stop seeing the worry in her Nan's face when she made her promise not to tell anyone. It didn't make sense.

Still frowning, she put the note aside and picked up the small parcel. It was heavy but no bigger than the palm of her hand.

It was only loosely wrapped in the same paper and it quickly unravelled and fell into her hand.

A pocket watch.

"Oh," her heart dropped a little.

A gold pocket watch. A scratched one at that. Nothing more. She'd fixed plenty in the clock shop. She knew that they used to be popular before the Second World War, when men would wear them in their waistcoat pocket with a chain that attached them to a buttonhole. Nowadays, they were mainly antiques, or just for show.

Barely had she looked at the cover for more than a second than she felt the cold of the metal replaced by a strange, welcoming warmth.

A small dot of light began to glow in the centre, and then gradually widened before spreading across the casing. It moved around the surrounding watch and warmed her hand.

The cover became transparent and the golden lines spread around a strange, horizontal figure of eight, as the molten, yellow lava ran through the tiny gulley. The outline of a star appeared, then a moon and then the sun before it too became transparent, revealing the face and the numbers of the watch itself.

She stared at it. Unblinking. Unable to let go.

Within no more than a few seconds she could feel it. Actually, feel it. The movement of the hands and the workings becoming part of her. Within her. A ticking and a whirring that she could hear inside her head and feel deep inside her chest. She felt the *fuzziness* rise like a cold snowball, and the molten gold embraced it. The frozen *fuzziness* was engulfed and melted, to reveal a newer, smaller, glowing version of itself. Like the *fuzziness* had been waiting to get started. Waiting for the Tumble Thunder.

Chapter 8

The floorboards were wet on his bare feet.

The first light of dawn crept around the sparse room. On the wall was a solitary picture he hadn't bothered to move. A probably long-since dead relative of some former owner. He neither knew nor cared.

A cold wind whistled through the draughty house. Outside, wet snow swirled and occasionally broke the silence with a sludgy splat on the window. The room was small. And it was cold. It had been a perfect hiding place while he waited.

He rubbed his filthy black stubble and yawned, making his jaw crack. He hadn't slept well, and it still felt like night. He'd grown thin over time.

Thinner than he'd like. His search for the girl, through the different times, had left him older than his years. So much so that he didn't even know his true age anymore. He felt old, but somewhere deep in the back of his mind he was sure he was just a teenager. None of it made sense.

There it was again. A rhythmic beat pulsing through his body. It had chased him from sleep.

The creeping light of dawn had been replaced by a glow from beside the bed. A collection of old boxes he'd piled up to act as a makeshift table. The light sent long shadows into the corners where damp floorboards met mouldy brickwork.

Picking it up, he felt a warmth spread across his hand. The molten trickle lit up the lines of his palm and his claw-like fingers spread around it, in a semi-fist, revealing dirty nails. The veins and tendons in his wrist bulged against his thin, almost translucent skin. The energy surged through his body, leaving him reinvigorated by a power he couldn't control.

He smiled, cracking his dry, pale lips and revealing yellowing teeth. His dark brown eyes reflected the golden glow of his own Tumble Thunder.

Now, finally, after years of searching, he could complete the task he had been given. The final act was upon him. Only then, would he have the true power over everything.

It had been such a long time since he had killed the others. He was anxious to finish the job.

"At last," he said, as a small drop of blood emerged from his cracked lips. "I have found you."

Chapter 9

Her eyes fought the sleep glue as Izzy emerged from a lazy fog. When light eventually crept in, she blinked hard to fight it off. A huge yawn and a stretch brought her body and senses to order. Almost.

The room swam into focus. The door, the walls, the sunshine glaring through the window. The desk, her notebooks and tools.

The new desk. The Tumble Thunder.

The room spun like a fairground waltzer when she jumped up. The bedpost helped steady her. She scrunched her eyes closed and started again. Her body ached from exercise it hadn't done.

She couldn't remember going to sleep. Or anything after the Tumble Thunder had almost attached itself to her. She sucked in a big gulp of air and felt for the *fuzziness*. The snowball that had become a golden, molten ball, wasn't there. At least, if it was, she couldn't feel it.

The *fuzziness*, her nan, her dad, the weird note he'd left her. No wonder she felt sick. And what did the note say about being the only one left? That scared her.

She dropped into her chair and re-read it.

> 'Dear Isabella.
> This is a Tumble Thunder,
> It is for you, and you are for it.
> Yours to complete,
> To complete you.
> Three times you must go.
> Beware the Time Shadow
> For there is only you left.
> It ends where two worlds meet.
> Find me.'

There it was again: 'There is only you left.'

She didn't like it. And what was the Time Shadow?

She was desperate to find her dad, but the note and the Tumble Thunder thingy left her feeling more alone than ever. The hairs on her neck stood up and she shivered.

Whatever it had done to her, she didn't feel ready for it.

She had no idea what, 'where two worlds meet', meant, but at least it felt like some sort of clue to where her dad was.

"Why don't you just tell me?" she said to the note in her hand, feeling lost and dejected. "What's the point of all of these clues and mysteries?"

Patting the top drawer of her desk to make sure it was closed, she headed downstairs, one slow step at a time. The sleep fog still hung in her head and her stomach was churning.

Her mum would know what to do.

The kitchen clock said after nine. She'd slept for more than 11 hours and she was still wearing yesterday's clothes with a bedraggled look to match.

Izzy's mum was serving pancakes. "Morning. No clock fixing. Just breakfast and a lazy Sunday for you sleepyhead and, oh," Izzy's mum stopped in her tracks at the appearance of her daughter. "Are you okay? Did you sleep in your clothes? You look terrible. You did, didn't you? Are you okay? You don't look it."

Izzy loved the way her mum would have a conversation with herself when she was worried. No matter how much she jumped to conclusions, she always seemed to land on exactly how her daughter was feeling.

"I feel really tired, mum. Something happened," she replied as she pushed her long hair out of her face. She stretched and yawned, and her shoulders clicked.

"Well, why don't you tell me about it?" said Jane. "You know, you can tell me anything you like."

Her nose twitched at the sweet smell of the fresh pancakes. She was hungry but felt sick, too. It was the strangest feeling.

Mum was looking at her, patiently. Izzy didn't know where to start.

Sliding a chair back, she sat down and took a deep breath.

Don't tell anyone. Not even your mum. She's not special like your dad.

Nan's words had come to her like a low whisper just as Izzy was about to begin.

"Well?" said Mum. "Come on then. Spit it out."

Izzy fidgeted in her chair. Normally, she'd tell her mum everything. There was nothing they didn't share. But there were bags under Jane's eyes that weren't normally there. Her hair needed brushing. The more Izzy looked, the more she realised her mum looked like she had enough on her plate. She worried about making it worse.

"It doesn't matter, Mum," she said, swallowing the words that were desperate to pour out. "Don't you worry."

Izzy was stuck. She needed to share everything about the Tumble Thunder and the note from Dad.

But she couldn't. She was scared about what might happen if she did.

She's not special.

It was such a strange thing for Nan to say. It was an even stranger way to say it.

"Well, if you want to tell me," said her mum, taking a sip of coffee, "then you know where I am. Any time you like."

"I know, Mum. Thank you."

In her chest, the small, spinning ball of gold had reappeared from its slumber. Something about the *fuzziness* wasn't happy either. It brought a feeling of dread.

Izzy realised it wasn't just that she couldn't tell her mum, but that she might put her in danger if she did.

Her mum smiled back as Izzy desperately tried to silently apologise with her eyes.

"I better get some homework done," she said, escaping back up to her bedroom.

If anger, sadness and confusion were all fighting in her head, she was convinced she felt them reach down and kick her in the stomach every now and again.

Find me, the note had said. No, her dad, had said. It was like the culmination of weeks of strange dreams and things she'd written down in her *Scramblings*.

The *Scramblings*!

She grabbed the pile and began to leaf through the pages, momentarily convinced that the answer might be within them. She re-read the most recent one. She tried to picture the shiny black buildings and the storm, but it was nothing she had ever seen or imagined.

Outside, the hubbub of shoppers and tourists below brought a steady buzz to her attic room, even three floors up. Carnaby Street, at the end of Foubert's Place, was one of the busiest in London and was rarely quiet. Silence wasn't something to be enjoyed in this corner of the capital.

The noise didn't help. But neither did her books.

She closed her eyes and tried to remember her dad in the dream. It had felt so real. She remembered how he'd stopped running and looked at her in the window. His eyes had shone as he smiled and moved a huge medallion from his right hand to his left to free him up to write 'find me' on the window.

It hit her like a thunderbolt.

What she thought had been a huge medallion, wasn't at all. It was the Tumble Thunder!

She'd caught the briefest glimpse at the time and hadn't thought anything of it. But Dad had had the pocket watch in her dream when they had been running together. Except it wasn't a dream, it was real. It was a *Seeing*. Dad had the Tumble Thunder, and now he had sent it to her.

So she could use it to find him.

She slumped on her bed. Terrified. She couldn't even tell her mum. She couldn't explain it, but it felt obvious.

Her *Dad Dreams*. The *Scramblings*. The Tumble Thunder and the note. Even what Nan had told her. None of it was for sharing. She was as sure as she could be, that this task was hers alone.

Running her hands over her desk, the smoothness of the wood seemed soothing.

"Ow." The pain interrupted her thoughts, and she glanced at her little finger. A splinter. The desk was perfectly smooth oak, aside from the small splintered panel where it looked like something had been scratching at it. She pulled the splinter out, sucking in air through gritted teeth.

She gently ran her fingers over the ragged wood. Down the ornate craving that led from the desktop to the side of the drawers and the stem of the lavender and disappeared underneath. There were a series of short scratches, about five centimetres long, down the panel that hid the secret drawer.

Her fingers found the catch underneath.

There was just enough room for Izzy to get her fingers between the edges of the drawer and the shiny gold pocket watch. She pulled it free and held it. The note sat, folded neatly beneath it.

The small, thick case of the Tumble Thunder opened easily despite its obvious age, and the face stared back. Izzy had seen plenty of old watches, but none like this one. It was perfect.

On the inside of the casing, were the indented shapes of a star, moon and sun, and a horizontal number eight, just like she'd seen earlier when it had almost melted into her hand. Her fingers felt the edges of the shapes. They were set back, as if they'd been deeply engraved into the metal.

The face itself was an off-white. The roman numerals and the hands were made from the same gold as the casing.

Inside the main clock face were two more dials, like on an old-fashioned stopwatch. A chronograph. Izzy had fixed plenty of watches in her life, but nothing like this. It was the kind of thing that would make Professor Wigglesworth do a cartwheel, even with his aching hip.

The smaller face was numbered 0-24, with a single, golden hand. Its partner on the right counted to four.

Below the centre of the Tumble Thunder was an eight-digit counter reading a full line of zeros. On the right side were three dials. The middle one stuck out furthest.

She pushed it in with a satisfying click, and the Tumble Thunder whirred. The eight zeros gradually began to turn. One by one they settled again. 18081860.

The two hands that had pointed directly at 12 reset themselves to half past 11.

A second hand she'd missed at first began gliding silently around the face. It was beautiful.

Slowly at first, and then more quickly, a warm glow shone through the centre and spread to each and every hand on the pocket watch. It spread out from the face, it engulfed the casing and reached her skin. But it didn't stop. The lines on her palm filled like tree roots of molten gold as the Tumble Thunder attached itself to her all over again.

It was like drinking hot chocolate on a cold day. The warmth and the light seemed to spread up her arms, her stomach, her body, down to her toes, and across her neck and face until everything in her room had a golden glow around it.

She was scared but felt strong. She took a deep breath and her vision went hazy.

But almost as soon as she felt the surge, it slipped back, like a tide racing from the shore. In its place was cold air, the sound of birds and the buzzing of insects. The golden tide receded from her vision into a single speck in the centre of her sight, and then was gone with a pop.

The Tumble Thunder was cold in her hand.

The rain was cold on her face.

Chapter 10

The warmth and strength that had flowed through her when she opened the Tumble Thunder had gone.

In its place was a bitterly cold chill. The hairs on her neck stood on end. She whirled around in a just-in-case-there's-someone-behind-me pirouette. But there was nothing. No-one.

Her heart was pounding. What had happened? Where was she?

She was surrounded by trees and close to her feet saplings had fallen, broken at the base.

"Hello?" she called out, half-hoping she might get a response and that she'd wake up from a weird dream. "Mum?"

Her voice drifted into the cold air. Rain ran down her face. She wiped it and swatted a group of tiny flies from above her head.

Around her the trees were as tall as the clock shop. They grew in perfect rows, creating a murky passage in between and stretching out in every direction like secret tunnels into an unknown darkness, the light suffocated just a few metres in.

"Helloooo!" she shouted more loudly, beginning to panic. "Anyone?"

Nothing. Wherever she was, it wasn't London.

The Tumble Thunder was still open in her hand. It was ten past nine. Her wristwatch told her the same.

Glancing back and forth from her wrist to the Tumble Thunder she noticed the second hand on the old pocket watch gliding silently. On the smaller face, the hand had moved from zero, to one – a quarter of the way around. She slipped it into her pocket.

"Where am I?" she asked the clearing, as if expecting an answer from the trees. "Ow!"

She slapped at an insect on her neck. The midges that had descended around her head, were now beginning their buffet. The tall trees almost leaned in her direction, closing off the light from above like staring strangers.

She was alone. And she had no idea where she was.

Is this what the Tumble Thunder did?

A branch snapped in the darkness of the trees. Her heart skipped a beat before thumping into life again.

Instinctively, she dropped to a crouch and tried to stay quiet.

The darkness stared back at her as she watched for the faintest movement. Her heart pounded.

The birds chirped and the trees swayed gently. Nothing moved. Another few seconds passed.

As she pushed herself back up there was a rustle in the undergrowth and a rabbit darted across the clearing ahead of her. It disappeared as quickly as it had emerged from the bracken.

"Hey!" she shouted and pushed out a huge breath. "Stupid rabbit!"

She folded her arms to stay warm, her tracksuit top damp on her hands.

It was then she noticed the smell of burning.

A small wisp of smoke was coming from beneath her feet. The pine needles around her trainers were smouldering.

There was a waft of smoke as she lifted her left foot to reveal a perfect, scorched footprint on the otherwise damp needles. She twisted her ankle to look at the bottom of her foot. Water squelched out of the hole in the heel where she'd worn her trainers out. But there was nothing black on them. No foot-shaped flame thrower. No black paint. Just water and a bit of mud.

None of it made sense.

The trees in the clearing had broken neatly near the base. Each one snapped as if partially sawn through at ankle height and then pushed over. Turning slowly, she saw they had fallen away from where she stood, like spokes in a bicycle wheel, with her at the centre.

Weird.

Despite the disappearance of the rabbit, she still eyed the darkness of the trees nervously. The branch she'd heard snap was loud. She wondered if a rabbit would really have been big enough to break it.

She could feel the rain seeping through her top to her bare skin beneath, she shivered. She was cold. Cold and alone, and being watched.

Despite the fear and the cold, the *fuzziness* had begun to spin in her chest like a warning.

She scanned the trees, her eyes flitting from trunk to trunk, dark passage to dark passage.

The words from the note her dad had left her in her birthday desk, drifted back.

Three times you must go.

Is this what Dad had meant? And if it was, where was she?

Tears came like warm taps, running down her cheeks.

Beware the time shadow.

The warning in the note had passed her by at first. But now, alone in the woods in the middle of nowhere, it came rushing back.

She had no idea who the Time Shadow was. Yet a strange foreboding was creeping from her chest to her throat. She shivered again and wiped tears from her cheeks.

What did this have to do with finding her dad? And how was she supposed to get home from wherever she was?

Taking another step backwards she squinted into the woods that stretched up the hill on the opposite side of the clearing. Her eyes were slowly adjusting to the gloom. She saw shapes of low bushes and piles of branches. There was nothing there, but the sense of being watched was growing.

Crack!

"Too big for a rabbit," she whispered and instinctively began to back up.

She scanned the shadows, her eyes flitting left to right. A broken tree stuck into her calf and she fell backwards, her hands digging into the thick pine needles as she scrabbled backwards.

Panicking, she scrambled to her feet and ran down into the alleys of planted pines.

Sharp branches grabbed at her, scratching her face. Pushing the branches aside she raced downhill through the trees.

The pine needles and mulch gave way under her feet until she was sliding faster and faster. She grabbed for branches that gave way in her hands and fell back, skidding downwards. The trees thinned out as the hill got steeper. Her bum hit a tree stump, propelling her headfirst into a huge pine. She felt a sharp pain in her shoulder as the impact sent her hurtling downwards, tumbling over and over. Until, suddenly, the trees and the scratchy branches released her and she was falling, twisting through mid-air.

The wind rushed past her face as she fell. She opened her mouth to scream just as she hit the water.

Chapter 11

Hidden in the darkness of the trees he had watched her examine the Tumble Thunder. She didn't know how it worked. She would soon learn.

The imitation he had built was cold in his pocket. He didn't need to check it. He knew it would have flicked over from zero to one. The warmth and its empowering glow had disappeared almost as quickly as it had arrived.

He felt weak and his legs struggled to hold him. He leaned against a tree and looked at his hand. Almost right *through* his hand. His skin was so pale it was almost translucent. His bones ached and he knew the years of searching had taken their toll. He'd lost count of the time slips he had made. Lost count of the amount of Tumble Thunders he had constructed, used and then discarded. He had paid a heavy price. His body could now barely withstand the pressure of each journey.

The girl was lucky. After a rest he would be at full strength again. As it was, she was guaranteed an annoying head start.

It had taken him years to learn how to build an imitation Tumble Thunder like her genius father had been able to do so famously. Building one of any kind had been near impossible. Only a Time Child could use the true relic that had passed down the generations.

Just being this close he could sense it. He had never been so sure; this girl had the potential to complete the one true Tumble Thunder and bring everything together. Alone she had the once in a millennia ability to save humankind from extinction.

For her, understanding her power was only the beginning. For him, it was the culmination of a lifetime of searching.

He had travelled from a future where the Earth was dying to find her. To stop her.

If he could steal the completed Tumble Thunder and kill the final Time Child, he could hold power over the very future of the planet.

In the clearing, she slapped her neck against biting insects. The branch had snapped under his foot as he shifted his weight in his tired leg. He held his breath.

The girl had dropped instantly into a defensive crouch. He was impressed by her instincts, but not surprised.

Around her, small trees were laid out in a circle. He knew they had snapped with the force of her arrival. Never before had he seen the evidence of such power. It never happened when he slipped through time.

He was sure she had looked right at him as she scanned the woods. His chest was straining for air but he resisted the urge to breathe, hoping the darkness of the trees would be enough to keep him hidden.

The inquisitive rabbit had been a slice of luck. It glanced up at him, no more than two metres away, lifted onto its haunches and raced into the clearing. A full-throttle bunny, running for its life from a transparent man who looked like a ghost with bad teeth.

The rabbit's noisy escape looked to have covered his presence.

But the respite was brief. The girl stared into the trees, slowly, left to right. She could sense him, even if she couldn't see him.

Shifting his weight again, another branch gave way and a louder crack made her twist in his direction, before she stumbled backwards, and fled.

Behind her, the air shifted and shimmered. It was like a heat haze with a purple tinge. It hung in the air before falling gently to the floor. To the watcher in the woods, her aura trail was unmistakable - it wouldn't be around for long.

He needed rest to recover his strength. In his current state he could barely stand. Time was both his friend and his enemy. Waiting would allow his full strength to return, but he knew they didn't have long in this place.

As the girl crashed through the tree-filled-gloom on the other side of the clearing, her aura glowed on the pine needles.

The man with pallid skin and his own Tumble Thunder smiled. He dabbed at the blood he could taste on his cracked lips.

He had dealt with the others, but she was stronger than all of them. The final Time Child.

Chapter 12

She kicked upwards and broke through the surface gasping for air like a rising salmon. Her lungs filled as she bobbed along on the fast-moving current. The water swirled and crashed around her. The river was fast, and as wide as a tennis court. It was framed on either side with pine trees up steep banks. Above the swirling rapids the trees gave way to a clear blue sky. Clouds of midges hung above the surface.

She strained to keep her head above the foam. But however hard she kicked, the current and her waterlogged clothes and trainers pulled her down.

Spun around by the torrent she spotted a log a few metres away and thrashed for it in a panic. Swimming as hard as she could she closed the gap and flopped her arms over the trunk. Her hands slipped from the bark as it rolled, and she was dunked below the surface. Clinging on she came back up and wrapped her arms around her slimy lifeline.

Fighting for breath between waves she spotted a small beach downstream and kicked for it, forcing the log to turn.

The bank drew nearer. Her legs ached from the effort, but her temporary raft wouldn't budge from the current.

Exhausted and terrified she tried again with all her might. Closer, but not much.

She hooked her hand around a broken stump of a branch on the trunk and a rock scraped against her shin.

Her scream was lost in the roar of the raging river.

The small beach was just 10 metres away. It was her only escape route. Sheer rocks led to a steep bank of trees along the rest of the bank.

Her shoulder ached from the fall through the trees. Her shin was sore and her fingers were starting to go numb. Her teeth chattered and she began to panic. But despite her rising fear, the *fuzziness* remained hidden.

She pulled in another deep breath and was jerked around as the log hit an eddy.

Spitting out water she clung on as the river threw her past a rock and she dropped under the surface. Bobbing back up, the log was ahead of her. Out of reach. The beach had passed. Her chance had gone.

I'm going to die, she thought.

But just as she began to fear the worst, the river turned a corner and calmed.

The rapids had been replaced by a flat, fast-flowing body of shimmering glass. Treading water was easier but every two or three strokes she had to stop to ease the growing cramp in her calf. When she did, she bobbed under, only to kick back up again.

Behind her came a growing rumble that rose into thunder. Her heart jumped as she twisted around. The shimmering glass was disappearing out of view and plunging downward over a waterfall as wide as the river.

Frantically, she tried to claw her way up the river as it dragged her nearer the edge. A scream stuck in her throat. As she kicked her legs found fresh air and the water pulled her over the edge.

For the second time that day she felt like she was flying.

The bottom of the waterfall hit her in the middle of the back like a swinging spade. It kicked the breath from her and she sank. She rolled like clothes in a washing machine, thrashing against the current as the light from the surface faded and the edges of her vision closed in. Her lungs screamed for air she couldn't give.

In the blackness she saw the Phoneys, heads buried in their mobiles. There was a swirl of black and silver water, and a telephone box came into view. Another swirl and a man with wavy brown hair talking through an old phone she'd seen in museums... Another swirl and from the darkness a familiar voice: "He is the first. Help him."

"Dad," she shouted into the water, but the voice was gone.

The words and the pictures drifted away and she was rolling again. Her chest convulsed as she fought the deadly urge to breathe deep underwater. Blackness was creeping in. She thrashed upward with a final, almost hysterical effort to reach the surface.

The visions of the man with the phone disappeared into a foggy haze as she felt the life slipping from her body.

Her chest began to spasm as she pushed upward.

But just as easily as it had taken her, the water spat her out.

Breaking the surface, air rushed into her chest as she took an almighty breath. Her feet found the bottom and half wading, half swimming she vomited cold water as she made it to the shallows and threw herself on the grassy bank.

The blue sky stared down at her. To her right the waterfall roared along its merry business as if nothing had happened.

Scrunching her fingers her hands began to hurt as blood rushed back into them. Her feet throbbed and she was colder than she'd ever been. Her body hurt. Her shoulder ached from hitting the tree and there was a sharp pain in her side. She wriggled her toes to bring them to life but it only sent a sharp pain up her shin. All alone, cold and scared she pulled her legs into her chest and cried. Her teeth chattered as she sobbed. She was lost. Pebbles on the bank bit into her backside and her legs. Thinking of her mum and her mission to find her dad, she felt totally helpless. Helpless and alone.

She felt a lump in her zipped pocket. The Tumble Thunder. It clicked open easily. The water hadn't bothered it. The second hand glided effortlessly round. It was almost 11 o'clock. Almost two hours since she'd looked at it in her bedroom and ended up in the middle of nowhere. How had the time disappeared so quickly? Her own wristwatch stood still at ten past nine. The second hand had stopped at the moment the old pocket watch had come to life.

She rubbed her eyes with the palms of both hands, wiping away tears and river water. Her nose was running and she sniffed loudly.

"Hey!"

She jumped back on the grass, scrambling away from the direction of the voice.

"Are you okay?"

Instinctively, she pushed her hair across her face and pulled herself up, leaning back on her hands.

A boy about her age, was standing in front of her, leaning on a long walking stick. He looked warm in an old tweed jacket and shorts with long socks. He had wavy, brown hair that seemed familiar.

"Are you sure you're okay?" he said in a thick Scottish accent. "Who are you? What are you doing out here?"

"Erm," her numb lips refused to make words. She shrugged instead.

After a few seconds the boy's face relaxed, and a warm smile spread across his face before he added, in a softer voice: "What are you wearing?"

"I could ask you the same," said Izzy, her lips shivering through the words. As she got up, her shoulder and her shin both gave her a sharp reminder of her adventure with the river.

He was slightly older than her, by maybe a year or so. He was taller too. Not by much, but he was.

"I'm Aleck," he said. "I saw you go over the waterfall. I didn't think you were coming back up for a minute."

He took off his jacket and wrapped it around her.

"I didn't think I was either. My name's Isabella," she said, thankful for the warmth. Pins and needles were buzzing around her hands and feet as she slowly warmed up. “But everyone calls me Izzy.”

“You’re lucky you’re still alive. You should probably have died going over that. Where are you from?”

“I don’t think you’d believe me if I told you.” She said, honestly.

“You don’t know?” he pulled a disbelieving face. “You are lost. This is Abernethy Forest, Scotland.”

“What?”

“Scotland,” he said, taking his cap from his head and brushing his hand through his hair.

Somehow, after she’d looked at the Tumble Thunder in her bedroom above the clock shop in London, she had been transported to the middle of Scotland. To the middle of nowhere.

She’d fallen in a river while being chased by someone who wasn’t there, thrown down a waterfall and almost drowned.

Her shoulder hurt as she adjusted the jacket, feeling the Tumble Thunder against her side.

The note from her dad came back to her.

> Yours to complete.
> To complete you.
> Three times you must go.

She didn’t know why, but just when she was going to die in the waterfall, her dad had spoken to her and a man with wavy brown hair had appeared. Now a boy who looked like the man's son was giving her his jacket to keep her warm.

The *fuzziness* bobbed slightly in her chest but she ignored it, angry at herself for not fully understanding.

"Aleck," she said, "Is there somewhere we could go to get dry. Then I really need to find a way home."

He looked her up and down.

"Come on, but we won't have any of those," he said, pointing at her tracksuit top, jeans and trainers. "Let's get back to the cottage. Mary will know what to do."

He set off across the field, his feet leaving footprints in the dewy grass as he strode away from the river. Izzy followed, and kept her eyes on the floor, deftly dodging piles of sheep poo, as their owners scattered in their path.

The walk with Aleck was long but, eventually, she partially dried out and warmed up.

"Here we are," he said, swinging open a gate that led into a huge garden. It was bordered on all sides by a tall, stone wall and a path that led to a back door of a large cottage. Smoke swirled from the chimney.

The kitchen had a bare stone floor and a woodburning stove. The smell of food hung in the air and Izzy's stomach rumbled loudly.

"Get down, Trouve," said Aleck, as a Skye Terrier noisily jumped up, muddying Izzy's damp jeans with his paws.

"Hey," said Izzy. "Get off."

Another dog, a sleek black and white collie, had decided to try and pull her across the stone floor by the bottom of her jeans. He was thinner than Trouve, and at Izzy's shout, he let go of her trousers and started weaving excitedly between her legs.

"Greysock, calm down," said Aleck, turning to Izzy. "Sorry, Mary found him in the woods last week on one of her walks. We're not really sure where he's from but he's full of energy. He doesn't stop bouncing around."

Greysock stopped and looked at them both, his tongue lolling out on one side. A white stripe ran down the middle of his face between his eyes and three of his legs were all black. But the lower part of his front, left leg was a light grey. His white tail wagged excitedly.

"We couldn't think of what else to call him," said Aleck, noticing Izzy looking down at his leg. "He looks like he's wearing a grey sock. We think he might have escaped from a farm nearby. He's a border collie. They're the smartest dogs you'll find."

Greysock bounced over to Izzy and sat at her feet. He looked up at her attentively and she rubbed the top of his head.

"That's the best behaved he's been so far," said a voice behind them. "Hello Aleck, and who this is?"

"This is Izzy, Mary. She got lost in the woods and fell in the river. I thought she was going to drown."

"Oh, missy, are you okay?" Mary butted in, in a thick Scottish accent, as she rushed forward to put her arm around Izzy.

"Yes, yes she's fine," said Aleck almost ignoring the near-death experience in the icy cold water. "Izzy this is Mary who I told you about. She goes everywhere with us."

Mary wrapped her arm around Izzy's shoulder and hugged her close like an old friend. She smelled of smoke and cooking. Her face glowed and her hair was scraped back in a convenient bun. The white, frilly apron she wiped her hands on hung loosely above stout boots.

"Well, hello dearie," said Mary. "Lost, eh? In the river you say? Well, that's nae good is it? At least that little tyke has taken a liking to you. Let's get you some fresh clothes and some warm food."

"Thank you," said Izzy in reply, straining her ears to understand. "I hope you don't mind me asking, but do you have a phone I could use?"

"I beg your pardon?" said Aleck.

"A phone. So I can call my mum and tell her I'm okay. I can't stay here."

"Well, I dinnae what you're talking about, but maybe we could send a telegram once we've eaten," said Mary.

"O-kaay," said Izzy, frowning. She'd heard of a telegram but didn't know what it was. The waterfall vision of the man she presumed was Aleck's dad with the old-fashioned phone came back to her once more.

She ate until she couldn't eat any more. The sleeves of Aleck's old jumper were so long they hung over her hands, but she was warm at least.

Izzy picked up the plates and walked over to the sink.

As she did, she noticed Mary looking at her back as if there was something behind her.

"What's up?" she said, spinning around.

Mary quickly glanced around Izzy, and then looked straight at her with a widening smile.

"Nothing dear. You're here now. Everything will be just fine. We'll look after you," she said, reassuringly. Aleck hadn't looked up from his healthy serving of seconds.

"O-kay," said Izzy, glancing at the air around her, and then looking back at Mary. She then put the plates in the sink to wash.

"Och lassie, leave those. I'll sort those out later," said the housemaid, ushering her away from the dirty plates. "You sit down there and tell us what happened to you this morning. It must have been terrifying when you arrived."

"What do you mean? Arrived?" said Izzy, as she was shooed toward her chair.

"You know," said Mary quickly. She looked around and tugged her apron before adding: "Being up there in those woods all on your own. It's a good job Aleck found you."

Mary's face was impossible to read and Izzy smiled back. Even if Mary somehow knew more than she was letting on, Izzy didn't think she was dangerous.

"Well, I went for a walk, and I just, well, I fell in the river," she said, pursing her lips as she reverted to her reluctant lies of earlier.

"That's strange," said Aleck.

Seeing the uncertainty and anxiety in Izzy's face, Mary changed the subject.

"Well not to worry, maybe we can sort a telegram for you," said Mary, putting her hand on Izzy's.

Greysock was nudging Izzy's leg and sniffing at the Tumble Thunder in her pocket.

"What's up boy?" she looked down at the dog and back up at Mary. One of his eyes was blue while the other was brown.

"Go on, missie, take him in the garden. He wants to play," said Mary, turning to Aleck. "You, young man, can help me finish clearing up."

"Aleck," said Izzy, before she headed to the garden. "Do you know what a phone even is?"

"A what?" he said with a confused face. "Not a clue."

"Okay," said Izzy, and followed the bouncing Greysock out of the kitchen. She stopped and leaned against a pile of logs as a stone dug into her toes. She pulled off the trainers she'd refused to swap for some boots and retrieved a small pebble.

Though she was warm, her feet were cold in

her still-damp socks.

She launched the pebble down the garden and Greysock raced after it.

"Is this where you're meant to be, Dad?" she asked the empty garden.

She remembered his voice in the river when she thought she was about to die: "He is the first. Help him."

She had no idea what he meant or where she was. Though she felt lucky to be alive after her adventure in the river.

When she'd seen Aleck's dad in the water, he had been talking down an old-fashioned telephone. But Aleck and Mary didn't have a clue what a telephone actually was.

She leant against a pile of logs next to the back door and knocked them loose. The two on top tumbled down the pile, loosening a pile of kindling and landing on a newspaper that had been folded for the fire pile.

The headline caught her eye.

Slowly, she unfurled it. It felt new. The name at the top was *The Scotsman*, and the headline, in bold, old-fashioned letters read: 'Dreadful Railway Accident: Four lives lost.'

She read the first line: 'On Sunday night an accident of a melancholy nature occurred between Edinburgh and Glasgow on the line of the Central Edinburgh Railway, by which four lives were lost and five or six persons seriously injured.'

There was a drawing of the accident instead of a photograph and the whole front page was full of other stories, like newspapers she'd seen in libraries.

Reading the headline again, she looked at the date and held her breath.

Chapter 13

Tuesday, August 18th, 1860.

She read the date again.

August 18th, 1860.

A pan fell noisily to the floor behind her. Aleck laughed. Aleck with his old-fashioned clothes and long socks. Mary with her frilly apron and huge, billowing skirt. On the stove a kettle was boiling.

Her eyes flitted around the kitchen.

There was no electric kettle. No microwave. No plug sockets. No fridge.

That's why there wasn't a telephone. It hadn't been invented yet.

She was in the past. It was impossible. But it was true.

Ducking out of sight of Aleck and Mary, she took the Tumble Thunder out of her pocket.

It felt smooth in her fingers but there was no golden glow when it opened this time. No strange feeling of strength that came rushing through her body.

At the bottom of the face were the numbers she'd been looking for. Eight digits that had confused her when she first opened it in her bedroom.

18081860.

18-08-1860.

The 18th of August 1860.

The Tumble Thunder had taken her 150 years into the past and hundreds of miles from home. It had warned her and she hadn't even realised.

Was this where she was supposed to find her dad? In the middle of Scotland?

Rubbing the Tumble Thunder between her fingers, she thought of the old, brown note in her desk. She'd looked at it so many times it was etched on her memory.

> 'This is a Tumble Thunder.
> It is for you, and you are for it.
> Yours to complete.
> To complete you.
> Three times you must go.
> Beware the Time Shadow.
> For there is only you left.
> It ends where two worlds meet.

Find me.'

"Three times," she said to herself. "I get it, Dad. This is the first one. And I need to help Aleck. But help him do what?"

Some kind of magic in the Tumble Thunder had transported her here. And there was something that she was supposed to do.

It was slowly beginning to make some kind of sense. But not much.

Finding herself here - in the past! Mary. This cottage. Aleck.

Aleck with his weird clothes.

She didn't understand. It was like she had all the clues but couldn't put them together. The *fuzziness* began to build and she swallowed the lump in her throat as her frustration grew.

"I don't know what to do. How do I get home?" she asked the empty garden.

But just as she could feel the molten *fuzziness* spinning, and her heart speeding up, Greysock barked. His puppy-like yelp ended with a slight whine. It broke her attention.

He was standing in front of her now. His oddly coloured eyes wide and attentive. His ears were pricked up. His black coat was shining and his fluffy white tail looped in a perfect curl, like a squirrel's.

He barked again, with his whine to finish. It made her smile. Looking straight at her he spun around in a tight circle. In spite of everything, her smile cantered into a laugh. The *fuzziness* receded.

"What is it, you silly dog?" she asked. "What do you want? You think you know what to do?"

He cocked his head, barked again, then ran off into the garden to join Trouve. The pair of them set about chasing a combination of fallen leaves and birds in the bushes.

"I don't think my dad is in those bushes," she said. "And neither is the way home."

"Izzy, are you okay?" it was Aleck.

"How long have you been standing there?" she said, feeling her face going red.

"Long enough to see you talking to the dog. Are you okay?" he asked again. "Don't get upset. I'm sure we can get you back to your parents."

There was something about Aleck that made her feel comfortable. Her gaze fell to the floor and then back up at him. He had freckles on his cheekbones, and a scar in the middle of his chin. When he smiled, his face came to life. He had the look of someone who didn't get much chance to have fun. Izzy decided there was nothing much to lose.

"Aleck, can you keep a secret?" she paused, looked at him, and decided to continue. "If I tell you something, promise me you won't say I'm going mad? It will sound like I am."

"Okay. I'll try."

"I wasn't out walking this morning," she said, and paused. "I'm not from around here at all."

Aleck raised his eyebrows: "Go, on."

"I'm from the future," she said, and waited for a reaction.

Aleck's eyebrows took the staircase to his hair line, and his mouth dropped open slightly.

Over the next five minutes she told him everything.

From when she'd first got the Tumble Thunder and the note, to how she'd ended up in the woods, and then the water. She didn't mention her *Seeing* in the water. That bit felt like it was only for her.

He listened without interrupting. When she told him she slept in her trainers - after she'd explained those were what her shoes were called - he almost laughed. But he held it in.

By the time it was over Izzy felt relieved. Her fear had lifted. Aleck's eyebrows had slowly succumbed to gravity.

"Okay. Well, maybe you are a little bit mad," he said, in a matter-of-fact tone. "But I could tell you were different when we met. I've been to London with my da once, and there was no-one dressed like you. I just couldn't quite work out what it was. I thought you might be a foreign spy or something."

"A foreign spy," she said, laughing. "Probably more believable than the truth."

"Da says the French are always trying to get into the country some way or another."

"Well, I'm sure they'd send a 13-year-old girl to check everything out first. In the middle of some woods. In a random part of Scotland." Izzy was laughing again. So was Aleck.

"Yeah, okay. Good point. Could I see the tumble thing?" he said, changing the subject. He pointed at the watch in her hands.

"Look, see the long number?" she said. "It's today's date. Look at the small face. It's ticked over to one."

"The time is right," said Aleck, checking it against his own watch. "And the other counter goes up to 24. That's nearly at seven now. What time did you say it said when you… found yourself here?"

"The Tumble Thunder said it was just after eight o'clock."

"Well it's almost five in the afternoon. Eight hours. I think that hand is counting up to a full day. I wonder what happens when it makes it to 24?"

The question hung in the air. Some rooks took off noisily in the woods nearby, as if spooked. Neither of them bothered to look.

Aleck handed Izzy the Tumble Thunder. She slipped it into her pocket.

Mary came out of the cottage waving a towel in the direction of the dogs who had started digging.

"Away you little mongrels. Away!" she shouted. At the sound of her voice, the dogs looked up. They paused and then ran off toward the bottom of the garden.

"As well as her amazing pies, you should see

her chop wood. She often picks up my brothers by their collars when they're horrible. And that's a lot," Aleck whispered to Izzy out the side of his mouth as Mary picked up a log and threw it into the pile. "My da told me she turned up one day at the house in Edinburgh looking for work when I was about two. She's been with the family ever since. We couldn't get by without her these days."

Mary turned from staring down at the dogs and walked back up the garden to the teenagers on the porch.

"It's a nice afternoon, but it'll be getting dark before long, so it will," said Mary, wiping her hands on her apron. "Looks like we won't be getting you back tonight at any rate. Maybe in the morning when Mr Bell is back. You'd better stay here the night. We need to keep you safe."

It was a statement rather than an offer, and she disappeared back into the cottage.

"Aleck, do you have a map?" asked Izzy. "I want to understand just where we are. Maybe my dad is around here after all."

"I don't," said Aleck, "and I doubt it. It's 60 miles to Edinburgh, Izzy. It takes a good half a day by coach and horses. There's nothing here but hills, sheep, deer, and us."

"Okay," said Izzy. She was more confused now than anything. "I'm here to do something. I'm just not sure what it is. I think I have to help you somehow."

The sun had dropped behind the trees and the

warmth had dropped from the day. At the bottom of the garden, the dogs were still looking for somewhere to dig.

"Trouve! Here boy!" Aleck summoned the dog. "Well, I don't know what it is. I don't see how I'm supposed to be any use to anyone in the future."

"In the water, there was a man with a phone, but you don't even know what one is," said Izzy. "I don't even think anyone has made one yet."

"What do you mean? A phone? Tell me what that is again," said Aleck.

"Well, it's a thing that helps you talk to people in a different place. Even if you're miles away."

"I don't understand."

Spotting a pile of old cans, she undid the washing line from a hook on the back door and tied a can to it. She passed it to Aleck and followed the washing line down the garden to an old post. She undid the string and tied it to a second can.

"Put it next to your ear," she shouted down the garden to Aleck who raised it to the side of his head. She spoke quietly into her own can: "Can you hear me?"

"Wow!" he shouted down the garden.

"You try it," she said into the can.

"Try it? Like this?" he said into his own can as she listened.

"Just like that," she responded.

Greysock bark-whined twice more and laid down excitedly in front of Izzy.

"I heard it," said Aleck. "I heard your voice in the can."

"Me and my dad used to do it when I was little," said Izzy. "It'll work from a fair distance away so long as you keep the string tight. That's basically how a telephone works. Well, how they used to work. They don't even have wires where I'm from."

"That's incredible. I think you're on to something," said Aleck.

"It's basic physics. Makes perfect sense. The tighter the string, the better the sound waves move along it."

"It's clever," said Aleck, "I think it could be really useful."

"Ha! That's the understatement of the year," she laughed, thinking of the Phoneys in her school and how phones had changed the world.

As she said it, the molten *fuzziness* turned over in Izzy's chest. She felt a rush of something like achievement, and the vision from the waterfall returned. She saw the man with an old telephone again and she realised. The man was Aleck - only older. She understood. She had helped him. Just like her dad had told her to.

Chapter 14

He moved slowly at first.

He had waited as long as he dared and urged himself to his feet. Too long and there would be no trace of her aura. Too soon, and he wouldn't have the energy to track her anyway.

He walked slowly into the clearing where the trees had broken at the impact of her slipping through time. She had arrived with phenomenal energy. It was unlike anything he had ever seen. The scorch-marks from her feet were still clear in the grass. The rain had stopped. The grass was beginning to dry despite the cool August air.

A buzzard screeched overhead as it flew by the small gap in the otherwise thick woods. The clouds were beginning to break. He crouched and examined the floor. The remains of her aura were faint but visible. It was like a fine purple dew on the ground where she'd walked. He followed the trail with his eyes into the downward darkness of the pine forest.

Standing, he felt stronger. The rest had worked, his energy had returned. As weak as the years had made him, he had felt slightly stronger since the girl first activated her Tumble Thunder. He followed the faint purple path before him. As he made the tree line, the hazy track became brighter on the dry pine needles.

"Damn flies," he said, wafting away a cloud of biting midges.

The buzzard screeched again as it turned. It caught a raft of warm air and climbed on outstretched wings.

"Damn bird," he said, looking up at the huge bird of prey effortlessly gliding through the sky. He took a step into the darkness of the trees. "Be easier if I could fly."

He pulled the collar of his black trench coat up against his neck. Pushing the thin, pine branches aside, he stepped down the steep bank.

"I'm coming for you," he said to the purple trail in the empty wood.

Chapter 15

The barking dogs yanked Izzy into the world of wakedom. Her eyes blinked open heavily and she rubbed them.

Initially she'd wondered why they were in her attic bedroom. There were never strays in this part of central London. Then she'd remembered the woods. Aleck, Greysock and Trouve.

Dark blue streaks of early morning light reached across the room from the cracks behind the curtains. The dogs' barking went up a notch as she rubbed the sleep from her eyes. It ended in Greysock's trademark whine. Mary had prepared the bed in the guest room at the back of the cottage that overlooked the garden. Having changed out of

Aleck's old clothes, she'd been glad to be back in her dry jeans and trainers.

"Shut up Trouve," it was Aleck. His voice was muffled by the heavy door between them. He didn't sound happy about being woken up before the sun.

Peering through the curtains, Izzy strained her eyes at the garden gloom.

The dogs briefly stopped barking. In the slate-grey light, the high garden wall stretched toward the back of the garden. It ran past the shrubs and an old bench to the foot of the woods beyond. Above it, the shadows of the trees held the dawn at bay.

As her eyes tracked back, something moved. A shadow that hadn't been there just a second before. She scanned left and right, looking for the edges. The longer she looked, the more her eyes adjusted to the gloom under the trees. The shadow was tall and thin, just on the edge of the trees beyond the back wall. Tall and thin with shoulders and a head!

Her goosebumps returned and her blood ran cold. She ducked back behind the curtains.

Peeking out, she was convinced the figure moved. Ever so slightly, as if shifting its weight from one leg to the other. Greysock and Trouve began snarling. She heard them scratching at the back door, desperate to get out.

"Okay, okay, I'm coming yer noisy wee doggies," this time it was Mary. She sounded grumpy at being woken. Izzy heard her bang into the kitchen from the hall.

The dogs whined as Mary dropped a heavy bolt free on the top half of the back door. It was split in two like those in a stable. The bottom half of the door scraped along the floor as she pulled it open.

At the slightest hint of an escape, the dogs scampered and skidded on the stone floor to get out into the garden, barking and snarling. Greysock's whiney finish hung in the air longer than Trouve's yappier shouting.

But when Izzy looked toward the far wall, the shadowy figure was gone. The dogs charged around and round. They dropped their front legs in an attack position and growled in the direction of the woods.

"Shut up yer daft brutes," shouted Mary down the garden. "There's nothing there."

Mary strode out onto the grass, still in her nightdress and long dressing gown. Kneeling alongside Trouve she stroked the top of his head as he snarled. But Greysock stopped barking and sprinted over, sat at her side and waited.

"Easy boys. There's nothing there. Calm down. It's just the woods," Mary said the words, but didn't sound sure. She stared into the gloom, watching.

Izzy stared too. She was convinced she'd seen someone watching the cottage. Whoever it was, the dogs had scared them off. If it was even anyone at all.

She opened the curtain just enough to throw a glimmer of daylight on her. Checking the Tumble Thunder she saw it was just after six o'clock.

The counter at the bottom had made it all the way around to 21. It had been 21 hours since she arrived in 1860. In London in 2013, she disappeared almost a day ago. Her mum would be more than worried. She had been here for nearly 24 hours and still felt exhausted. She wondered if her mum had already rung the police, and if she'd ever find anything more from her dad.

The Tumble Thunder clicked closed.

Sitting back on the bed, she rearranged her pillow, and laid down. Without meaning to, she fell asleep.

The smell of cooking woke her. Her stomach grumbled.

Less than five minutes later she was eating breakfast with Aleck. Blackened sausages with crispy fried eggs. It tasted as delicious as it smelled, and tasted a lot better than it looked. Mary had set a fire under the old stove. The kitchen had quickly warmed up to the point of being too hot.

Unlike Aleck, Mary was dressed. More sausages and eggs sizzled angrily in a large black pan on the stove. Aleck was still in his pyjamas.

"Was there anything in the garden, Mary?" asked Izzy, through a mouthful of sausage. "These are amazing," she added, pointing at her plate.

Mary turned from pushing the huge sausages

around the pan. Her face was red with the heat of the oven. She wafted her face with a cloth, before wiping her hands.

"No miss. The dogs heard something, but there was nothing there when I went out. There's all sorts that lives in these woods. Could've been a fox or a badger. Blimey, it could even have been a wildcat up here. That would have sent them potty." She laughed as if she didn't believe herself and turned back to the rapidly blackening sausages.

Izzy glanced across the round wooden table and looked at Aleck. He was stuffing a large crust of bread into his already half-full mouth.

"I think there was someone in the garden," she whispered to him. "I'm sure I saw someone, standing near the wall at the bottom. I think that's what the dogs were barking at."

"No, I don't think so dear," Mary said loudly over her shoulder without turning around. "Otherwise, the dogs would have been over the wall and out into the woods to have their heels. They wouldn't have let that wall stop them."

"And anyway," said Aleck more quietly so Mary didn't hear, "We need to think about how we're going to get you home. I think we could get up to Edinburgh and find a train to London."

Izzy pursed her lips. She wasn't convinced. She didn't think she'd somehow time travelled 150 years into the past to a remote part of Scotland just to go back to London on the train.

The vision of an older Aleck in the water with the phone came back to her again.

"Come on," she said to him, and headed toward the back door and the cool Scottish morning. "Let's check out that phone thing I showed you."

Aleck got up and followed. Izzy sat on a low wall at the top of the garden while Aleck went a little further along. They experimented with the can and the string before the dogs appeared, eager to investigate the smell of sausages.

While Trouve noisily pestered her to release the tasty goods, Greysock sat in front of her. He looked straight at her and didn't move.

"Hey boy," said Izzy. She held out a small piece of sausage. The collie took it from her gently.

"He's a funny dog," said Aleck. "We need to get him back to his owner today too."

Izzy reached out to stroke his head. As she did, he turned to the bottom of the garden and the hair on the back of his neck stood on end. He bared his teeth with a snarl.

Izzy pulled back her hand and followed the dog's gaze to the back of the garden. The morning was still and the woods beyond the wall were dark despite the early sunshine.

"What's up, boy?" said Aleck. He stroked Trouve, scanning the trees. "Is there something in there?"

"I don't like it," said Izzy, looking at Aleck and then back to the collie. "What is it, Greysock?"

Then, on Izzy's hip, a familiar feeling of warmth. She pulled the Tumble Thunder out of her pocket and opened it.

What followed felt like slow motion. In truth, it took little more than ten seconds.

The golden glow emanated from the centre of the pocket watch just like before. The warmth began to spread through the face of the old pocket watch. Izzy felt its energy seep into the palm of her hand.

"Izzy? What on earth?" exclaimed Aleck, looking on. Then, pointing at the time on the Tumble Thunder, "Look. You've been here a full day."

It was just after nine o'clock and the smallest hand on the watch face had almost reached 24. Beneath it, the counter that had showed 18081860 had reset. 00000000.

My full day is up.

As Trouve barked, Greysock growled. A low, grumbling warning from deep in his stomach aimed at the woods.

At the bottom of the garden in the dense darkness of the woods, there was a small golden glow.

Straining to see, branches cracked above and beyond the wall.

The light from the Tumble Thunder began to spread through her body. The empowering hot chocolate feeling seeped into her bones.

"Izzy. Are you okay?" it was Aleck, but his voice was like a distant shout in a tunnel. The light from the Tumble Thunder began to spread across her vision.

"It's okay. I'm okay," she told him, softly.

At that moment Mary came crashing out of the cottage. Out of breath she scooped up Greysock and thrust him into Izzy's arms.

"Take him with you missy. You need him," she said, stepping back and putting an arm around Aleck. The dog was heavy but he had stopped growling. His warmth merged with that of the Tumble Thunder, and he nestled into her.

The small hand ticked silently over to zero. Everything went golden and strength rushed through her body. An impenetrable haze descended and she closed her eyes. Greysock whimpered and pressed himself into her side as she held his collar.

* * *

The pile of *Scramblings* was on her desk, where she'd left them. Her chair felt cold.

Her desk was just as she'd left it. The light was streaming in through the old window and her rucksack was by the door.

Her eyes felt heavy and her stomach grumbled loudly.

A cold wetness on her hand made Izzy jump. A border collie with one blue eye and one brown looked up at her. He nuzzled his wet nose against his new owner and his collar jangled.

* * *

In the garden of the cottage in Scotland in 1860, Mary stood with Aleck. She had seen the glow in the woods too. More, she had seen the man in the dark coat desperately trying to get through the branches and toward Izzy as time ran out.

Now, as only scorched footprints remained where Izzy had stood, she looked back at the trees. He had gone too. She didn't need to check.

"What on earth?" said Aleck, staring at the floor. Then up at Mary.

"Don't worry, Aleck," said Mary, picking up the cans and the string, handing them to him. "She did what she came to do. Don't forget her. Don't forget the things she showed you."

Chapter 16

Izzy leapt down the stairs two at a time. Her heart bursting. She was desperate to see her mum and tell her everything that had happened.

"Mum! Mum! I'm here. I'm okay," she said as she rushed into the kitchen. "Don't worry. I'm sorry."

Jane only half turned from washing the dishes.

"If you've come to talk, Izzy, then give me a minute," said her mum, casually, without turning. "Just let me finish these."

Izzy frowned. She'd been expecting to find her mum printing missing posters and surrounded by police. But there was no intrepid detective at the kitchen table. No posters. Just her mum. Washing up.

Greysock nudged her leg. He had chased her down the stairs thinking it was some kind of game. He looked up at her and his nose twitched. His head swivelled toward the smell.

On the table, her breakfast was waiting. The orange juice and fresh pancakes were right where she'd left them the day before. Her chair was even pushed back from where she'd gone upstairs, 24 hours ago. Before Scotland.

"I thought you'd be down before too long, so I thought I'd wait for you and we'd eat together," said Jane turning around. She dried her hands on a tea towel from the drainer.

Izzy didn't move. She'd been gone a day. But it seemed like nothing had changed. Even her breakfast was still waiting for her. Her mum hadn't missed her at all.

"And what on earth is that doing in here?" Izzy's mum pointed at Greysock. Her eyes were wide.

"Oh," said Izzy thinking on her feet. "I saw him out of my bedroom window and went down to see if he was still there. I think he's a stray or something. Isn't he cute?"

The young dog ran over to Izzy's mum and sat down. He looked up at her, cocked his head, laid down and rolled onto his back. It was enough to melt Jane. She resisted for a second but then dropped into a crouch and rubbed Greysock's exposed belly.

"Well, aren't you a gorgeous little boy," she told the dog. "Though you shouldn't be in here."

"Mum," Izzy said. "Weren't you wearing that top yesterday? Haven't you missed me?"

"What are you talking about? You stormed off upstairs five minutes ago. I'm surprised you had time to go down and let this boy in. We need to find his owner. And no, this top was clean on this morning. Don't you like it?"

"Huh."

"My top. Don't you like it?" her mum asked again.

"Oh, yes, I love it, Mum."

Izzy looked at her wristwatch. It was just after ten past nine. Just a few minutes ago she'd been in Scotland. In the past. The Tumble Thunder was in her pocket. She could feel the cool metal against her hip.

Her mum rubbed Greysock's belly. Izzy wondered about Aleck and Mary. The dog didn't seem to have a care in the world and her mum was none the wiser.

She'd been in 1860 for 24 hours. But nothing here had changed. If there was ever any doubt that it had all been real, the proof was lying on his back in her kitchen. Quite simply, it was the most bizarre thing that could possibly have happened to anyone ever. Full stop.

But while no-one seemed to have missed her, her stomach was less than happy. She was starving.

Travelling through time had left her so hungry she actually felt a little sick. Sick and drained. Yet it was less than an hour since she'd eaten Mary's blackened sausages and eggs.

She pulled up a chair and gulped down her orange juice. Stuffing a pancake in her mouth she saw how filthy her hands were.

Her mum didn't seem to notice. She was too distracted by Greysock.

"He's a gorgeous little dog, Izzy. But he can't stay. I don't think we could have a dog in the shop."

Her mum sipped her coffee, carefully blowing it first. Izzy remembered watching her pour it.

How was it still hot? That was 24 hours ago.

"Does he have a collar?" asked her mum as Izzy set about her second pancake. She offered a small piece to Greysock.

"Yes, but there's no name tag on it," she said. "But I think he's called Greysock," she lied, clumsily.

"So how did you know his name, if he hasn't got a tag on his collar?"

That one had Izzy stumped. Should she explain to her mum how she'd time travelled to the 1800s and met a boy called Aleck in some woods? Was given a dog by a lovely Scottish lady who liked to burn sausages? Her Nan's words came back to her. Whatever she had to do for her dad, it felt like sharing it with her mum might put her in some kind of danger.

"Well, I saw he had a grey sock," she said, remembering Aleck's explanation. "I thought it just kind of suited him."

Izzy's mum looked under the table at the dog and threw him a piece of pancake.

"I think you're right," said Jane. "Let's keep hold of him today and see if anyone comes looking for him."

"Thanks Mum," said Izzy, slightly shocked.

"You'll have to walk him though," said Jane. "I haven't got time and Professor Wigglesworth is going away today so I'll be extra busy in the shop."

"Where is he going now?"

"He said something about a water clock that's been found in Egypt. A real one this time. They're exceptionally rare, and worth a fortune. He'll be gone a few days."

"I think he's mentioned them before. Aren't they basically just a clever bucket?"

"Something like that. It's called a clepsydra or something," said her mum, rolling her eyes, and sipping coffee. "You sure you're okay? I know you slept in your clothes, but you look more tired now than when you first came down this morning. You're filthy too. I didn't notice earlier. You're 13 now, Izzy, you need to have a shower at least once a day. Probably about time you stopped sleeping in your trainers too." She let the final point drift off.

"I know, Mum," said Izzy, rolling her eyes. "This has been the longest Sunday ever."

"Well, make sure you have a shower and get changed before Porter comes round later."

"Porter?"

"He's coming round for tea, remember?"

Izzy hadn't remembered at all. Though she felt like she couldn't tell a grown up about the Tumble Thunder, she wondered if she could tell Porter without putting him in danger. She wished she could, but decided against it.

"Don't worry Mum, I'll make sure I look presentable. Come on Greysock, you can help me with my homework."

"Then maybe you can try and find his owner," her mum shouted after her.

The dog looked at them and followed Izzy out of the room. He stuck close to her heels. They headed upstairs and Izzy flopped at her desk. Slowly, Greysock inspected the skirting boards with a cautionary sniff before doing the same to everything in the room. Satisfied, he walked over and jumped onto the bed. He turned three times, plonked himself down next to Izzy's favourite teddy, and went straight to sleep.

"You're tired too, are you?" Izzy smiled and grabbed an empty notebook from her pile of *Scramblings*. With a black pen she wrote "THE TUMBLE THUNDER" on the front of a new book and opened the first page.

Over the next hour she made notes about everything she could remember. Every detail of the past day she'd spent one hundred and fifty years in the past. Everything that seemed important. From the scorched grass in the woods, to visions of Aleck with the phone when she thought she might die in the river, to the way the shadowy figure had moved in the dark.

By the time it was done she had filled nine pages. Her hand ached. She flexed her fingers. It was the most she'd ever actually written, even at school. But it wasn't every day she had to remember going back through time. It still didn't seem to make that much sense.

Greysock had slept the whole time. He was snoozing proof she wasn't either dreaming or going crazy. Every now and then his legs twitched as if he was running. He gave a muffled bark, as his mind raced through whatever dog dream he was enjoying.

In the note he'd left, Dad had said she must go three times.

"Well, I guess that's one, boy." she said to the dog. He didn't react. "I didn't find Dad, but I found you. I don't get it. I think I helped Aleck, whoever he is, understand what a telephone is. But why?"

Greysock opened one eye, glanced over at her, and closed it again.

"Thanks," she said, smiling. "Really useful."

She reached into her pocket for the Tumble Thunder. It clicked open easily. Though it was cold, there was something about holding it that made her feel better. It didn't glow, or warm up. It just gave her a slight sense of reassurance. Every time she opened it, it was the same - a mental hug.

The counter at the bottom still showed a row of noughts. The hand that counted to 24, was pointing neatly to zero. The smaller face that went from one to three, was pointing slightly off to the right at the number one.

Three times you must go.

"Well, one down," she repeated to herself. What next?

Slowly studying all of the hands, she turned the watch over in her hands. Thanks to Mum and Dad, and Professor Wigglesworth's shop, Izzy was an expert in timepieces. It wasn't exactly what most girls dreamed of, but for Izzy it made her feel like she had a knowledge that hardly anyone else had - especially 13-year-old girls. It was like a secret superpower.

Eyeing the roman numerals through a magnifying glass she used for fixing clocks and watches, convinced her it was a rare antique. That just frustrated her more. She had never seen anything quite like it.

Listening closely, the noise of the inner workings was faint, but perfect. It always amazed her mum and the professor that she could even hear the inside of a watch. But to Izzy it sounded like the faintest tinkling of a piano. Sometimes she could almost feel it. Except she couldn't place this tune.

On the back she expected to find some inscription about the maker or the year it was made. But there was nothing. On the face itself, where watchmakers liked to show off by adding their names in gold leaf, there was nothing. The indented patterns on the inside of the front casing intrigued her. A number eight on its side. A star, a crescent moon and the sun. Pretty, but weird. And fairly useless, she thought.

"Hey, boy," she said, as Greysock nuzzled his head between her arm and her side. "What do you want?"

The collie nudged the Tumble Thunder with his nose, then looked at Izzy. He cocked his head.

His brown and blue eyes were sparkling. So was the tag on his collar.

Izzy frowned. The tag was a small silver disc. Inside it was a small star that she hadn't noticed before. Slipping the collar from Greysock's head she held the tag up in the light.

A four-pointed star.

On the desk, the Tumble Thunder lay open and the four symbols in the casing glinted. The moon, the sun, the sideways eight and the star. A four-pointed star.

She thought she understood.

She slipped the tag off Greysock's collar and compared the two.

The stars were equal in size. The one in the dog tag was slightly raised from the surface. She flicked it with her thumbnail, but it wouldn't budge.

She reached over and picked up the smallest screwdriver. Laying the collar flat on the desk, she attempted to prise it off. It was stuck.

She tapped it lightly, nothing. Then she hit it harder. It didn't move.

"Come on!" she said, getting angry. The *fuzziness* grumbled, but didn't move.

Frustrated she held the tag just above the Tumble Thunder to compare the size again.

As she did, it popped free. Except it didn't so much pop, as slip out of its own accord.

It almost hovered at first, and then began to slowly settle into the Tumble Thunder. The casing glowed golden and welcomed it.

As it sank into the old watch, the molten *fuzziness* began to slowly turn in Izzy's chest and she closed her eyes to welcome it.

A slow golden wisp rose from the now encased star and she felt the molten *fuzziness* in her chest reach out for it. Instinct forced her to take a deep breath and she pulled in the haze, deep into her lungs where it bonded with the *fuzziness*, which swelled and turned a deep orange. The same glow emanated from the whites of her eyes as she opened them, before settling back to normal.

Her senses felt heightened. The room was in sharper focus than before. Something inside her had grown.

The first part of her Tumble Thunder quest was complete.

Chapter 17

It was almost six hours later when she woke to the car horns on the busy London streets. She was used to sleeping through the hubbub of shoppers, but she couldn't usually hear the traffic. Her window was closed, but everything felt louder. She could make out small children giggling and adults talking. Bus engines, a car horn, and pigeons gently cooing amongst it all.

She listened, half enjoying, half mystified by her new ability.

She rubbed sleep from her eyes. It was almost three o'clock.

"I guess we needed that boy. You feel better now too?" she asked the collie, who jumped up to sit up on the bed. The dog's eyes looked brighter than before. His smooth coat was more sensitive on her hands. He seemed to smell worse too. It was as if putting the star into the Tumble Thunder had turned her senses up to 100.

Ten minutes later, with the Tumble Thunder in her pocket, the smell of shower gel buzzing in her nose and minty toothpaste sharp in her mouth, she headed downstairs with Greysock at her heels. Mum wasn't in the kitchen. The table was set for Sunday lunch. The smell from the roast in the oven filled the room and ambushed the scent of coconut shower gel in her nose.

Pans were boiling on the stove. She could hear the bubbles. The small lounge beyond was deserted. It had been a while since they'd been in there. When her dad was around they would sit in there every night. They'd listen to him making up stories about adventures and trips to the future that she was convinced he'd never had. She couldn't remember any of them.

Her mum had always watched with a disapproving look on her face, like he was telling her things he shouldn't. She'd never actually believed any of them. They were just stories. At least, that's what she thought at the time. Now, she wasn't so sure.

Leaving the kitchen, she passed her mum's closed bedroom door and paused. There was no noise inside at all. Maybe Mum was sleeping.

Though it would be strange with Sunday lunch underway.

Greysock nudged her and spun round in a circle.

"What"? she asked the restless dog.

Greysock whimpered and spun around again and again.

Izzy had always wanted a dog, but she didn't have a clue how to look after one. The border collie continued to whimper and sat down. Then he stood again and Izzy finally understood.

"You need a wee?" she laughed at herself. "Sorry boy. I don't speak dog. Come on."

They headed downstairs and through the shop. It was empty as usual.

"That you, Professor?" she said in the direction of the clattering in the storeroom behind the counter.

"Be out in a minute," came a muffled reply.

The bell seemed louder than ever in her sensitive ears and she caught the door as it swung open. It was all the invitation Greysock needed.

Quick as a flash, he scampered through the gap and out of sight.

"No. Greysock. Wait!" his speed surprised her. His back legs skidded on the path as he headed left into the narrow street. Disappearing between the legs of startled shoppers he zipped around the corner. He'd been so placid and obedient since she'd found him, that it didn't occur to her to put him on a lead.

"Greysock! Come back! Come here, boy." She called into the narrow street in despair. "Come back!"

Foubert's Place was only three metres wide and full of Sunday shoppers. It was only ever a way to get somewhere else. A family of tourists huddled around a mobile phone were arguing about which way to go next. Scooting past two old ladies chattering about the weather, she sped around the corner and ran straight into Porter.

"Ooof," he said, as they slammed into each other. "Watch my crisps! What's the rush?"

Porter had crumbs down his jumper and around his mouth but didn't seem to care.

"Where are you going?" he asked, licking long, skinny fingers casually.

"Soz" she said, pushing herself off him. "I'm chasing a dog. It's a border collie. He came this way. Have you seen him?"

Porter nodded and cleaned his thumb with a slobbering suck. He stepped to one side.

"This one?"

Greysock was sitting behind Porter, wagging his tail. He had a, 'what's the problem?' look on his face.

"There you are," she said. "I thought I'd lost you."

"He came flying round the corner, had a wee like a madman, then sat there."

"Come on, you silly dog. This way," she said, then turned to Porter. "Crisps? I thought you were coming for tea?"

"It's just a snack," he said. "I missed lunch. I need to stay fuelled."

Izzy laughed and the pair of them dodged through the crowds and made their way back to Wigglesworth and Son. This time, Greysock stayed at their heels as the family around the mobile phone continued to argue about the correct way to Big Ben.

"Where did you get him from anyway?" said Porter as they closed the door, shutting off the noisy street. "I'm sure you didn't have a dog yesterday."

"I didn't," said Izzy who had the beginnings of a dull ache in her temple. "I found him. He's been following me ever since." It was mainly true, she thought.

"That's a cute dog. Hello Izzy. Hello again Porter," said Professor Wigglesworth from behind the counter.

"Hey Professor, I thought you were going to Egypt today?" said Izzy.

"I am. Just got a couple of things to do first," he said. "Flying from Heathrow. Leaving in a minute. There's talk it could be one of the oldest clocks ever found," he added, going back to his favourite subject.

"Sounds cool," said Porter.

"It is, young man. It is. Clepsydras were ancient water clocks that were used in Babylon and Egypt more than 3,000 years ago. Apparently, there's an ancient legend that it has mystical powers," said the professor.

"Yeah? Like I said, cool." Said Porter, politely. He forced a smile and nodded.

Misreading Porter's feigned interest, the professor seized on the opportunity to share more.

"Some believe that they used them in China in 4,000 BC but I've never really believed that. For me the secret of the oldest timekeepers lies in Egypt. It never ceases to fascinate me. A mystical people the ancient Egyptians. I sometimes think they had the answers that could unlock the mysteries of time itself. By my reckoning, Isabella, that would be quite a handy thing to know, don't you think?"

His eyes were dancing as he spoke. In that one moment, Izzy thought he somehow looked years younger and older at the same time.

The professor took a breath to go on but was deterred by the vacant look on Porter's face and switched back to the present. He gestured to the collie who had now rolled onto his back for a free tummy rub. "Did I hear you say you found this fine fellow?"

"Well, I suppose he found me. I don't think we'll find his owner," said Izzy, thinking back to Aleck and Mary.

"Well, someone must own him. He's clearly housetrained if he knew to go outside for a piddle in a strange place."

"And he likes crisps as much as I do," said Porter,

as the dog grabbed a tossed crisp from mid-air and crunched it triumphantly. "Why don't you keep him Izzy? We'll have to find a lead though."

"Well, there's not really much room for a dog around here," said the professor. He took off his round, wire-rimmed glasses and produced a handkerchief with a flourish. "But if your mum says he can stay, at least until we find his owner, then that's fine with me."

"Thanks Professor. I'll try."

"Mind you do. In the meantime, there is a stash of old pieces in the storeroom. I picked them up at auction. Do you think you could have a look at them for me while I'm away?" asked the professor, pocketing his handkerchief and righting his glasses on his nose.

"Are they actual antiques this time? Or did they come from Switzerland via China like the ones you sold the Americans?" said Izzy with a smile.

"Smart girl," said the professor, with his customary wink. "All antiques are antiques in this business. The quality depends on who's buying them. There's only one box. They're old pocket watches."

Izzy's eyes widened.

"Don't worry, Professor. I'll sort them," she said, wondering if any were like the Tumble Thunder.

"Thanks Izzy. I'll be gone a few days I would expect, so your mum is going to be watching the shop for me. I've told her I'm not around for lunch today. Try and help her out as much as you can."

He pulled on his coat over his three-piece suit.

"Good luck finding that Clepsy-wotsit," she said.

"Isabella," he replied with a flourish, picking up a walking cane and slipping on a trilby, "I shall do one's best. Toodle-ooh."

With that he was out of the door and limping into Foubert's Place.

Mum was back and clanking around in the kitchen as they headed upstairs. Her hair was tied back, matter-of-factly.

"Hello Porter," she said. "Lovely to see you again."

"Hiya," he said, nervously.

"There you are, Mum," said Izzy. "Where have you been?"

"I just had to do a couple of things," said Jane, before turning to Porter. "I hope you're hungry. I forgot that the professor wasn't staying, so I've got an extra portion of Sunday lunch going spare."

Porter smiled from ear to ear. Greysock responded by walking over to Jane and sitting at her feet. He cocked his head to one side and gently pawed her leg.

She looked down at him and smiled. "Ah, yes. I'm sure I've got enough for our other new visitor too."

Greysock padded over to a corner of the kitchen so he could see all of them and laid down. His eyes open, watching his new people.

Izzy looked at Porter. He seemed untidy today. Like he'd slept in his clothes. She tried to remember if he ever looked any different. Maybe she hadn't noticed before because he was in school uniform. But today, with a tatty t-shirt and jeans that looked a little too frayed at the seams to be fashionable, she found herself wondering if he was okay. His hair was messy as always. His nails were dirty. His white t-shirt looked grey.

Noticing her examining him, Porter pointed towards the dog and leaned in towards Izzy.

"So," he whispered. "Where did you really get him from? It's hardly like border collies wander around the middle of London is it? And he doesn't look like a stray."

She looked at her new friend and bit her lip. She looked at the dog, and then back at Porter.

"You wouldn't believe me if I told you." She said honestly. "He kind of found me. I've no idea where he's actually from, but I don't think he wants to leave."

The dog raised his ears and looked at them both.

"Better stop talking about him. I think he knows," said Porter, and threw Greysock one of his remaining crisps.

Considering there was so much to talk about, the three of them ate their late afternoon lunch in relative silence. Jane served Porter the largest plate of food Izzy thought she had ever seen. He attacked it like he was going to win a new t-shirt if he managed to finish. It was no contest really. Izzy and her mum were barely halfway through theirs when Porter ceremoniously slipped the knife and fork onto the empty plate.

"Did you enjoy that?" said Izzy's mum, with a glint in her eye. "I hope it was as good as you get at home."

Porter stifled a huge, satisfied burp behind a hand. Izzy giggled.

"Oops, sorry," he said. "It was awesome. I don't get meals like that at home. My mum and dad work away a lot so it's just me and, err, well, my big sister mainly. Takeaways are a speciality. We get them most nights."

"Lucky you," said Izzy. "I mean, about the takeaways."

Porter made an attempt to smile but didn't finish it. Instead he gave a little shrug and a, "hmm."

Izzy glanced over at her mum, unsure what to say to break the awkward moment.

"Well, don't you worry about that, dear. I've got apple pie and custard for pudding."

The sunshine broke through the clouds on Porter's face at the thought. It remained that way through another massive serving. When Izzy's mum promised him a home-cooked meal any time he liked, he beamed.

"I mean," she said. "Izzy's friends are always welcome. It's not like she actually has time to make any with the number of schools she's been to."

"I don't like making friends," said Izzy, and the clouds dropped over Porter's face again. "It doesn't always end well."

"Izzy, you can be rude sometimes," her mum chided.

"It's okay, Mrs... Izzy's mum. I don't tend to like people either, so I know what she means. Izzy just seems different. She's nice to me."

Izzy blushed and gave Porter a smile. Porter just made things seem easier. Like he would be there for her without wanting anything in return. She'd never had a friend like that before. Not even Hattie.

Fifteen minutes later the kitchen was tidied. Jane headed downstairs to clean the shop.

The children retreated to the attic. Greysock followed, just two to three steps behind.

Throwing the rucksack against the door to keep it closed, Izzy turned to Porter.

She was desperate to show him the Tumble Thunder, how she ended up nearly drowning and all about Aleck. She even wanted to describe the *fuzziness* to him. To talk about her *Seeings*. But even replaying it in her head it felt totally crazy. Worse, it felt like telling him everything would somehow put him in danger. So she went half in.

"I need your help," she said. "I need to find my dad. And I don't think I can do it on my own."

"Okay. But I thought he was dead?" said Porter bluntly, before quickly adding, "sorry."

"Well," said Izzy, brushing aside her friend's clumsiness. "I was always told that. But I never quite believed it. Now I'm sure he's still alive and he's out there somewhere. I need to find him. It's important."

"Because he's your dad?" asked Porter with an isn't-it-obvious tone.

"Yeah, that. But more," said Izzy, looking Porter dead in the eye and remembering her dad's note:

You're the only one left.

"Like?"

"Like something really important relies on me finding him. It feels bigger than just me and my dad. It's just, well, I don't know what it is yet, and I don't think I can do it on my own."

Chapter 18

Izzy's dad shields his eyes as he runs. The huge lightning strike momentarily illuminates the huge black square. In a split second the darkened world has been polished. The light bounces off the floor and the skyscrapers.

His eyes sting with the intrusion as the blackness consumes his surroundings once more.

His hair is matted against his face with the relentless rain. Oily griminess runs down his cheeks and into his mouth. It's gritty between his teeth. Gloopy puddles soak his feet. He speeds on, his lungs heaving with the effort.

What have we done? How did it come to this? There is no time.

With another huge crash of thunder and a flash of lightning, it stands before him. An enormous pyramid, as black and shiny as his entire surroundings.

Seconds later he runs into the torrent of water cascading down the huge steps that lead directly to the top.

Each block of the pyramid is the size of a family car. At its centre are a series of waist-high steps. He follows the fury of the water up with his eyes, straining to see the peak.

Another momentary whiteout precedes more thunder.

They're here.

A line of people, at the very top of the steps, wearing long, black cloaks.

Slowly, he climbs. Each step a challenge of oily, slippery stone. He hoists his knee onto the next platform and then rolls forward into the torrent of rushing water. Again and again, desperate to avoid the slip that would send him crashing to the bottom.

The monotony of the rain and the climb weakens him. He must make it. So much depends on it.

The people above wait silently. As he nears he sees there are only ten. Someone is missing. There is no time to wait.

The Temporatii are assembled. Soon it will begin. They will all, soon, begin again. They must lay a path before the girl and separate the pieces. Only she has the potential to bring them together safely.

She must put right, what humankind has done so badly wrong.

The nearest figure turns. One-by-one, they all do. Low hoods obscure their faces. The water runs off their perfectly waterproof cloaks.

Izzy's dad rushes to the summit and stands before the queue. He has no time to wait for the missing member of their group.

"When the portal is open," he shouts above the rain, "You must be bold. We must move quickly. It is now or never. For all of us. We believe time slipping through a portal like this destroys the memory. If you do it again, it will kill you. You will remember one thing: your mission. You are each going to your pre-ordained time. You must help the Time Child. You will know her when she comes. Watch for the Time Shadow. He will follow her."

He turns and opens his hand. An object glints in the darkness and he waves his arms in front of him.

As he does, a silver light appears in thin air above the top step as if summoned. It fizzles like a sparkler and races downwards, before stopping at knee-height.

A small, stocky figure steps forward. A grey beard betrays his attempt at anonymity and Izzy's dad recognises him instantly.

The old man reaches for the hanging line of silvery light. For a moment his hands seem to disappear into the brightness. He pulls it open, like a heavy pair of curtains, and is engulfed by a dazzling white beam.

For a second the world itself seems to bend. The line of people appear distorted, as if reflected in a curved mirror. The pyramid protrudes slightly from the source of the light.

The rain is illuminated like tiny crystals now falling in an arc, repelled by the beam. The very fabric of the world has been pulled apart at the seam. A gateway to another place. A portal opened to another time.

The man heaves and stretches the opening further. He looks down the line, nods and steps into the opening. And disappears.

The hanging line of light pops back into place and everything around them appears to ripple and shimmer. It settles like a pond and normality is restored.

At the top of the pyramid, the queue of people climb to the next step.

Robert opens the Tumble Thunder in his hand and the golden glow illuminates his face in the darkness. He walks down the line of the group, stopping three times to remove something from the Tumble Thunder and pass it on to his people. With the last, the pocket watch's glow fades.

One-by-one they pull open the fabric of the world and climb through it, into the blinding light. Each one causing reality to first distort, and then shimmer back into place.

Izzy's dad knows they will forget everything about this world; this time. Only the memory of the coming child will remain in their new timelines. That's how they had designed it. Just the select few of the group would be allowed to travel back through time with their memories intact. It was the only safe way.

Eventually, only Izzy's dad remains.

The rain remains heavy. He can still taste it. A lightning strike illuminates the desolation of the square. It is almost surgically devoid of life and humanity.

He puts his hands into the light and begins to heave it apart.

"Robert! Robert!" a faint and desperate voice calls over the rain. He lets go of the portal and turns.

"Robert. Wait."

"Where have you both been?" he asks. "I had given up on you."

Chapter 19

Izzy could feel the rain on her own face as she watched her dad. It was wet, cold and, it smelled…

"Urrrggghh! Stop it, Greysock."

The dog's tongue was rough against her face as she opened her eyes. She pushed him away in disgust and used her sleeve to wipe her cheek clean of his sticky drool.

"Ewwww. Don't do that again. That was gross," she said, blinking against the light. She was still getting used to how heightened all of her senses were.

Greysock wagged his tail excitedly and bark-whined. It made her smile. She'd never heard a dog do that before.

Pulling herself up onto her elbows she yawned and stretched.

What was her dad doing? Who were the people and what was the portal? Who was the Time Child and who had shouted at him?

When her dad had first gone away her *Seeings* had disappeared too. But since her birthday, since the Tumble Thunder, things had changed quickly. Now it felt like she was struggling to get through a full day without something changing, or her powers - *yes, my powers* - getting stronger. She was beginning to understand, that her dreams weren't dreams at all. She was seeing the future. But a future where her dad had already been.

"But try explaining all of that to someone, Isabella. They'd think you were bonkers," she told her attic bedroom. "Including Porter."

But it wasn't just that. She felt that sharing it with anyone, even her mum, would put them in danger. In truth she didn't know what to do for the best. It was like she was making it up as she went along.

Greysock plonked his head on her bed. She was sure he was listening.

She picked up *Dad Dreams* from her desk and wrote everything down. It had started as a way of ordering her thoughts. It had become a journal of everything odd that had happened to her. It seemed everything was linked, but she was only now beginning to understand what it all meant.

Greysock drank greedily from a bowl of water she'd brought up the night before. He sat next to the door and watched her write. He didn't move as she dressed or performed her pre-breakfast watch-fixing routine. When she ate with her mum, he sat by her side in the kitchen.

"That's the most patient dog I think I've ever seen," said Jane, over their porridge. "He must have been trained by someone. Leave him here today. He'll be fine with me."

"I know. Sometimes I think he's just watching me," replied Izzy, pulling on her school blazer and grabbing her bag. "See you later, Mum."

Greysock followed Izzy out of the kitchen, padded to the top of the stairs and bark-whined at her.

"What's up boy?" she turned, smiling at the whine that followed the bark. "Sorry. I keep forgetting that you'll need a wee too."

He scuttled down the two flights of stairs, passed the professor's flat, and into the shop. Her schoolbag over her shoulder, Izzy held him by the collar as she opened the old shop door. It was before eight, but the street was busy already. People in suits and smart clothes looked miserable as they made their way to work through the Monday morning drizzle.

Greysock looked out and slowly walked through the open door. Tentatively he sniffed the ground and then sat bolt upright. His eyes were fixed dead ahead.

"What's up, boy?" she said.

The dog didn't waiver.

"Hey! You okay?" she added, and momentarily let go of his collar to bend down.

Greysock darted two metres into Foubert's Place, turned, barked at her, and ran off towards Kingly Street. He dashed left and away from the busy traffic.

"Hey!" Izzy ran after him and splashed in a puddle from a drain as she turned the corner. "Eeww." She wiped the dirty water from her legs and looked up.

There, standing obediently next to George, was Greysock. He circled the old man's legs, seemingly being careful not to knock over his morning coffee, and nestled at the side of his new friend.

"Hey, Izzy. Is this little man yours by any chance?" said George, offering the dog a small piece of a morning croissant without looking down.

"Well, kind of," she said, as she came to a stop. "He found me yesterday and now he won't leave my side. Well, at least not until I let him out for a wee. But I've got to go to school and I can't take him."

"Well, let me see," said George, pushing his hand into a deep coat pocket and producing an old piece of rope. "Now what have we here?"

Much to Izzy's amazement, Greysock didn't move. George made a simple loop with the rope and slipped it into the dog's collar.

"There. Perfect. Why don't you leave him here with me and get him later? I'm sure he'll help me make conversation with a few more folk. I'll pop by and let your mum know."

"I didn't know you knew my mum," she said, slightly taken aback.

"Oh, Izzy," he said reassuringly. "I know everyone. I've been here forever."

Izzy frowned but didn't mind, "Okay," she said, and quickly replaced her school shoes with her old trainers, before heading off.

She didn't see Porter until the second lesson of the day. It was science with Mrs Mainwaring.

Neither of them had been in trouble with her since they'd ended up in front of the headteacher, together. Even the Phoneys seemed to have settled down recently.

After Izzy had covered Harriet and Georgia in pudding and almost committed a custard assault on Ellie, an uneasy stalemate had descended. When they passed in the corridor there was the occasional snigger or comment. But unless Ellie had both of her Phoneys with her, she generally just passed with an indignant silence.

Izzy felt they were bound to stage something sooner or later. But she also thought that they had become wary of her. They were scared of Porter too. When it came to it, he was bigger than any of them. Either way, it meant that things had been easier.

Until that morning.

Izzy and Porter had taken their seats alongside each other when the Phoneys strolled in. Ellie had an air of malevolence about her. Harriet and Georgia followed close behind, arm in arm and giggling to each other.

"Morning weirdos," said Ellie as she passed. She kicked Porter's bag under the desk with a flick of her shoe. Her ponytail looked even more severe than normal. Her hair so tight her eyebrows were pulled back and up giving her the air of a surprised cat.

Izzy rolled her eyes but otherwise ignored her. Porter clenched his fists on the table. Under his white school shirt, Izzy noticed a gravy stain. He was still wearing the white t-shirt from Sunday lunch the day before.

"Get lost Ellie. And you two idiots," he said to her disciples behind her. "I can't be doing with you lot today."

"Just ignore them," said Izzy as the Phoneys settled three rows back.

They were sneakily bombarded for almost the entire lesson. A variety of rubbers and rolled up paper mixed with spit landed on their desk, heads or faces when Mrs Mainwaring wasn't looking.

Izzy ignored it. But after the fifth rolled up piece of wet paper had stuck to his face, Porter picked up his textbook and turned to throw it. Izzy grabbed his arm just before he launched the missile.

His eyes were bulging. His face was red. Izzy shook her head and lowered his arm.

"And that, is how soundwaves work. Now anyone care to explain it back to me?" said Mrs Mainwaring turning from the whiteboard. She'd been scribbling incoherently and rambling for the best part of two minutes with her back to the class. "Erm, what's going on Izzy? Porter? Everything all right?"

"Fine Miss," said Porter, through gritted teeth, still looking at Izzy. Then, smiling, he added, "I think Ellie knows the answer."

"Good, then I'll be delighted to hear it. Ellie?" She looked at the head Phoney expectantly.

Ellie looked up with a blank expression. She looked to Harriet and Georgia for inspiration but found nothing. She looked down at her page of empty notes and doodles of puppies' faces, and then back up at the teacher.

"Well. I think. Erm. That. You know," she muttered, her face flushing red. "I don't know."

"Then I suggest you pay more attention and stop messing about in my class, you silly girl!" snapped Mrs Mainwaring. Her voice was cold. Ellie looked like her head was trying to shrink into her neck.

Izzy and Porter smirked. It was a small, but satisfying, triumph.

Mrs Mainwaring clapped her own textbook closed and wrapped up the lesson while the bell was still sounding. Izzy and Porter grabbed their bags and were the first down the corridor. They had just passed the geography block, when she heard Ellie and the Phoneys behind them.

"Oi! Tree Trunk! Think that was funny, do you?"

It was Ellie. Her lips were pursed and her eyes raged.

At the sound of her voice, everyone else in the corridor backed up against the wall to get out of her path.

Ellie was flanked by Harriet and Georgia. They took their lead from the friend they adored and dropped their bags to the floor with a thump. They crossed their arms.

"Well," said Izzy before Porter could respond, "it was actually pretty funny, yes. But if you just want to carry on throwing spit balls like you're in nursery then feel free."

"You shut up. Shouldn't you be at home crying over your missing daddy? Why don't you take Tree Trunk with you and cuddle up together? Maybe your dad has shacked up with his parents. I hear they've all run off too."

"Why don't you just get stuffed, cat face?" said Porter, clenching his fists at the mention of his mum and dad. His face had turned a slightly darker shade and Izzy was sure his eyes welled up, ever so slightly.

At the sight of her new best friend's hurt, Izzy felt the molten ball of the *fuzziness* rise up in her chest in an almost protective reflex. She glanced up at the white plastic clock on the wall and concentrated as the red second-hand ticked idly past 12. The minute hand clicked onto five. She took a deep breath, searching for the calm Dad promised would come.

Ellie pulled her ponytail tighter, put her hands on her hips and tilted her head at the pair of them. For a few seconds the groups stared at each other.

"Why don't you try and make me, Tree Trunk? Or you, daddy's little weirdo?" said Ellie, turning to Izzy.

At that, the *fuzziness* spun into life and demanded to be set free. Izzy's vision went temporarily hazy and she closed her eyes.

The pure rage reared up her chest from the depths of her stomach. She was ready to explode. But instead of losing herself, Izzy took a deep breath and held it steady. Unlike she'd ever been able to do before, she forced it not to move.

Her eyes fixed on Ellie who was, in turn, staring at Porter. Izzy allowed herself a smile as the *fuzziness* curled up like a ball of energy next to her heart. She could feel it pulsing, like a caged comet. She felt its heat and glanced up at the clock. The second hand ticked idly past… the 12 and the minute hand ticked silently to five.

Again?

Izzy had watched it do that already, just a few seconds ago.

A wave of dējā vu rushed over her.

Like before, Ellie pulled her ponytail tighter, put her hands on her hips and tilted her head at them.

Just as Ellie opened her mouth to speak, Izzy cut in. She was smiling. She knew what was coming. She'd seen it.

The ball of *fuzziness* and energy in her chest hovered in place. Izzy couldn't hide her delight at controlling it for the first time ever.

"Before you start, no, we don't want to make you. His name isn't Tree Trunk and I am most definitely not daddy's little weirdo. So, erm, goodbye," smiled Izzy.

With that, she quickly turned Porter round and the pair walked off, arms locked in defiance. Ellie and the Phoneys were left without the fight they'd been craving.

"Coward!" Ellie called after them in desperation. Her face shocked. Her body tense for a fight that wasn't going to happen.

Izzy turned and waved at the three phoneys.

"Bye then," she said with a beaming smile.

She pushed the *fuzziness* down into her stomach. In a split second she felt the molten ball contract, and then disappear, with its tell-tale pop.

"Izzy," whispered a clearly confused Porter. "What just happened?"

"I saw her say it before it happened. I've never done that before."

For the first time since her dad had left, she'd experienced a *Seeing* while she was awake. Even better than that, she'd controlled the *fuzziness*. Usually, it exploded and led to her being expelled from another school. Not today. Today she had put it away as a wave of control and reassurance had washed over her; through her. Just like when she used the Tumble Thunder.

Her smile was so wide her face ached. She felt she was beginning to understand.

They passed the headteacher's office just as he appeared from his own lunch break.

"Oh, hello you two. Are you okay?" said Mr Tomkins, adjusting his red waistcoat.

"You know, Mr Tomkins, we're just fine," said Izzy, glancing into the office and noticing the grandfather clock she'd admired on her last visit was gone. "In fact, we're better than ever."

"Are we?" said Porter to Izzy, who was almost carrying him down the corridor in her state of triumph.

"Yes," she said. "Yes, we are."

"Okay," he said, and shrugged.

Ducking round the corner past the headmaster, Izzy stopped them both and looked around.

"Porter," she whispered. "Are you okay?"

"Course I am. Why wouldn't I be?"

"It's just what Ellie said about your mum and dad. Is that true?" asked Izzy, hoping she hadn't upset him.

"Kind of, not really," said Porter. "They just work a lot. It's really just my sister and me."

"Okay, if you're sure," said Izzy, tightening her own ponytail. "Porter, will you cover for me this afternoon? Tell the teachers I'm not well or something. I need to get home and try something. I think I know what to do."

Chapter 20

Dodging out of the school gates and out of sight, she ran almost all of the way home.

Porter had looked wounded when she hadn't asked him to go with her. It wasn't that she didn't need him. It was more that she felt the next step was one for her to take alone. For both of their sakes.

Out of breath from her run home, she barely shouted a proper hello as she passed George. Greysock bark-whined what seemed like an apology at the old man and scampered after his new owner. She rushed through the clock shop with the dog at her heels and bounded up the stairs. With a cursory greeting to her mum, she almost crash landed into her chair at the desk.

Adrenaline pumping through her body she took the Tumble Thunder from its secret drawer, the familiar *clunk* presenting it to her. Holding it in the palm of her hand she stared at the face. The warm, controlled *fuzziness* was still faint in her chest. It was the key to everything. It must be. Being able to control the *fuzziness* at school had convinced her she'd be able to control this too. All she had to do was focus.

Then she'd be able to complete the next task and find her dad.

The timepiece sat in her hand. The fine gold leaf detail and pointed hands stared back at her. She felt the edges of the warmth that had consumed her when she'd first ended up in the woods in Scotland.

She waited for it to happen again. For the strength to wash over her as she slipped through time.

Greysock sat beside her and nuzzled into her hip. Her hand slipped through his collar, and she took a deep breath.

Nothing.

She waited. Her eyes and mind focused on the face of the old pocket watch.

Nothing.

She fiddled with the dials on the side and closed her eyes, attempting to summon the *fuzziness* from her chest.

Nope.

Frowning, she held the Tumble Thunder up grandly in front of her. She took another breath.

"Take me through time," she commanded.

Nothing happened. Greysock yawned.

"Make me slip through time," she said again, her voice faltering at the edges.

Greysock laid down and sighed.

Izzy caught herself in the mirror. Her hair was messy. Her school uniform was crumpled. Her arm was high in the air and she was commanding a pocket watch to make her time travel.

"What are you doing?" she asked her reflection. Her arm dropped. So did her mood.

The heady mixture of adrenaline, empowerment and elation that had jet-powered her home and made her ignore her new friend, shrivelled into a tiny black spot in her chest. Silently, it stepped into the shadows.

What replaced it was Porter's disappointed face and an overwhelming feeling of guilt at how she'd treated him.

With the guilt pangs pulling on her insides, she tried again the next morning before school. And the next.

"Take me there." Concentrating. Nothing.

"Now: Work." Gritting her teeth and staring hard at the second hand to calm herself. Nada.

"I command you," didn't work either.

"Please?"

Not. A. Thing. She wanted to cry.

By Friday morning, she'd given up. The *fuzziness* was in hiding. Hibernating deep in the cave behind her chest. She'd gone from a feeling of total control, to total helplessness and desolation.

The rules of the Tumble Thunder and the *fuzziness* were a mystery to her again.

She didn't understand why she couldn't call it, or why it didn't work on her command. Having begun to believe that she was special, she suddenly felt very ordinary. The sharpness it had brought to her vision and her keener hearing, seemed to have faded too, as if her lack of belief affected them.

"Fine then. See if I care," she said, in frustration.

She opened the secret compartment in her desk. The Tumble Thunder clanged as it landed, then she slammed the draw back on its hidden latch.

* * *

Despite the start of the weekend, Izzy walked home from school feeling gloomy that Friday afternoon. She hadn't seen Porter since she'd sprinted home and left him in the corridor on Monday. He'd been off ill since then and she hadn't heard from him. Without Porter she was friendless again. She knew she'd upset him and felt terrible. Though he had a slightly odd passion for crisps, she'd never met a friend who had looked out for her in the way he did. She hoped she hadn't ruined their blossoming friendship.

Without Porter, she went out of her way to avoid people as much as possible. It had been her mission to be invisible and avoid any more trouble with Ellie and the Phoneys. She'd just about managed it.

Crossing Great Marlborough Street, she passed under the stone arches into Kingly Street. Strangely, for a Friday afternoon, it was largely empty away from the hustle and bustle of Oxford Circus. A few tourists were taking pictures of the old Clachan Pub, just up from the clock shop. They didn't give Izzy a second glance.

Opposite the pub, George was sitting, leaning back against the wall. His gloves were off. They lay neatly folded on top of his old fedora. Greysock was sleeping beside him, his head on the old man's thigh. She realised she'd never actually seen her homeless friend sit down in all the years she'd known him. It was worrying.

"Hey George," she said quietly. Greysock opened his eyes at the sound of her voice and his tail wagged furiously.

"Well, hello Isabella," said George, with a huge smile, and his familiar, gentle warmth. "Today has been a fine day. Your little pal here has been keeping me company. I was given the tastiest sandwich for my lunch. Hey, where's your smile? You left it at school?"

Izzy pushed her mouth wider, in a flat, fake attempt.

"I don't know, George. I just don't feel like it."

"Well, you know miss, nothing is ever as bad as you think. Nothing. I've been living out here for as long as, well, for longer than you'd understand. And I'm okay."

Izzy had never understood why George was always positive. She realised too, she'd never actually asked him anything about himself.

"George," she began, tentatively. "Why are you always in a good mood? It must be horrible being outside all the time. Sleeping in the cold and stuff."

He smiled again and untied the makeshift leash from the neck of the now wide-awake border collie.

"Well, Isabella, things aren't always as bad as they seem. Or as bad as they look. Take me. I don't sleep outside little miss, oh no. Now, don't tell anyone, but a few years back, when I was just strolling around, I found a secret way into a disused basement. It's not the Ritz, but it's free and no one seems to care. I've slept there every night since."

"But what if someone finds out?" asked Izzy, feeling guilty that she'd been feeling sorry for herself.

"Maybe they will," he said. "But I doubt it. I think it's just meant to be. Some things are. I'm just grateful for what I have and I like being around here. I feel like it's my neighbourhood. Reckon all these folks would be lost without Old George, maybe even you too."

"If you say so," she said, shrugging. "Come on Greysock. See you tomorrow, George. Thanks for looking after him."

The old man got to his feet slowly. He picked up his hat and fingerless gloves with dirty hands and bowed extravagantly in front of her.

"It was my pleasure for a special friend. Adios, farewell, au revoir, ta-ta for now," he said, and patted Greysock on his flank as the dog also stood.

"Aww, thanks ," she said and smiled for the first time that week. Giving George a friendly wave, she turned for home.

"I'll be looking out for you," he shouted after her.

Her Mum was just polishing the Churchill picture when Izzy appeared at the counter. Greysock was at her heels.

"Hey Mum. Hey Professor. How was Egypt?" she said, as the door closed behind her, causing the old bell to jangle. The professor looked up from the clock he was fixing. He gazed at Izzy through a magnifying glass attached to his spectacles. It made his eye seem twice as big as in real life.

"It was illuminating, Izzy. Illuminating," he said intriguingly, and went back to his work.

He didn't offer any more. Izzy wasn't in the mood to ask.

"You okay, Izzy?" her mum asked. "Have you remembered it's Nan's special weekend? We're on the six o'clock train. You'd better get a move on."

"Oh, yeah," said Izzy, her mood lifting at the mention of Nan. "Of course."

She rushed forward and hugged her mum. Holding her tight. Greysock sat at Izzy's side and looked up at them both.

Jane looked at Professor Wigglesworth over her daughter's shoulder as she held her. The professor gave a single nod of acknowledgement.

"Come on," he said, breaking the moment. "Let's see how ready you are."

"Ready for what?" it was a strange thing to say.

"Never mind," he said, hurrying on. "There's a couple of tourists who look like they're coming our way. See if you can guess what they're after Izzy. You've always been good at that. Let's see if you're getting any better now you're older."

Still hugging her mum, Izzy moved them around like a pair of dancers.

"You're on," she said, with a smile.

There was nothing like a challenge to focus her mind. Before her dad had disappeared, Izzy had always thought that Professor Wigglesworth was aware of her *Seeing*. He used to challenge her to guess things she had no right to know. Things she shouldn't understand. But this was the first time he'd done it since the day she'd waved goodbye to her dad. He'd been smiling when he left. It was the main thing she could remember about him.

The tourists in Foubert's Place, looked to be in their mid-40s *and probably American*, she thought, judging by the combination of trainers, combat trousers and fanny packs. He was taller than she was and was undoubtedly more lost. She seemed to have an air of confidence about where they were. She was staring at the window. Examining the corners. Izzy concentrated, searching for any kind of feeling.

"Hmm, I'm not sure. Definitely American," she said, smiling. "I don't think they want anything beyond some free wifi. They definitely don't want one of those dodgy Chinese clocks."

A smile returned to her mum's face. She rolled her eyes and went back to cleaning the collection of cabinets that housed the shop's meagre displays.

The shop doorbell was followed by a question in broken English and a heavy French accent: "Exsqueeze me. Iz zer weefee I can use?"

The woman hung from her husband's arm, as if trying to attach herself to him. He held her tight. They moved forward clumsily, as if they weren't used to walking together.

The man leaned on the counter and took several deep breaths. It was like he was grateful to be sucking in the air. The professor didn't seem to mind and almost waited for him to finish.

After explaining that they didn't have broadband of any kind, the professor ushered the blonde-haired French woman out of the shop, though he allowed her to stop momentarily at the door while she glanced at the picture of Churchill. Usually, he didn't have time for people who weren't going to buy anything.

Before the couple headed out to Foubert's Place, the pair paused. Like the man had just seconds before, she seemed to take several deep breaths like a runner before a race. Whatever it was, both of them looked fresher than when they had entered the shop.

Izzy frowned at them. The breathing thing was weird.

"American, eh? At least you got the wifi bit right," he smiled at Izzy. She'd been sure they weren't European. They may as well have had 'American' stamped on their foreheads. Their accents weren't quite right either.

Izzy slid up to the window, hanging back just enough to stay out of sight, and watched them stroll down Foubert's Place. They walked quickly side by side, no longer arm-in-arm. They were a good metre apart. She watched them reach Kingly Street where they paused. The man said something to someone she couldn't see - in the direction of where she'd left George - and they both nodded. They turned toward Great Marlborough Street and disappeared out of sight.

Izzy stared in their direction for a few more seconds. She was puzzled. Nothing about them felt right.

Next to her, the professor flipped the sign that hung on the door from 'Open' to 'Closed'. He pulled down the blind that covered the glass. The professor and Izzy's mum went about covering the glass counters with red felt sheets to protect the watches from dust. Carefully, they put the shop to bed.

There was little that was modern about Wigglesworth and Son. The black and white stone tile floor reminded Izzy of an old-fashioned barber's shop. From the cabinets to the pictures on the wall, pretty much everything was old. The electronic till was the only semblance of the 21st century.

As far as Izzy could tell, the professor had spent almost his entire life worrying about keeping the clock shop going, and travelling the world looking for antiques. He loved the shop like it was a part of him. It was like his life depended on keeping it going.

Izzy looked out of the window again. There were more people about now. The odd French-American couple had gone.

Chapter 21

By half-past-eight their train was slowly pulling into the station at Great Chardan. The journey from London to Salisbury took less than an hour and a half on the train. Yet, the short distance to the little village where Nan had lived as long as Izzy could remember took another hour on the smaller rural line. She didn't think she'd always lived there, though Nan never talked about anywhere else. To Izzy it felt like a place that Nan had ended up, rather than loved to live. From her cottage, it was just a short walk to Salisbury plain and the ancient Stonehenge, the reason they were here.

Whatever the truth, Izzy couldn't wait to see her. She was desperate to ask Nan what she knew about the Tumble Thunder; and how it could lead to her dad.

Nestled between West Amesbury and Great Durnford in a small valley on the River Avon, Chardan was a blink-and-you-miss-it kind of place. Izzy didn't know how many people lived in the tiny village. She'd once counted only eight buildings. The train stopped here just twice a day; once in the morning and once in the evening. Even that felt too often. If you came by car, the turning from the main road was masked by high hedges that must have been four metres tall. It was easy to drive past it. Most people did.

Izzy and her mum had been the only people on the train. Now they were the only people on the platform. As the carriages disappeared around a slight bend on the single track, edged by thick trees, Greysock gave a bark-whine in the train's direction. He hadn't left Izzy's side for the entire journey. First, he'd padded in her footsteps through London. Then he sat nestled against her legs on the first train, before curling up in an empty seat next to her on the second.

The three of them stood in momentary silence. In the trees behind the platform a blackbird was in full song.

"It's beautiful, isn't it?" said Izzy's mum, picking up her worn, brown rucksack. "The sound of the countryside. You forget how noisy London is. No wonder your nan chose this place rather than to live with us. Come on."

She set off down the platform slope without explaining. Izzy looked after her, wondering what she meant, before following. Greysock fell in behind.

They pushed through a white gate that gave a miserable groan from its old hinges. The pathway that led to Great Chardan and Nan's house was just beyond. It was flanked on both sides by overgrown hawthorn bushes. They had joined at the top to create a tunnel, concealing the path from the rolling hills either side. It was a village that did its best not to be found.

The evening sun was just beginning to dip in the sky as they emerged onto the single road that led down into the village.

As the road dipped to the left and down a hill, a handful of cottages appeared before them. Like everything here, they seemed old and forgotten. They were all painted white, with thatched roofs. A gentle stream of smoke whispered from each chimney.

"Now, which one is it?" said Izzy's mum, stopping dead in the centre of the narrow road, but looking away from the cottages. Izzy and Greysock stopped too.

Her eyes scanned the left side of the hedges. They were covered in lengthening shadows from the evening sun.

"Aha," she said, and headed for a narrow opening just smaller than a doorway and easily missed. Unless you knew where to look, it was practically invisible. Through it there was a stony path that ran parallel to the line of hedges but hidden from the road.

They turned left again as the path led away from the hedge and the road, following a small stream that babbled towards the Avon. The thatched roofs were now all that could be seen of the rest of Great Chardan, a few hundred metres away.

As the stream turned right to gently disappear into a small valley, they came to Nan's cottage.

"There you are. Where on earth have you been?" came a loud but familiar voice.

Nan was standing on the red, painted doorstep wiping her hands. She wore a large apron and an even bigger smile. Around the front doorstep were two enormous plant pots filled with flowering lavender. Her dogs, a pair of overweight chocolate Labradors named Arthur and Bert barked a half-hearted welcome and disappeared back inside.

"Hello Betty," said Jane, greeting the old woman with a warm, but weary, smile.

Izzy rushed to her nan and they wrapped their arms around each other.

"I missed you, Nan," said Izzy, feeling relieved but unsure why. "Can I smell cake?"

"Course you can," replied Nan. She released Izzy and opened the doorway with a sweeping, welcoming arm that stopped at the third member of the travelling party. "Who's this chap?"

"He's Greysock, Nan. He kind of found me, and now he follows me everywhere," said Izzy. She rubbed the dog's head before heading into the small kitchen to investigate the smell.

"Found you, you say? Well, Mr Greysock," she addressed the dog directly. "Don't be stealing food from my boys. And no peeing in the house."

Greysock stared at her, and the pair considered each other for a moment. His ears stood up and he leaned forward on his front legs in an extravagant bow. Satisfied that the old lady covered in flour was a friend, he stood up and dashed inside. He brushed against her legs as he went.

A huge Victoria sponge was waiting on the stonework surface in the kitchen. A generous slice was on a smaller side plate, with some ice-cold milk.

Nan had prepared the same thing for Izzy for as long as she could remember. Her annual visit for midsummer's day always began the same way: the warmest of greetings and an amazingly fluffy cake. The summer solstice on June 21 was special for her Nan. Though Izzy always enjoyed being part of the crowds when they visited Stonehenge to see the sun rise, for Nan it was the highlight of the year. It was as if being around the old stone circle on this one day refreshed her. It had been the same with her dad. Izzy felt it too. She always left feeling invigorated. That there was something like magic in the air, just for a few hours. Strangely, it never affected her mum in the same way.

Izzy wasn't sure exactly how old her Nan was. She'd asked her once without getting a straight answer and Izzy had settled on, 'around 80'.

Whatever her actual age, Nan became practically giddy when midsummer's day came around. She daubed their faces in bright paint, dressed them all in garlands of fresh lavender and lilies and made them wear flowing white lace dresses. In truth, they were barely recognisable.

Jane had once whispered to Izzy that it was just because Nan was a hippy, stuck in the 1970s. Izzy just thought it was an excuse to pretend to be young again. Because it clearly made her Nan so happy, she went along with it.

But for the last two visits, things hadn't quite been the same. Nothing had been the same since Dad left. Izzy still felt excitement at being around the huge circle of stones and she felt invigorated just like before. Yet the joy had gone, despite the smiling and the dancing. Izzy never understood why Nan still enjoyed it so much with her only son missing.

Except that he wasn't totally gone. The note with the Tumble Thunder in the desk had proved that.

Halfway through a mouthful of cake, she almost choked.

The desk! The desk that Nan had brought because her dad wanted her to have it.

That led to the Tumble Thunder.

Because Nan knew her dad was still alive - and THAT'S why she doesn't miss him. She knows.

Why didn't I realise before?

Because Stonehenge reminds her of him. And he's still alive, isn't he?

"Tuck in, Isabella. Tuck in." Nan watched her eat the cake and pulled out one of the even older chairs.

"Thanks Nan," said Izzy, as best she could through jam, cream and a wide grin.

The molten *fuzziness* in her chest had risen up to say hello. But it wasn't through anger or fear. She felt happy. For the first time in a long time, she wasn't just hoping her dad was alive. Suddenly, she could feel it more strongly than ever.

Her senses responded too, rushing back to full throttle like before. The strengthened smell from the cake was like a heady nectar.

Being with Nan in her strange little cottage, she felt closer to her dad than ever.

The kitchen, like the rest of the cottage, was basic. There was an oven of sorts. A line of cupboards against the wall near the back door and the small table at which Izzy sat. Nan lived a simple life. She only had a cold tap and no washing machine. When she needed hot water for a bath or to wash some clothes, she boiled an old-fashioned kettle or a pan on the stove. The only warmth in the cottage came from a portable gas heater she moved from room to room.

Izzy loved Nan dearly. But even she thought her lifestyle was a little, well, odd. She forbade Izzy and her mum to visit at any other time apart from the summer solstice at Stonehenge. It was like she was trying to live without disturbing the world.

"I love you all, dears, but I do like my own space," she'd told Izzy once. Instead, she visited London when she could, but Izzy still wished she saw more of her.

The cottage consisted of the kitchen, a small lounge and two bedrooms. There were old fireplaces in every room, but none were ever lit. There were very few ornaments or decorations. Just a big, simple vase of lavender in every room. It was Nan's favourite and smelled so strongly that it filled the whole cottage. There were a handful of pictures on the wall; Nan was the only person who seemed to have pictures of Izzy as a baby. She had one of Nan and her dad holding her wrapped in a blanket. There were no baby pictures of her with her mum. Neither were there any of the grandad she had never met. Nan never spoke about him.

While Izzy finished her cake and tried to work out how to get Nan on her own for some gentle questioning, Nan prepared some sandwiches and a picnic for the next morning.

Her mum unpacked what few things they'd brought with them in the spare bedroom. There was just one bed. Izzy always slept outside in the small garden in an old tent. Her dad had stowed it in the spare bedroom years earlier. Despite being away from home, Izzy still brought the teddy Dad had bought her. She hated sleeping without it - when she'd found herself in Scotland with Aleck she'd missed its familiar smell as she drifted off.

With everything put away and the picnic ready in Nan's old wicker basket, the three generations of the Latimer family sat in the garden and watched the sun go down.

Nan insisted on hearing every last detail about the shop and what Professor Wigglesworth had been up to. She always asked lots of questions about the professor, even though she seemed to enjoy not getting on with him. She virtually interrogated Izzy about 'that nice boy', Porter. Jane seemed to spend her entire time defending both the professor and Porter from her questions. The more Nan asked, the more Izzy giggled. It felt like being in the cottage had taken all of her worries away, though she was still desperate to get Nan on her own.

The evening sun changed from its golden glow, to an orange hue as it dipped below the horizon. The few clouds in the sky lit up a pinky-red. Just before it finally gave out on the day, Nan gently took Izzy's hand.

She pulled an old, battered envelope from her apron, and handed it to her granddaughter.

"I found this the other day," she said. "I thought you should have it. It will help." She smiled widely through reddened eyes, and rubbed the scar on her neck. It was at least five centimetres long and ran from underneath her jaw toward the centre of her throat. Izzy had asked her once how it had happened.

"I had a fight with a bad man when I was very young," she'd said and her blue eyes had sparkled. "He thought he killed me. But your old nan is still hiding out here. Still a part of things."

Today, her blue eyes were ringed in red. Izzy knew she'd been crying.

In the envelope was a photograph. It was slightly faded at the edges.

"Oh my God. What do I have on? My hair!" said Izzy.

"I thought you'd like that. You loved those dungarees, and those pigtails," said her nan, wrapping an arm around her. They laughed gently. "You're about six there. Your dad always took you to Greenwich. He loved it there too. Do you remember?"

Izzy stared at the picture and thought hard. Concentrating. The *fuzziness* flashed by, like a shooting star, bright and fast, then gone.

Though the colour was faded from the picture, her dad's blue eyes still shone out. Just like they did in her dreams. They were almost as bright as the dungarees she was wearing.

"I remember," said Izzy, as it gradually came back. "We went there so often I think I could even remember the way. He was obsessed with the place."

In the picture her dad had one arm around her shoulder. With the other, he was leaning against a wall beneath a clock.

"He's doing that thing," said her mum, leaning in. "Whenever he leaned against something, he'd tuck his outside three fingers in. Never understood that."

Izzy remembered how her dad would do that, too. As if he were about to shoot her with a finger gun.

Without thinking, she kissed the picture and held it out for Nan.

"You keep it. He'd want you to have it now, I'm sure of that," said Nan, pushing it back in her granddaughter's direction.

Izzy's mum stood up abruptly. She briefly turned away to wipe her face.

"Right," she said, taking a deep breath and pushing it out noisily. "I think it's time for bed."

Izzy caught her wiping an escapee tear from her left cheek as she headed inside. She dabbed at her face again just before she disappeared through the back door.

"Nan," said Izzy, breaking the momentary silence, and deciding to chance it. "You know he's alive, don't you?"

Nan's eyes flickered slightly in the fading daylight. She toyed nervously with the apron she'd worn all day. Gradually, the thinnest of smiles appeared.

"You're beginning to work it out," she said. "I can't say more. It's down to you. Wherever he went. I know he misses us. I know he misses you. What he did, he did for you."

"Okay, but why?" the question trailed off in the cooling air. "If he left on purpose, then why doesn't he just come back? I miss him, Nan. I miss him so much."

Her Nan smiled and looked straight at her granddaughter.

"You'll work it out," she said, with a confident smile. "It's more important than you know. But you must do it alone. For all our sakes'."

"But Nan," Izzy began in protest.

"No Isabella," interrupted Nan. "It's not for me to say. It's for you to work out. It's well past my bedtime, and tomorrow is a big day."

With that she got up, walked over to her dogs, patted them both goodnight and followed Jane into the cottage.

"She knows," she said to Greysock, as the sun finally gave up on the day and dipped below the horizon.

Chapter 22

Slightly bleary-eyed from less than four hours sleep, it had taken less than half an hour to walk up to Stonehenge.

Izzy had woken to the sound of Nan shouting into the garden at the dogs.

She'd barely felt awake when she'd put on the white flowing dress and smiled as Nan painted her face. She didn't even complain when Nan put three sprigs of lavender in her hair. Secretly, she liked dressing up like this. It felt right, somehow.

"Here we are. Our favourite spot," said Nan, twirling around like a teenager. She threw a picnic blanket onto the damp grass.

Betty had clearly been up longer than the rest of

them. Her short hair was braided against her head. She wore a garland of lavender around her neck, while a straw hat that was decorated with even more of the scented, purple flowers was perched precariously on her head. Her face, like Izzy's and her mum's, was daubed in butterflies and painted petals. Greysock had refused to stay at home with Bert and Arthur. He was also sporting some lavender around his collar, just for good measure.

There were thousands of people there. Izzy didn't think she'd ever seen so many at Stonehenge before.

In the past couple of years, after her dad had disappeared, being back here had felt hard. This year though, she wasn't sad at all. She felt closer to her dad than at any time since he'd disappeared. She was going to see him again. The *fuzziness* in her chest wasn't spinning, it was dancing a waltz.

Ahead of them, the sky was brightening. The giant rocks that made up Stonehenge stood black against the dawn.

Izzy's Nan always set up their picnic on the south-western side of the outside circle of the main monument. It meant that when the sun rose over the famous stones, they would get the best view. The actual main circle of stones was always crowded. Stonehenge was made up of almost 100 huge rocks with some that were as high as a double decker bus. How they'd been built, without any modern machinery, impressed Izzy as much as it baffled her.

The stones were so tall Izzy worried they might fall on someone. She always avoided going too close, even though they'd been in place for 3,000 years.

This year the crowd seemed denser than ever. Though it wasn't quite light enough to make them out properly, figures moved around in the distance. Some were dancing. Where the fields opened into Salisbury Plain beyond, a low white mist hovered above the ground.

"Ah Betty, there you are darling. I thought you weren't coming," said a tall woman, appearing out of the receding gloom.

"Hello Emma. You look splendid as ever," said Nan. They hugged as if they were long, lost friends.

Nan turned and introduced Emma to Izzy, and then Jane.

"Pleased to meet you," said Izzy, politely.

"Hello," said Jane.

"Ah, you must be the famous Izzy," said Emma, largely ignoring Jane. "Your nan talks about you all of the time."

Nan and Emma hushed their voices while they talked, amid the general hubbub and laughter in the crowds around them. Emma was much younger than her nan, even than her mum. She wore a garland of bright yellow flowers that matched her blonde hair and a white lacy dress. It was similar to the ones Nan insisted they all wear. Izzy wasn't sure if she remembered her from the previous year, but she was sure she'd seen her somewhere before. Annoyingly, she couldn't place where.

After a few moments of hushed talking, Emma said goodbye. She wandered back into a small crowd of people just out of earshot. One of them, a stockily built man with a thick moustache, watched her return. Emma whispered something to him. He caught Izzy's eye. They looked at each other for a second and the couple disappeared into the gloom.

"Who was that, Nan?" asked Izzy. She rubbed her neck uncomfortably where the face paint had begun to irritate her skin.

"An old, old friend. I've known her a long, long time. More years than you'd know," said Nan, with a mischievous smile.

"Hey. It's almost sunrise," said Jane. "The sky's really clear. It's going to be beautiful. There are so many more people here this year, too."

Izzy took it all in. The sky was brightening. There were all sorts of people. Some looked like they'd been preparing for a year, with flasks, hiking boots and waterproof walking coats. But there were a healthy handful of others, like Izzy, her mum and Nan, who looked like hippies from the 1970s. They were adorned with purple flowers. The women wore flowing dresses and the men wore loose-fitting white shirts and linen trousers with sandals.

Despite the silly clothes Izzy always felt at home here. Since her dad had disappeared, it was one of the few times and places where she still felt happy, despite it being where he'd left. It was a feeling of belonging she only normally got from the clock shop.

As she looked around, the morning broke over the horizon and a strange hush descended on the huge crowd.

For what must have been a full five minutes, not a single person spoke. The skylarks welcoming the dawn from high above offered a backing track to the rising sun. A brilliant light spread across Stonehenge and the crowds looking on. Izzy saw the shadows dip away as a golden hue washed over the stones. Some people shielded their eyes. Others wore sunglasses.

"Good morning, Starshine," said Nan, in a distant, cooey voice.

Suddenly there was a crash of breaking wood and shouting in the direction of the main stone circle.

Izzy strained her neck to see what was going on. The shouting turned quickly into a muffled, heated argument. Greysock barked. Within seconds, things were flying through the air near the main circle 50 metres ahead of them. People began to panic and barge others out of the way.

"Shush, Greysock," said Izzy, stroking down the raised heckles on the back of his neck.

"Come on, Jane. Izzy, we need to move. I don't like this. Let's go," said Nan. She hastily swept up some of the picnic things into the basket she'd brought.

"What's wrong?" asked Jane, shocked at Nan's changing mood.

"Hurry, Jane," Nan snapped. "She can't be found!"

"What's going on?" asked Izzy.

"Move," said her mum, picking up the picnic. "We need to go."

The tone of her mum's voice was enough to spark her into action.

Her mum didn't say anything else and Izzy followed, without hesitation. Nan held back, briefly, quickly finishing picking up the picnic they didn't have chance to enjoy. Izzy saw her remove her garland of lavender and scrunch it up in her hand. She scattered them on the floor all around them, as she walked back toward Izzy and Jane, ushering them away.

Izzy, her mum and Nan headed back to the cottage a different way from which they came. Her nan was out front, striding. Izzy was puzzled but knew better than to ask questions when her Nan was in a mood like this. They zig-zagged across fields and through valleys as the shadows grew shorter from the rising sun. No-one spoke. Finally, they emerged from alongside a hedgerow into Nan's garden. It had taken them an hour to walk back. The sun was fully up. Bert and Arthur wagged their tails happily as they entered the gate.

"Ok," said Izzy, as she sat down at the kitchen table. "What was that all about?"

"Jane, put the kettle on," said Nan, ignoring the question. "We need some tea. Then you need to think about your train home. It's almost time, Izzy."

Chapter 23

He'd arrived before the crowds. It was still dark but he didn't bring a torch. Instead, he had walked the entire perimeter of the old, grassed ditch that surrounded Stonehenge. He felt sure that she would be here. He had chuckled at the sight of so many people at the ancient stone circle. They thought it was mystical. He doubted many of them actually realised it's true magic. It's unique place in time. It was the same magic that he knew would bring the girl here. It had to. Her followers too. No matter the danger of them all congregating, the power of the stones on this single day was too big for them to ignore. He had returned every year looking for her. He had almost reached her once, but her father had led him away. It took an hour for him to understand he'd been tricked. When he returned, the girl was gone.

This time, he felt confident he would finally find her.

The journey had been long to reach Salisbury Plain. It had been many days since the time slips to Scotland that had left him drained. He was fully recovered and felt strong. The stone circle had that effect on those who understood it. Wherever he was, in whatever time, he could always return to Stonehenge on midsummer's day. It was like a beacon of energy for his kind. Still, he was keen to remain as hidden as possible. Not everyone understood it like him.

He stuck to the dark shadows near the biggest stones. His long, black trench coat kept him warm from the mist that hung in the air. As the sun came up, the crowds fell silent. Forced to stay still to avoid standing out, he scanned face after face.

Previous years had been like searching for a needle in a haystack. He knew he was looking for a girl, but he'd been unsure of exactly how old she would be in this time.

But after her 13th birthday, her coming of age, she had activated the Tumble Thunder. His own Tumble Thunder, constructed to mirror the use of the original, had drawn him to her through a connection he didn't fully understand.

It was only a matter of time before he would

find her. He knew she was here somewhere. And now he knew what she looked like. Her long, curly, blonde-brown hair was unmistakable. Turning slowly, he leaned against one of the old stones. He was so full of energy he was restless. In the sky, birds were singing. He wiped his face with his thin hands and stared around the crowd.

"Daddy. That mister looks weird," said a small boy, no older than five. A piece of chocolate was melting in his hand as he shoved it in his mouth.

"Shush, Mason," said a large woman through a mouthful of sandwich. She was wearing pink dungarees that looked a little too small.

"But he does, Mummy. Look. He's funny," added the boy, more loudly.

Several heads swivelled to look at the man with grey skin and the black trench coat. He stepped to his right, to dip behind the stone and out of sight. But instead of dipping out of view, he trod on the hand of a small girl who was ignoring the sunrise and sitting playing with a well-worn doll.

"Owwww," she shouted. "Dad!" She looked up at him with childish outrage.

"Hey! Watch where you're going, mate," said a gruff voice, nearby.

"Mason! You've made me spill my coffee now!" said pink dungarees woman. She stood up quickly, wiping her legs, and bumped roughly into her husband who sent another man sprawling as he tried to keep his own balance. As the second man landed, he went head-first into two deck chairs that cracked and splintered under his weight.

The serenity of the sunrise was replaced with an immediate chaos.

The solstice forgotten, a full-on shouting match erupted within the stone circles. Pink dungarees woman who had spilled her coffee, attempted to quieten well-worn doll girl, who was crying and holding her fingers. At the same time, gruff voice dad was now arguing loudly with deckchair man, who wore long shorts and hadn't taken kindly to being sent flying across the grass. People began shouting. A couple of things were thrown.

The weird mister in the black trench coat sidled around the stone, and away from the melee.

Not far away, a dog barked, and ended with a whine. That barking whine. He'd heard it before.

In a garden. In a garden in Scotland when he'd been hiding in the woods. The dog. Her dog!

Ignoring the hubbub behind, he began making his way in the direction of the bark as fast as he could through the crowd.

After 15 metres or so, he tried to pick up his pace, worried the dog and its special owner would be long gone. Pushing his way through, people began to turn in his direction. A woman with long blonde hair shook her head and refused to move. He ignored her, but a man with a thick moustache stepped into his path. For a moment they were locked in a dizzy dance. The man in the trench coat tried to skirt round the moustachioed blocker who briefly ducked and mirrored every movement. Then, as if bored of the gesture, the man stepped aside and allowed him to pass.

He followed the direction of the dog's bark-whine until he stumbled on a small, cleared area. On the floor was an empty picnic blanket, with a sprinkling of purple flowers. A cup from the top of a flask lay on its side, next to a fresh tea-coloured wet patch. The crowd around were oblivious.

The dog was gone. If the girl was here, she'd also disappeared.

He picked up some of the petals and rubbed them between his thumb and forefinger. Lavender. He hated lavender. For some reason he had never understood, the smell of lavender was the only thing that made a Time Child stop releasing their aura. It was the stuff of legend with the Temporatii, the name given to her followers. They wore it as a sign they wanted to help the special one stay hidden. *Most of them probably don't even know the Prophecy was actually true*, he thought.

He crumbled the petals in his hand and looked around. A legend it might be. But the girl's aura was gone. He had missed her again.

Chapter 24

For the first time since Izzy could remember, they'd taken the early train out of Great Chardan and back to London on Midsummer's Day.

The atmosphere in the cottage had been weird after their hurried exit from Stonehenge.

Neither Mum nor Nan had spoken much. Instead, they'd gulped down their tea. Jane had hastily packed up their things and they were ready to go.

"You be careful. Safe home. Mind the time," Nan had said, hugging Izzy and her mum and throwing crunched up lavender on them.

"Nan," moaned Izzy, spitting out lavender. "Stop it."

"Keeps the smell of the dogs off you," she replied, and hugged them both. Her eyes had been wide. Glassy.

In fact, after that long farewell hug and a goodbye belly rub for the dogs, Izzy and her mum made it to the station a full 30 minutes before the 8am train was due.

* * *

As Izzy, Jane and Greysock turned the corner into Foubert's Place, Izzy saw her mum's shoulders drop. For the first time since leaving Great Chardan, she smiled, and extravagantly blew out a lungful of air.

"Well, that was an adventure, wasn't it?" she said, looking at Izzy.

"Something like that," said Izzy. "I'm shattered. And I'm starving."

Greysock bark-whined in agreement.

The brass bell on the door of Wigglesworth and Son jangled loudly as her mum pushed it open.

It was a little after 10 o'clock. They had been awake for the best part of eight hours and had travelled halfway across the country, on two train journeys and one tube ride. Izzy's belly rumbled loudly, none-too-happy about the amount of effort that had been put in today with little breakfast reward.

Though the shop was open, it was empty as usual. Professor Wigglesworth was nowhere to be seen. Speckles of gold floated around the shop as the sunlight streaming through the window illuminated dust in the air and gave it a magical feeling.

The jangling of the closing door brought the professor from the storeroom.

"Hello, you two," he said, smoothing down his creased trousers with both hands and looking quizzically at them. He ceremoniously pushed his wavy, white hair back over his head. "I thought I'd missed a customer. What are you doing back so soon? How was Betty? Still as terrifying as ever?"

"Oh, Professor, you love her really," said Jane, smiling naturally now. The frown lines on her forehead had relaxed.

"Maybe. I see you're still with us." The professor looked at Greysock, emphasising the "*you're*" with mock indignation. "Izzy, I thought you were going to find his owner?"

"I think we're his owners now, Professor. You don't mind if he stays with us for a few days, do you? Just a few days?"

Greysock nuzzled up to the professor, demanding attention.

"Well, he can stay," said the professor, patting the dog on his head. "He is a good-looking fellow. But don't let him get too settled, eh? Now, I don't know about you, but I need to eat. I've been rushed off my feet this morning. And you can tell me why you're back so early."

Izzy and Jane nodded in agreement and 10 minutes later they were sitting together in the kitchen. A huge pile of toast and jam was laid out on the table. Izzy devoured as much as she could as Jane told the professor what had happened at Stonehenge.

Amid "uhuhs," and "hmms," Izzy slipped Greysock her crusts in his hiding place beneath her chair. The professor raised his eyebrows every time she fed the collie, but didn't really seem to mind.

The dog, as if aware that the professor wasn't overly keen on his presence, stayed close to Izzy.

"And then we got the first train back this morning," finished Jane, reaching for her cup of tea. "I've never seen so many people at Stonehenge for the sunrise before. It was an incredible sight, until Betty dragged us away. She's really starting to have some funny moments in her old age."

She glanced quickly at Izzy, as if to make sure she'd heard.

"Or something like that," said the professor. "Not everyone can stay young indefinitely."

He ran his hand through his white hair again and smoothed his shirt with both hands.

"Aren't you older than her?" Izzy laughed.

"I'm older than all of you put together," he said, winking. "Oh, go on. One more of those delicious pancakes, and I'm done."

Jane reached over to pass them and, as she did, her sleeve caught her cup of tea. It went tumbling over the table, spilling everywhere. It covered a pile of junk mail, turning the fliers a milky-brown.

"Oh, bloody hell!" cried Jane, grabbing a tea-towel and mopping up the tea. The professor stood up and moved the cups and plates. Izzy grabbed the soggy leaflets and moved them out of the way. Some were wet through and she put them in the bin. One caught her eye and she stuffed it in her pocket. A flyer for 'Paws for Thought', addressed to Professor Wigglesworth, a new pet shop that said it had 50% off for that weekend only. She decided she'd check it out later and get something nice for Greysock.

The tea flood over, Izzy and Greysock headed up to her room. The adrenaline of Stonehenge and the morning dash across country was fading.

She threw the rucksack against her door and laid on her bed. Her eyes were heavy. Greysock snuggled into her side. His warmth was comforting but she'd been unable to find her favourite teddy. She worried she'd left it at Nan's cottage.

As a result, sleep had been slow to creep up on her. Eventually, just as it began coaxing her into darkness, she was snapped awake. It was as if someone had thrown a bucket of cold water on her face. Or black, grimy rain.

"Dad?" It was as if she felt him close by, but her room was empty.

But beneath the piles of *Scramblings* on her desk, something was glowing. Greysock whined. Where the top drawer met the bottom of the desktop, there was a tiny slit where wood met wood. Through the thinnest gap, there was a yellow light. She thought she could actually hear it. A low hum.

The *fuzziness* began to bring its warmth up her chest as the Tumble Thunder called her.

Opening the bottom drawer and being careful of the scratches, her hand found the hidden lever that opened the secret compartment.

Pushing her fingers inside she pressed the wooden button, and heard it activate against the springs. There was a light clunking, and it opened.

It stared up at her. The casing had flicked open. The roman numerals, the hands and the details of the old watch glowed with a perfect gold. Its power reached out to her and she picked it up. Like before, the lines on her palm filled like rivers of gold. With it the empowering warmth swept across her body.

Beside her Greysock bark-whined a warning, and she wrapped her free arm around him. Pulling him close, she felt the golden warmth spread from her to him. Her own golden glow reflected in his blue and brown eyes.

Using her forefinger she pushed the middle of the three dials on the side, and there was a click. Then a whirr. The two hands on the clock face that had pointed jointly to 12, span forward to just before seven o'clock.

The first time she had used it, it felt like she had woken it up. This time, it had been waiting.

The golden glow was replaced with a familiar warmth that overtook her body. It brought with it a surge of fulfilment, like the first taste of hot chocolate on a cold day.

Compelled, she concentrated on the six digits on the face of the watch. They stared back: 000000.

The warmth grew stronger. It reached up and merged with the rising *fuzziness* in her chest. She could feel them bind, becoming a hundred times stronger. A hundred times more reassuring.

Like melted chocolate heaven.

Her vision went hazy. She closed her eyes as the six digits began to slowly move. Instead of being scared, she hugged Greysock and embraced what was coming.

A second later, she wished she hadn't.

Chapter 25

An overwhelming stench assaulted her recently improved sense of smell. She instinctively bent over and retched but her breakfast stayed put. It smelled like a toilet that hadn't been flushed for a year.

The warm air stung her eyes. At her feet, Greysock whined.

The six digits at the bottom of the Tumble Thunder showed 22061830. She clicked it shut.

This time, she understood.

22nd June, 1830.

She was in a small alley. The floor was cobbled and grimy. Ahead of her, a jet-black horse and carriage bounced by on huge wheels. A suited man, in a top hat, flicked a whip at the horses in front.

The passageway was barely three metres wide. The walls were made of brick, and a narrow open drain ran from the back to the wider road. Water ran down from the gutter and behind her, three men were asleep against the back wall. They looked half dead. One of them was dressed differently to the others. He wore a long, black coat. His skin was pale, almost grey. Izzy stared for a second, until the man groaned loudly. Startled, she backed away and stepped in a puddle.

Where she'd stood, she saw two blackened footprints. The grimy pebbles were unmistakably marked with soot. It was like in Scotland, the first time the Tumble Thunder had worked. Except then, the scorched earth had been blackened undergrowth.

On her right, two huge wooden crates lay smashed. Like they'd been thrown at the wall. Rotting food had spilled out. A barrel lay broken; the metal rings that encased it lay twisted and mis-shaped.

A huge rat emerged from a hole in the wall, beneath the crates. She jumped. Instinctively she shoved the Tumble Thunder into her pocket. As she pulled her hand back to her face, the flier for the pet shop fell out of her pocket and onto the floor. Distracted by the rat, she didn't even notice.

The rat ignored her. It carried a small piece of food alongside the dirty stream to the road. Greysock bark-whined and shot after it.

"Hey! Wait!" shouted Izzy at the disappearing dog.

It was too late. He was out of sight before she had finished calling his name.

She chased him into the street, but he was gone. The road was wide and busy; the air felt clearer here but not by much. Dark carriages pulled by darker horses streamed down the road like a horde of tadpoles in a stream.

Men and women walked arm in arm. The women wore huge billowing dresses, carrying parasols and holding handkerchiefs over their mouths and noses. The men, in suits, waistcoats and ties, all had red faces beneath a tall, top hat. One dabbed at sweat from his temple.

She was puzzled, yet strangely reassured. She knew this place.

It was June, in 1830. The Tumble Thunder had told her that much.

Watching the perfectly dressed passers-by, Izzy suddenly felt conscious of her jeans, trainers and t-shirt. A group of teenage boys on the other side of the street prodded each other and pointed at her. She headed left, in the opposite direction. Sticking to the side of the path away from the road. Glancing over her shoulder she saw the boys cross the road to follow.

A news stand had posters about the weather and the smell. A huge pile of dried and slightly yellowed newspapers fluttered briefly in the breeze.

"Standard. Get your Standard. The Big Stink carries disease!" shouted the vendor, waving around a rolled-up newspaper. "London hotter than Africa! The Thames is a killer. Get your Standard!"

He wasn't as well dressed as the suited men with their wives. He wore a flat cap and a dirty white shirt beneath his tweed jacket. Rivers of sweat ran down his lined face as he shouted.

Izzy agreed it was hotter than Africa and she couldn't escape the Big Stink. But she didn't understand why the Thames was a killer.

She turned left away from the main road into a familiar street with market stalls all around.

A butcher was hanging meat on an enormous hook on a stall. Along the front sat bunch after bunch of sausages. There were lots of flies. Next to that, an old woman in a bonnet leaned on a wooden cart filled with vegetables. Both the butcher and the woman looked tired, and hot. Everyone looked hot.

She checked behind her just as the boys turned the corner. The look on their faces made her nervous and she pushed into the market to avoid them. Among the throng of people, it was even hotter and smellier than in the street. She dodged past a couple carrying baskets of bread and there was a temporary break in the crowd.

Her jaw dropped.

The Shakespeare's Head pub, on Carnaby Street.

In 2013, at home, she saw it every day. It was just down from Wigglesworth and Son where she lived with her mum and the professor in Foubert's Place. Above the entrance to the pub, the bust of William Shakespeare stared out across the market. The pub had been owned by relatives of the great writer himself. It had stood at the top of the famous Carnaby Street since the 1700s. She'd read it once on the plaque on the side of the building.

Izzy was just 30 metres away, but 180 years, from her attic bedroom in the flat above the clock shop.

Not only was she in 1830, but she was in London. She was home. Kind of.

She paused, glancing from the market to the pub, taking it all in. Searching the passing legs and crowd for Greysock, she headed for Foubert's Place. She was desperate to see her home, as if seeing the clock shop would make everything feel okay.

"Hey. Come back. You little wretch!"

Izzy was spun around as a girl about her own age sped past, bumping into her as she tried to avoid the crowds. Two dogs carrying sausages were at her heels. Izzy recognised one immediately.

"Greysock! Come here," she shouted. But the normally obedient collie ignored her and continued after the girl and the other dog.

"Oi! You with them?" shouted the butcher who'd she'd just seen. "Someone, get the Peelers! Get those dogs!"

He was heading in her direction at top speed with a face like thunder.

Without a second thought she turned and ran after Greysock and his new friends.

In front, the young girl in the pretty dress headed straight down Carnaby Street, away from Foubert's Place. Izzy followed, glancing once in the direction of the clock shop. It would have to wait.

The angry butcher was still shouting and chasing. At full speed, Izzy soon caught the younger girl. They ran together. An odd quartet. Izzy in trainers and jeans, the girl in a lacy dress and shoes, and the dogs, both carrying sausages, just ahead of them. They weaved between legs as they went.

They turned right toward Regent Street, and there was a loud whistle in the distance.

"It's the Peelers," shouted the girl. "Come on."

She grabbed Izzy by the arm and they ducked into a passageway. She whistled through her teeth. The smaller dog, a King Charles spaniel, turned and ran back to her. Greysock followed. They headed to the back of the alley and took some stairs down next to an old cellar door. They were below street level and hidden.

They waited in silence for what seemed like ages. Izzy held Greysock and stroked his head to keep him quiet. The girl held a finger to her lips and the spaniel stared straight at her. He didn't make a sound.

She was prettily dressed, and her hair was tied back in two buns. Her dirty clothes looked expensive.

Above them, there was another whistle. Raised voices. They seemed closer. Greysock flattened his ears to his head. The spaniel didn't move. The girl was looking up toward the street, her eyes fixed. Listening.

As they sat in the silence, there was a familiar sound as Big Ben chimed at the Houses of Parliament. She counted seven. It had been before noon when she had been in her attic bedroom.

After a few seconds, there was another whistle. Then more shouting. Now further away than before. Izzy let out a huge breath.

The girl turned and smiled.

"I'm Alexandrina," she said in a voice that Izzy thought was incredibly posh. Putting out a hand for Izzy to shake, she carried on, without a breath. "But people call me Drina. This is Dash. He's my best friend. My best friend in the whole world."

Hearing his name, the Spaniel wagged his tail, and nuzzled the outstretched hand of his owner.

"Pleased to meet you Drina. I'm Isabella," said Izzy, shaking hands. "But people call me Izzy. This is Greysock. He's not really my dog, but I found him and now he follows me everywhere."

Greysock sat next to Izzy and dropped the sausages he'd been holding the entire time. He gave a small bark, finishing with his trademark whine.

"He's pretty," said Drina, turning to her own dog. "Dash never leaves me. Ever. Do you boy?"

Dash and Greysock lay down together and began chewing on the raw sausages.

"Eeeww, Greysock," said Izzy. "That's actually disgusting."

Drina giggled. The two dogs continued to chew on their stolen food.

"Where are you from Izzy? Your clothes are peculiar," said Drina. Her speech was eloquent and posh, but curt to the point of being rude. Izzy didn't mind.

"Closer than you think," she replied, thinking of the clock shop and the Shakespeare's Head pub, 180 years in the future and only around the corner. "What about you?"

Drina paused and looked at Dash. The two considered each other for a moment.

"We don't live far away," she said, as if she too was being purposefully vague. "Just beyond Hyde Park. It takes about half of an hour to get there from here. I'll show you. But we'll need to careful. The Peelers will be looking for us."

"The Peelers?" asked Izzy, raising her eyebrows.

"Yes, you know, the Peelers. The Police? They're a new part of the government. They're supposed to catch criminals. And dogs who steal sausages."

She looked at the two dogs, still scoffing, and laughed again. Izzy laughed too. There was something about Drina that she thought was familiar. Her laugh was infectious.

Their giggling over, they made their way up the iron steps to the passageway.

"Come on. Let's go this way. Just follow me. Try not to do anything that makes people look at us," said Drina.

Izzy looked down at her t-shirt, jeans, and scuffed white trainers and back at Drina, with wide eyes. The pair of them shrugged.

"I'll do my best," said Izzy. She nervously rubbed one trainer on the back of her calf to clean it.

The smell was worse at street level; the heat still stifling.

As they left the passageway, Izzy felt the Tumble Thunder cold in her jeans pocket.

The note from her dad had said she had to use it three times. The first time, she felt like she'd helped Aleck. Mary had given her Greysock and the star on his collar had helped fix part of the Tumble Thunder. Did she have to complete the Tumble Thunder to complete herself?

None of it really made sense, like the warning about the Time Shadow.

'Three times you must go,' the note had said.

"Which makes this two," she muttered under her breath as she walked. "But how does that help me find you, Dad?"

She stayed close behind Drina as they crossed Regent Street, through Mayfair and toward Hyde Park, oblivious to the world around her.

The carriages and the people rushed by. No-one seemed to notice the girl in the strange clothes. For her part, the girl from the future, paid them no attention.

All she could think about was her dad.

The more she thought about him. About her *Seeings*. About the Tumble Thunder. The more her belief grew that she was going to find him in the end.

He had given her the Tumble Thunder for a reason. It had taken her to Scotland because she was supposed to find Greysock. Whatever the star had done to the Tumble Thunder it had done something to her too. She could see and hear better - even smell better. Given the stink, she wished she couldn't.

Now it had brought her to London, in 1830, and she was meant to be there. But why?

She followed Drina.

"I'll find you, Dad. I promise," she said, looking up and realising they were in the middle of Hyde Park, hidden by trees. Between the branches was the Serpentine. The huge lake dominated the centre of Hyde Park. Izzy used to come here with her mum and dad for picnics. She loved the place. Loved the open air amid the bustling city.

"Pardon?" said Drina. "I beg your pardon?"

"Oh, nothing," said Izzy. "Nothing."

Drina checked there was no one around and pulled a cast-iron key from inside her dress and proceeded to unlock the small wooden door. It faced away from the main park, hidden by the undergrowth.

"Splendid," said Drina, pulling open the door. The evening sunlight illuminated a staircase that led sharply down, before levelling out to a passageway. It was dim, but not totally dark. A gas lamp on the wall threw out enough light to make eery shadows.

Izzy looked at Drina and raised her eyebrows. "How do you know about that? Who are you?" she said, looking the girl up and down.

"Don't worry about it. Just get in. Don't worry. It's not dark even when I close the door. My governess, Madam Lehzen, makes sure that these tunnels are always lit by gas lamp. In case I want to… in case I want to go out on my own. She says it's important for me to meet people."

She motioned Dash forward and he tore down the steps. Greysock looked up from Izzy's heels and followed. Drina put her arm around Izzy and they crouched through the door. She closed it behind them and locked it with a clunk.

Chapter 26

He bent over slowly and steadied himself with one hand on his knee. He was still tired. He picked up the yellowed, scrunched paper. It was hard, like it had been wet and dried out in the heat. Next to him, there was scurrying as another visitor emerged from the wall.

There had only been one rat at first. Now there were several. Unabashed they sat, munching the rotting food that had spilled from the broken boxes. Her time slip seemed more powerful this time.

In the woods in Scotland, she had damaged some small trees and scorched some earth. Here, in a smelly back alley of wherever, she had thrown two grown men from their feet. They were still unconscious behind him. The pine boxes had been thrown against the wall and landed in pieces. An old beer barrel was lodged against a drain next to the men. The steel that encircled its wooden body bent out of shape. Her faint purple aura trail was still present on the floor. It led out of the alley and left into the road.

She was getting stronger. It was only a matter of time. Sooner or later, the Time Child would realise her true potential. He could sense her awareness growing.

Slowly, with thin fingers, he unfurled the paper. It tore slightly where it had dried. Some of it couldn't be saved and crumbled in his hands. Piece by piece, he unfolded what was left of the flier for the pet shop. It was smudged, but there was writing in the top corner. A date. An address. A name.

Professor Wigglesworth,
The Old Clock Shop,
12 Foubert's Place,
London.

More than that, a date. Though it was smudged, the year was clear - '2013'. He'd been searching in the right time, at least.

He smiled and his thin lips cracked. Blood trickled onto his chin. Half-heartedly he wiped it away on his sleeve. His head spun from the effort of the time slip. But he felt something else; triumph.

Not only had he found the Time Child. He had found another piece of the puzzle too.

His smile widened and he laughed quietly.

For now, he needed more rest. Stumbling to the side of the alley, he allowed his back to slide down the wall. It was hot. He closed his eyes and wondered about the terrible smell. As he did, he noticed more hansom cabs passing at the end of the alley. Not far off, he heard a man shouting about the "Big Stink" and the "Standard".

London? He smiled. *Perfect.*

But rest first. He must sleep. He needed to regain his strength. Then he would find the clock shop.

He knew that if the girl had a connection to London in 2013, she wouldn't be able to resist visiting in 1830. Who would? He had no idea where she'd gone since leaving the alley and turning left. But he knew exactly where she was going to end up.

He was determined to be waiting for her when she did.

Chapter 27

The room she was in was sparsely decorated and snug.

After walking down the tunnel for a few minutes the night before, Drina and Izzy had then climbed up a small set of steps that appeared before them. Opening a large, wooden door they emerged directly into this bedroom.

Drina had virtually shoved her into the room, quickly shutting the door closed behind them.

"We always have to do that quickly," she said.

There was a heavy clunk behind her. Izzy had turned to see Drina lift what looked like an entire bookcase, complete with dusty books, into place in front of the tunnel.

"Isn't that really heavy?" Izzy had asked.

Drina looked at her and smiled mischievously.

"It would be, if it was actually a bookcase," she had said, then knocked on the side with her knuckles. The wood responded with a hollow echo. "Quite convincing door, don't you think? It keeps my tunnel a secret."

After that, Drina had closed the curtains, shutting out the enormous gardens beyond the window. She told Izzy not to leave, and promptly left herself. She had returned a few minutes later with bread and cheese, and a jug of water.

"I told Madam Lehzen about you," said Drina. "Every day when I go out, she asks me if I've met anyone peculiar. I've never quite understood why."

Izzy ate everything, throwing Greysock the occasional crust and piece of cheese.

Almost as quickly as she'd appeared with the food, Drina had gone again. For a second time, she told Izzy not to leave. Izzy had tried to ask questions. She'd wanted to find out more about her mysterious friend. But as she thought about asking, Drina had almost floated elegantly out of the room.

Still exhausted from Stonehenge, Izzy had almost collapsed into sleep. One thing she was beginning to realise about travelling through time, was that it was exhausting. She had fallen asleep as soon as she sat on the huge bed in the room and didn't wake until a nearby crowing cockerel noisily interrupted.

Greysock had snored most of the night.

He rolled onto his back and half woke up when the door opened. It was Drina.

Izzy caught the briefest glimpse of the huge, walled garden before she closed the door behind her. There was a vast, perfectly trimmed lawn, and enormous bushes full of pink flowers. In the middle was a fountain, with paths either side that led to a huge mansion. It reminded her of the huge houses she saw when she was exploring the nicest parts of London. It was made of red brick and seemed to go on forever. She was sure she'd seen it before. Maybe in a book. But she couldn't place it.

"We can't let anyone see you," said Drina bolting the door. She gave it an extra shove for good measure.

Less than 15 minutes later, they were heading back out of the tunnel. They emerged in Hyde Park. Drina opened the main door slowly, just a crack, and peeked out. She waited a few seconds. Sure that no-one was around, she swung it open. The sunlight streamed in and Izzy walked up the last few steps and into the daylight. Dash and Greysock, who patiently followed in the tunnel, ran ahead and straight into the trees beyond. Somewhere behind them was Drina's huge mansion, but Izzy had no idea where it was. She looked around, but it was nowhere to be seen.

The morning sun was just warming up. It hid behind the clouds and a low misty, smog hovered above the park. There was hardly anyone around. The smell wasn't as bad here, but it still hung in the air.

The dogs were barking at each other and running around in circles in the park. Izzy and Drina laughed as they rolled around like long, lost friends.

"I think they missed each other after last night," said Izzy, as Dash took a pitstop in the trees for a wee.

"I think the excitement got to him," said Drina. She was still smiling. Her hair scraped back onto her head in a double bun. She was far better dressed than yesterday. Her shoes were perfectly shiny, without a single blemish. They looked like they'd been freshly polished just minutes ago.

Izzy hung back and took the Tumble Thunder from her pocket. She flicked it open. The counter that went from 0-3, had moved around to two. The hand that counted back from 24 to zero sat ominously before the 14. She had been here, in 1830, for just over half a day. Half of her time in this version of London was gone. It was just before nine o'clock.

She had only a few hours left before she would return to her own time, and she had no idea what she was supposed to do here. It seemed she was no nearer to finding her dad.

The second hand glided effortlessly as she tried to work it all out. She focused on it, reaching for the molten *fuzziness* that had bound itself to the pocket watch when she'd slid the star into place.

It stirred, slightly, and warmth rose. Concentrating, she tried to embrace it, as if it held the answer to what she was supposed to do.

The indented moon on the casing, glowed, ever so slightly. There was the faintest hum, and the warmth from the *fuzziness* and the glow stopped.

"The moon," she said to herself, and flipped the Tumble Thunder closed, looking up at Drina. "I need to find a moon to fit the Tumble Thunder." It was starting to make sense, kind of. She had three uses of the Tumble Thunder. Each time, she had to find a new piece.

She slipped it back into her jeans pocket and ran to catch up with Drina, who hadn't even noticed she'd dropped behind. Keeping close to her seemed important too.

What she didn't understand about it all, was why she had to be in London in 1830. Confused, she decided to head for the one place she did know: home.

The clock shop in Foubert's Place was a little over thirty minutes away. She explained to Drina that she needed to go there to see if one of her best friends was okay. The white lie came with an air of authority she hadn't thought possible.

"Splendid," said Drina. "That sounds like an awful lot of fun. But it's rather important we stay out of sight as much as possible."

Drina weighed Izzy up, as if making a final decision about whether staying with her was wise. The dogs had quickly tired of chasing each other in the morning haze and ambled over.

"Come on," said Izzy. "It feels like we've got a lot to do today. I need you to stay with me. It's already getting warm. And that smell? Eeeeeew." She wrinkled her nose and wafted her hand in front of her face.

"I know, it's rather awful, isn't it?" said Drina. She took a small tin out of a pocket in her dress and opened it. She dabbed her finger at a lilac-coloured cream inside and rubbed a small amount below each nostril and offered Izzy the tin.

"You should try some. It's just a perfumed lotion, but it takes the awful smell away. Everyone calls it the 'Big Stink'. I'm afraid it's been so hideously hot for so long that the Thames has just started to, well, smell. It's full of all sorts these days. Let's just say that the contents of people's bedpans only end up in one place. I've heard that people even throw dead bodies in there, though I've never seen any."

"What? Really?" Izzy wrinkled her nose as she rubbed cream on her own top lip. Then pulled in a deep breath.

"Ooh, you're right, that's better," said Izzy, carefully sniffing for signs of the stink. "Now it only smells like two buckets of poo and a dead body, instead of 10."

"You're amusing. And you're awfully peculiar," Drina said with a wide smile. "I do believe there's much fun to be had with you today, Izzy. And I, for one, need some more fun in my life."

Dash barked in agreement, and Drina patted his head.

"Okay," said Izzy. "If you're sure. I'm not sure what's going to happen today. What I do know is that I need to go back to Foubert's Place and find the clock shop."

"Well then, we better be off," said Drina, heading off across the park. "Come on Dash. Let's not go too close to the Serpentine, the smell isn't much better than the Thames."

Originally, Izzy had thought that Drina was just stuffy and posh. But the more she got to know her, the more she thought she just liked to get to the point. Greysock padded beside her as she followed her new friend. Drina seemed to just want to have fun, and it didn't sound like she got much in the house she lived in.

I've seen that house before, she thought. It is huge.

What Izzy did know, was that having Drina around gave her a healthy dose of inner confidence. Izzy hardly needed any help on that front, but Drina acted as if she knew every inch of London personally. It was almost like she owned it. She didn't know how but there was also something about Drina that she knew. That she'd seen somewhere before.

Chapter 28

After their run-in with the angry, sausage-deprived butcher the previous day, they approached Foubert's Place from the opposite end to the bustling, Carnaby Street market.

Leaving Regent Street with its army of carriages, Izzy, Drina and the two dogs had walked up Kingly Street from the quieter end, away from Oxford Road.

Ever since leaving Hyde Park, they had stayed close to the walls of buildings. They wanted to avoid as much attention as possible. It hadn't really worked. They had barely left the Serpentine when Drina apologised for not lending Izzy some of her clothes so she could blend in.

Izzy didn't mind. The occasional odd look from the passing women didn't really bother her. They looked positively dismayed at the fact that she appeared to be wearing boys' clothes. She couldn't imagine herself in a frilly dress for a second. Her trainers and jeans felt the lesser of two evils.

The dogs seemed less concerned than their owners. While Izzy and Drina had walked in single file for much of the way, the dogs had zigzagged through an obstacle course of human legs with glee. A couple of grumpy men had attempted a kick as they sped by.

When they reached Kingly Street, the crowds thinned and the girls walked side by side.

"Drina," said Izzy. "Can I ask you something?"

"No," said Drina, simply. "If you ask me too many more questions, I'm afraid we simply won't be able to be friends. Knowing too much about one's new acquaintances is a dangerous business as far as I'm concerned. Let's just be new friends who are both jolly determined to have some fun."

"Oh, erm, okay," said Izzy, slightly stunned.

They turned into Foubert's Place and paused. Carnaby Street was at the far end, like always, just beyond the Shakespeare's Head pub. But instead of the string of designer clothes shops and fancy bars she walked by every day, there was an old butchers with blue and white tiles. Next to that, a grocers with pies and vegetables on a stall out front and a bakers where a long queue snaked outside and up towards the Shakespeare's Head. But it wasn't that different. Cobbles replaced the diagonal stone paving she was used to, but even the bare brick frontages of the buildings above the shops were recognisable.

A tall man with a top hat almost bumped into the pair of them, and Izzy dodged out of his way. The cobbles were slimy and she stepped in a suspiciously murky brown puddle beneath a drainpipe next to the baker's.

"Eww," she said, grimacing at the residue on her trainers.

Her stomach turned over at the sight. When she looked up, it did a double back flip. "Oh."

She put an arm across Drina to stop her in front of the shop Izzy called home, almost 200 years in the future. Both dogs sat and waited.

Most of the buildings in the street were four storeys tall, but 12 Foubert's Place was modest in comparison. It was narrower and hidden in between two grander buildings that were bolder and a full floor taller.

The navy paint around the single window of the shop was bright and fresh. The writing above, in bright gold, gleamed the words, 'Wigglesworth and Son'. Just below, in letters that weren't faded in the way she was used to, it read: 'Clocks and repairs since 1825.'

The window was clean and the door was shiny. The gold number 12 shone and the handle looked immaculate. The only thing that made the clock shop stand out from those around it was, in fact, just how clean and new it looked. The others around them looked dirty and uncared for.

Someone clearly loved 12 Foubert's Place. Someone loved it very much indeed.

But something wasn't right. Peering through the window, Izzy could see the familiar glass counter. Everything looked remarkably similar to how she knew it. Then she realised. Red velvet covered the glass counters and the collections. It was exactly how Professor Wigglesworth would leave the shop every night at closing, or if he was going on one of his trips.

There was a small 'closed' sign hanging from a chain in the window. Something wasn't right. It was the middle of the morning and all of the shops around were buzzing and full of life and people. Yet the clock shop, despite its clean and welcoming appearance, was empty. Cupping her hand against the glass she thought the inside seemed eerily gloomy.

"So, what do we now?" asked Drina.

"I'm not really sure," said Izzy. She stepped back and looked up at the building.

Above the shop there were two rows of narrow windows. Above them, a small railing outside of the attic. For as long as she could remember, she'd leant on them watching the people in the streets below.

She'd been convinced that coming here would give her some answers. But now that she was here, she didn't know what to do next.

"Did you say your friend would be here?" said Drina. "Maybe they're upstairs. Do you think we should knock and see if they'll come down?"

Drina's words shook her out of her deep thought.

"Oh, yes," she said with a sudden urge she couldn't explain. "Upstairs. That's it. I need to get to the attic. There might be something there."

Looking around she tried the door. It was the same cast-iron door handle that she was used to. It looked newer, but it was basically the same.

It didn't budge. She tried it again, just to be sure. It was locked.

She gave it a shove at the same time, just for luck. Nothing.

"Erm, isn't it locked?" said Drina, with a smile. "We'll need a key. Is there another way in?"

Greysock and Dash had both been waiting patiently while the girls inspected the building. Greysock though, had seemingly had enough. He jumped up at the door, leaving grimy paw prints on the glass. Izzy thought he was looking in, but he jumped down a second later and walked around Izzy and sat beside her. She looked down at him, and he nudged her leg with his nose.

"What boy?" she asked the collie. "What is it? We can't get in."

Greysock nudged her leg again. Higher this

time, on her hip where the Tumble Thunder sat in her pocket. She didn't think it would help. Turning it around in her fingers she felt it clink against metal. Pushing aside the pocket watch she felt her key. Her front door key.

She pulled it out and held it up.

"Oh, my Lord! Why didn't you say you had a key?" Drina threw her hands up. Izzy felt the blood rush to her face. Greysock bark-whined his disapproval at her forgetfulness.

"Well, I do. I just don't know if it's the key," replied Izzy, and Greysock nudged her on the leg again.

"Well, you ought to try it," said Drina.

Checking no-one one on the street had noticed them standing in front of the empty shop for so long, she slipped the key into the old-new-old lock. It turned to the left with a smooth clunk she wasn't used to.

She smiled: "Everything has a time and a place. Thank you, Professor."

She pushed the door open gently, and Drina and the dogs followed. She did her best to be quiet until the door hit the entry bell and a loud jangling announced their arrival.

"Oh, hello. Hi. Good morning," said Izzy, into an unnervingly familiar, yet totally empty shop. "Hey there. Is anyone home?"

No answer. Greysock wasn't as patient. He shot ahead, cocked his head left and right, and disappeared through the back of the shop. Izzy didn't even have a chance to call him before his paws were thundering on the stairs.

"Come on," she told Drina, and they chased after the dog, completely forgetting to stay quiet. Behind them, the door clunked softly closed.

They charged up the stairs, passing the flat where Professor Wigglesworth lived in the present day - it was empty.

"Greysock! Come back!" Izzy shouted.

They passed the kitchen where her mum had made her breakfast - yesterday? - and crossed the landing, following the collie up the next set of stairs.

Izzy pushed through the old wooden door into the attic and stopped dead in her tracks.

She couldn't believe it.

The room, and so many things in it, looked, unbelievably, as if it was... no... her... it can't be... bedroom.

The *fuzziness* briefly fluttered in her chest as she forced herself to blink. She swallowed hard and took a deep breath.

It wasn't her room at all. But it did look a little like it. There were white blankets thrown over boxes where her bed would be. Instead of her pine wardrobes there were large wooden crates that were stacked neatly on top of one another.

"Izzy, are you all right?" said Drina, pulling on her sleeve. "You've gone grey."

"I'm fi…" the words stuck in her throat. There, just where she'd left it in 2013, was a desk like the one that Nan had bought her for her birthday. She couldn't believe it.

Greysock was sitting in front of it, whining and pawing at the drawers.

"Oh, Greysock," said Izzy, recovering her ability to speak. "You've scratched it."

A five-centimetre scratch now ran down the front of the second and third drawer. Izzy was dumbstruck.

Just like on mine.

She walked carefully toward the desk, eyeing up the detail. It was exactly the same as hers. Oak and seemingly hand polished. An intricate carving of lavender descended from the top of the desk and down around the left leg. Like hers.

The drawers sat to the right, two of them wide enough, "wide enough for notebooks," she said under her breath, before adding: "This is my desk. Just not yet."

"Pardon?" said Drina, who appeared bored at the lack of the fun she'd been hoping to find with her new friend. "Izzy, I don't think your friend is here. We should just go."

"Wait a minute," said Izzy. "Just one more minute." Her fingers traced the side of the drawer and down beneath the bottom one. She searched slowly with her index finger.

There you are.

She pushed her finger into the hole and found the wooden button. There was a familiar sound of gentle clunking and the springs groaned as the secret panel opened.

But the drawer was empty.

"So where is the friend you needed to see, Izzy?" asked Drina, now totally puzzled by her new friend. She'd been expecting to meet someone new and interesting with the girl in the strange clothes. So far, it hadn't panned out that way.

"I can't really tell you," said Izzy.

As she chewed on the words, a sudden feeling of dread rose from her chest. The molten *fuzziness* swirled and flashed like a police siren. It was a *Seeing* or the dḗjā vu she'd had before, but it didn't feel good. She couldn't explain it. She sensed danger was nearby. Something was coming. Or someone.

"I think we need to go," she said, heading for her bedroom door. "I think we need to go right now. Come on!"

The quartet had just reached the top of the spiral staircase on her attic landing when the bell on the shop door clanged loudly. They stopped. From two floors down came the sound of breaking glass.

Izzy peeked down the staircase, a hand on each rail. Someone was in the shop. The warning *fuzziness* left her in doubt of who it was.

'Beware the Time Shadow.'

"What on earth?" said Drina. But Izzy didn't answer. She grabbed her friend's hand and they tiptoed back into the attic room. Closing the door as gently as she could, she pushed across a small bolt, pausing briefly as the rusty metal ground noisily against the frame.

They were trapped.

Drina and the dogs looked at her. The spinning *fuzziness* was still flashing a red alert in her chest as she scanned the room looking for a way out.

For a moment she eyed up the window before remembering the 10 metre drop outside.

There was no other way out... except.

She ran to the corner of the room and moved three wooden crates piled on top of each other.

There, less than a metre high, was the familiar small door she was forbidden to use in her own bedroom. Now, it was their only way out. Whoever smashed the glass in the clock shop hadn't popped by to bring them presents and a friendly hello. More than that, she knew it was the Time Shadow. It had to be.

She swung open the door, gently, and peered down the murky staircase. The smell of damp, mouldy air wafted into her face.

"It's the only way out," she whispered to Drina. "We'll need to be quiet. Go gently and quickly, so the steps don't make any noise. I think we'll be okay. I think."

"You don't fill me with confidence, Izzy. We are

not amused," answered Drina, stooping into the opening and onto the top step. "Dash, Greysock, come on."

"Just keep going until you get to the bottom. It's covered all the way down apart from on the next landing. Be careful not to be seen when we get there. There's a door at the bottom. We can hide down there. I hope."

Izzy followed Drina into the gloom and slowly closed the small door behind them. It clunked into place. Feeling down the frame in the near darkness she found a small latch that felt rusty and old. She swung it over and felt it drop into a metal hoop on the other side of the frame.

"Please be strong enough," she whispered to the door.

But no sooner had she taken one step to follow Drina than the bedroom door handle was rattled loudly. She stopped. A second later there was a loud thump as someone gave it a hefty boot.

Izzy scurried down the stairs as fast as she dared behind her group. There was just enough light from the next landing to enable them to see where to put their feet. She caught up with Drina and motioned for her to go faster into the darkness below.

"Fast as you dare," urged Izzy.

They paused at the gap before the next landing, level with the kitchen. Izzy squeezed past Drina to make sure the coast was clear. She paused for a second and beckoned the group on.

They had just passed the first floor - home to Professor Wigglesworth's flat - when they heard a crash from above.

"My bedroom door," said Izzy, as she urged her friend down the final few steps.

"Get out of the way, stupid dogs," hissed Drina, her feet almost escaping from beneath her on the slippery stone.

The wooden door to the cellar stood before Izzy for only the second time in her life.

On the only other time she'd crept down here, the door had been locked with a heavy bolt. This time, the lock was gone - or hadn't been put on yet - and she pressed on the cast iron lever on the lock and pushed. It didn't move. A heavy shove and it screeched open a fraction of a centimetre, before slipping back into place.

Wincing at the noise she glanced up the stairs.

"Help me," she told Drina. "I think we can do it together."

Drina put her hands next to Izzy's on the huge handle. They heaved. The door moved the tiniest fraction and dropped back into place.

"It's too heavy," moaned Drina. "We can't do it."

Her eyes looked sad in the gloom.

Izzy took a huge breath and pushed it out loudly. She was out of ideas.

An almighty crash from above brought her back to life. Splinters and chunks of wood thumped down each step toward them from the now obliterated escape door above.

"Come on!" Izzy ordered Drina.

With a panicked shove they heaved at the heavy basement door and it screeched open five centimetres. They pushed again as descending footsteps echoed from the top of the stairs

The door screech again as it opened just enough for them all to squeeze through.

They emerged into a room with bare brick walls and a single window. Daylight streamed in. There was no time to take it in. They spun around and put their shoulders into the door. It screeched almost closed, and they shoved again. Just as it slid into place a black boot wedged itself in the bottom. Thin fingers wrapped around the edge of the door as it was pushed back.

The girls shoved with everything they had. Greysock barked and Dash snarled.

"Don't. Let. Him. In." Said Izzy through gritted teeth. Her trainers slid on the floor as she looked for a better grip, and she aimed a kick at the boot holding the door open.

"I'm trying. He's too strong," said Drina, her pristine shoes scuffing against the stone.

As the girls heaved, Greysock jumped and snapped at the fingers protruding from around the door.

There was a high-pitched scream as the hand withdrew. Emboldened by Greysock, Dash bit the foot that was still holding the bottom of the door open. The boot followed the hand and disappeared. The heavy door screeched into place with a thunk.

Izzy latched it while Drina frantically searched for something to wedge it closed. It didn't take long. Underneath the window was a huge plank of wood. Drina lifted it into place on the brackets that were attached to the wall on either side of the door. It reminded Izzy of the kind of barrier they used in castles.

"Phew," breathed Izzy. The pair of them lent back against the door and slid down.

"There's no getting through that," added Drina. She hugged her friend and smiled as she released her. "When I said I wanted to have fun today, I didn't expect to have to run for my life!"

They laughed and a heavy thump shook the door. They heard footsteps retreating up the stairs.

The pair looked at each other.

"I don't think we're finished yet," said Izzy, getting up. "There's no way through that door, but how are we going to get out of here?"

The cellar was brighter than Izzy expected. It was about three metres wide. There was an old wooden workbench down one side. Next to it was a single stool, and the walls were bare brick. It looked damp and felt cold. The 'Big Stink' seemed to be even stinkier down here. As well as being fairly narrow, it didn't seem to be very long. It ended just a few metres ahead of them. In the far wall was a cast iron fireplace that looked like it had never been used.

The solitary window was just below street level and she could see passing feet in Foubert's Pass above. It was a small alley that ran behind Foubert's Place and the clock shop. Three iron bars ran down the window, just a few centimetres apart.

There was no door in sight. They were trapped.

Having recovered from the excitement of attacking a hand and a boot, the dogs began sniffing every corner of the basement. The girls worked their way around, looking for anything that might help them escape. They discussed, briefly, whether they should open the door again but decided against it.

"We can't wait too long, though," said Izzy. "If that really was the Time Shadow, then it won't take him long to work out that the back of the building leads to Foubert's Pass. Once he knows we're trapped he's bound to come straight back."

"The Time Shadow?" said Drina. "Who on earth is that?"

"Erm, well," said Izzy before Drina cut her off and carried on.

"Whoever it is, he might still be there. Maybe he's sitting on the stairs. Maybe he's waiting for us to open the door and walk straight into him."

"Good point. Keep looking."

Between them they pushed the heavy bench out of the way. They found nothing but bare, smelly brick. They even pulled at the bars in the window. They were stuck fast. The brickwork and cement around them were solid, despite the damp.

"There's no way out," said Drina. "We're trapped."

Izzy pulled out the Tumble Thunder. It was already early afternoon. Where had the time gone?

The second hand ticked slowly by, and Izzy took a deep breath. She tried to calm herself down and relax. *'Make time to make time,'* Mum always said.

And then it hit her. She opened her eyes and put the Tumble Thunder back in her pocket.

"The fireplace," said Izzy. "There's no chimney at the back of the building. So, it can't be real."

Drina looked at her, not really understanding what she meant.

Izzy strode over to the black fireplace and looked at it. It was slightly rusty and sat back into the wall. She pulled at the black iron. It wiggled.

Encouraged, she gripped the surround and pulled properly. It groaned and almost came away in her hands. Free of its brick prison, it swung away from the wall on old hinges.

"I don't believe it!" she cried, as Greysock bark-whined his approval.

Where the fireplace had once merged perfectly into the wall, was a low hole that led into a dark nothing beyond.

"Oh my. Turns out that I'm not the only one who likes a secret tunnel," said Drina, and strode forward to investigate. She bent down and stuck her head into the gloom.

"Hellooooo," she said giddily, waiting for her voice to echo. "It appears we're not trapped, after all. Splendid work Izzy."

Before Izzy had chance to reply, Drina disappeared into the secret passage. Dash followed.

"Come on," said Drina from the darkness. A disembodied hand appeared and beckoned Izzy forward. Greysock ran through first.

Izzy stooped and squinted into the darkness. She hated the idea of a pitch-black tunnel.

Reluctantly she ducked through the gap and was almost sick.

"It's okay," said Drina, ignoring the stench. "There's room to stand. It seems to lead this way."

Their eyes slowly adjusting to the lack of daylight, they set off.

Every few metres some natural light came in through a drain. Occasionally it was followed by some dirty looking water.

Realising they were in the sewer, they walked carefully on the edge of the water that ran beneath their feet. The dogs followed.

The sewer ran left down Foubert's Pass, then right, following Carnaby Street and straight on.

Down here the smell from the whatever-it-was-that-belonged-in-a-toilet liquid that ran through the middle was almost unbearable.

"Izzy, wait," said Drina a few minutes in. She

leaned against a wall trying not to be sick. "This is positively disgusting."

Izzy was breathing slowly, as if to prevent the smell sneaking through. Though the Time Shadow was no longer right behind them, she could still sense he was searching for them. Carnaby Street was now way behind them and the streets above felt quieter. The *fuzziness* was still hanging around and she had goosebumps, despite the heat.

"Come on," she said, looking ahead. "I think we've almost made it."

A few metres in front of them, a small row of steps led up to a wider opening. The fresher air reached forward to greet them. They stuck their heads into the daylight.

The warm, yet still smelly, air of London was a relief compared to the stench of their escape tunnel.

They took huge breaths of air, like divers emerging from the depths. Free from the dark, they were at the bottom of some more stairs that led up to street level.

"I might be able to breathe now, but my mum is gonna kill me when she sees my trainers," said Izzy, wiggling her toes. A brief sense of worry shot across her mind. Then she remembered how the first time she'd used the Tumble Thunder, she'd returned at the exact same moment as when she left. Her mum wouldn't even know she'd been gone.

"If by trainers you mean those things," said Drina, pointing to Izzy's feet, "then I agree. Madam Lehzen won't be very happy with oneself either. Though she'll probably get one of the maids to boil my clothes and just order afresh from the tailor."

Izzy shot her a glance with raised eyebrows.

Drina ignored Izzy's quizzical look and ran up the steps. They had come out underneath one of the arches on Air Street; a cut through between the grand white buildings of Regent Street and Piccadilly that both led to the iconic Piccadilly Circus. Despite where it was, in the heart of London's busiest area, Air Street always seemed quiet. It was the perfect place to leave a secret tunnel and disappear discreetly into the crowds.

Drina looked down at her own feet and wrinkled her nose.

"I know just the place that will get us out of this predicament. At least for now," she said. "Come on."

Dash and Greysock walked obediently alongside them. If Scotland in 1860 had been strange for Izzy, then her hometown in 1830 was even stranger. Where huge neon screens, traffics lights and crowds of tourists dominated Piccadilly Circus in the 21st century, here it was carriage after carriage and the smell of horses mingled with the Big Stink.

Watching the traffic roll by she noticed they were being watched. A solitary figure in a hooded cloak stood next to a lamppost across the street.

She couldn't quite see a face, but she was sure it wasn't the Time Shadow. It looked like a woman.

"Where exactly are we going?" Izzy asked Drina, eyeing their watcher who had started following them, on the other side of the road.

"King William the Fourth square," said Drina, without pausing. "It's named after the King. And there are fountains where we can at least clean our shoes a little."

"I've never heard of it," said Izzy, looking over her shoulder. The constant chasing and following was making her feel tired. She wasn't sure how much more she could handle.

Over the next few minutes, they barely spoke as Drina walked with her head down. Izzy kept glancing back to see if she could spot their follower. She did. Every time. The figure in black flitted through the crowds, staring in the direction of the girls.

As they moved further from Piccadilly Circus, the throng of people and carriages eased and the streets opened up to reveal a huge open space.

"Ah," said Izzy. "Trafalgar Square."

"No, actually," countered Drina, looking around at the square's fountains. "This is William the Fourth Square, like I told you."

Izzy opened her mouth to reply, but movement in the corner of her eye caught her attention. She swivelled on the spot.

Unseen, their follower had closed in. Somehow the gap between them had closed to less than 10 metres.

"Drina, move," said Izzy.

She turned to grab Drina and tell her to run, to hide somewhere.

But her new friend was casually sitting on one of the grand steps at the top of the square, taking her shoes off.

"I can't. I need to clean these shoes or Madam Lehzen will be positively fuming. She despises it when I go out as it is," replied Drina casually, smiling at Dash.

"Drina," said Izzy, fear in her voice. The *fuzziness* was rising in her chest but she couldn't move. Time felt like it had stopped.

"You're right," said a voice. "Those shoes are a mess."

"Dearest Daisy, you found us," said Drina, her face lighting up. "This is Izzy, the friend I told you about."

"Madam Lehzen," the woman in a black cloak said to Izzy. "Pleased to meet you. I'm Drina's governess. Izzy, or is it, Isabella? Either way, it is delightful to meet you my dear. It is a privilege too."

Madam Lehzen was tall and thin, and dressed in black. She had a pointed nose and chin. She caressed Izzy's cheek and seemed to look at her back and behind them.

"Are you okay?" asked Izzy, turning around to look behind herself.

"Oh, yes," said Madam Lehzen. "I'm more than okay. I'm positively enthused."

Her smile highlighted by her bright red lipstick was matched by a scarlet brooch on her chest. She looked elegant but stern.

Izzy breathed out. Relief swept through her body. She'd been convinced that the woman that had followed them was bad news.

"Drina, my dear, I told you to be extra careful today. I couldn't find you for a long time," said the governess, as her eyes scanned the square.

Drina looked at Izzy and rolled her eyes: "Madam follows me everywhere when I go out. She's happy for me to leave, but always watches me. It was her who instructed the tunnel be built in Hyde Park. It helps me get in and out without being spotted. When I told her about you, and Greysock, and the way you dress, she expressly forbade me to come out of the palace gardens without her."

She stopped talking abruptly and shot a guilty glance at her governess.

"The palace?" asked Izzy, frowning, and looking between Madam Lehzen and Drina.

"It doesn't matter now. Another time," said Madam Lehzen, who had begun crumbling up some small purple flowers and throwing them on the ground. "I fear we might not have much time."

Izzy turned to see what the woman was looking at.

Across the square, a group of around 30 or 40 workmen were digging. Others were heaving huge stones attached to ropes. What Izzy knew as Trafalgar Square was still being built. Where Nelson's Column stood towering over this part of her London, here there was only a stone base. The workmen looked like they'd only just begun. The four lions were missing too. At least the famous fountains were just how Izzy was used to seeing them. They dominated the square, though the water looked dirtier than she was used to. Drina got to her feet.

"Come on, let's use the fountains," she said, and made to cross the road between carriages.

Madam Lehzen didn't move. She was scanning the square from one corner to the next, fiddling with the two tiny horns on her necklace. Searching.

There was something about the look in her eyes that made Izzy nervous. She felt in her pocket for the comfort of the Tumble Thunder. The *fuzziness* was rising.

Picturing the second hand sweeping slowly she took a deep breath. She felt for the *fuzziness* and tried to calm herself. It rose a little more and then stayed in place. Slowly it pulsed like in the cellar, but she held it. It was like a molten ball that literally made her heart feel warmer. She breathed out, and it didn't move.

A smile spread across her face with the triumph.

For only the second time ever she had controlled the *fuzziness*. It was like she was learning how to use it. Whatever this strange power was that she had, it was getting stronger.

Izzy was so pleased with her own self-control that she barely noticed Drina step out into the road. The girl was still smiling back at Izzy and her governess when the trotting horse ran into her.

Its front legs knocked her to the ground and its hind legs stood on her before the huge wheels of the carriage it was pulling rolled over her back. Her body was thrown to the kerb. Her head was twisted at a horrible angle on her neck.

She was dead.

Madam Lehzen screamed.

Izzy recoiled and turned away.

When she opened her eyes again, she saw Madam Lehzen scanning the square.

A huge feeling of dēјā vu washed over her as she recognised the *Seeing* for what it was.

She'd just watched Drina's death in the same way she'd seen Ellie and the Phoneys trying to start a fight with Porter at school.

Wheeling around as Drina stepped into road, Izzy grabbed her by both shoulders and pulled her back. They fell in a heap, just as a huge black horse rushed by, pulling an even bigger carriage. The breeze from the passing horse brought a wave of fresh stench from the foul, warm air.

"Drina!" shouted her governess.

"Whoa, there! Out of the way!" shouted the angry coach driver, who swerved the horse and carriage far too late. He was still shouting as he headed around the square to the Mall.

"You saved me," said Drina, and hugged her new friend. "That horse would have killed me. You saved my life."

Izzy was sure of it this time. Controlling the *fuzziness* had enabled her to see something before it even happened. It was her second seeing since her dad had disappeared, and stronger than ever.

Even more, she felt a sense of accomplishment. In that moment she was convinced it was why the Tumble Thunder had brought her back to this London; to save Drina. All she had to do now, was find the moon.

As the *fuzziness* receded, she held Drina and cried. The relief swept through both of them.

Greysock and Dash brought the girls to their senses. Licking at their owner's faces, the girls began to laugh.

"Izzy, you truly are a blessing for all of us. I'm so glad you came for Drina," said Madam Lehzen beaming. She pulled Izzy close and hugged her. Izzy was confused but didn't say anything. "Come on, we must get you both cleaned up properly," added the governess.

After crossing the road carefully and avoiding any more carriages, the girls sat by the fountain and attempted to clean their shoes. The dogs jumped in and splashed around.

The *Seeing* had drained Izzy. Her eyes felt heavy. When Drina suggested they begin the walk back to Hyde Park to get some dinner she happily agreed.

They left William the Fourth Square - Trafalgar to Izzy - and headed down the Mall, toward the grand Admiralty Arch and Buckingham Palace beyond.

Greysock and Dash had run off ahead and darted through the arches to the side. Carriage after carriage came idling through at a leisurely pace.

Madam Lehzen hung back, walking behind the girls as if chaperoning them. She was still glancing around. It made Izzy feel nervous.

"Is she always like that when she's out with you?" Izzy asked Drina, motioning back at the woman.

"Dearest Daisy? Always," said Drina, with a carefree smile that seemed to ignore the fact that she'd almost just died minutes earlier. "She's looked after me for as long as I can remember. My papa died when I was very young. She cares for me like I'm her own. I trust her more than anyone. Even my mother."

"Wow! Who are you?" asked Izzy. For the first time in hours, she thought of her own mum. She didn't think she would be worried. She doubted she'd even realised that her daughter had gone.

As tired as she was, Izzy knew she'd be back with her mum soon. She was convinced that saving Drina had also taken her closer to her dad. It was like everything was clicking into place.

Flicking open the Tumble Thunder, she saw there was less than one hour left in 1830.

"What's that?" asked Drina. "It's really pretty."

"It's a special watch. It's helping me. And, somehow, I think I'm helping it," said Izzy, looking at the shapes on the casing and realising she hadn't finished everything after all.

"A moon. I'm not finished unless I find a moon."

Chapter 29

It had taken him an age to find her again. After being bitten by the dogs in the clock shop, he made his way around the building to where the cellar must have been. There was no way out.

He was mulling over returning to the clock shop when he heard a noise beneath his feet. He stooped and listened. He followed the muffled voices of the girls from one drain to the next. He strained to hear over the hubbub of the smelly city.

After realising they were in a drain, he followed what he thought must be the direction of the tunnel. He soon lost their voices and had ended up in Trafalgar Square almost by accident.

It was then that he'd seen her properly for the first time. Her jeans and trainers made her stand out. Her long curly hair looked messy. But her purple aura was unmistakable, even from here. It still amazed him how only a select few could see it.

He watched as the Time Child pulled the smaller girl back from out of the path of the horse and carriage. She had almost certainly saved her life.

The woman with them had a keen eye and was almost certainly one of them. He watched as she sprinkled what could only be lavender all around – but she was too late. He could already see her. He hid among the workmen tending to Nelson's Column and watched the girls clean their shoes before heading in the direction of the Mall.

As they began to walk across the square, he knew this was his chance. He would have to be careful. The girl was becoming aware of her powers. Rushing in would be of no use now.

He glanced at his own Tumble Thunder. It was like Izzy's but looked older, more jaded, and made of a dull, dark steel, like pewter. The counter on the left that had been counting down from 24 hovered near the zero. The pocket watch showed it was just a few minutes before seven o'clock. He would need to be quick.

"I don't think you understand any of this yet, do you?" he muttered to himself under his breath. "Foolish girl. You have no idea what you're capable of."

He melted away into the crowds to get ahead of them. Once he was out of sight, he started running. But instead of heading straight down the Mall he turned right and took a passage that he knew would bring him out right in the middle of Admiralty Arch.

It had taken him longer than he thought. He turned into the passage just as the girls passed through the arches 10 metres ahead of him. The sprint had taken it out of him and he slowed, only to almost bump into the woman who had been watching the children.

"You?" she said, looking straight at him, quiet enough not to alert the girls. "Here? Now? You won't have her."

With that she jumped at him just as the dogs ran towards them barking. The woman's elegant appearance belied her determined strength .

"Run! Girls! Run!" the woman shouted, as he spun her around on his back. The dogs bit at his legs. The larger one, the collie, got a hold of his lower calf and wouldn't let go. The pain was excruciating.

For a second, the girls didn't move.

"Dearest Daisy!" shouted one of the girls.

"Run Drina. Run Izzy." The woman's voice was insistent but calm. A smile flickered on her face.

There was a thud and a crunch as she was pushed back against one of the stone arches. She cried out in pain but hung on. "You won't have her," she hissed in his ear.

The collie released his leg and his long coat prevented the smaller dog from doing too much damage as it snapped at him.

The girls had started running. He knew his time was short. With an almighty effort he pushed back against the wall again. Another crunch, and the woman screamed. She held on but her grip had loosened.

"You can't stop me," he snarled at the woman, noticing her black, lacy hat had fallen to the floor. "I haven't come this far, through so many times, for you to stop me now."

He pushed back again, and she hit the wall harder. The woman let go and slumped to the floor.

Looking up, he noticed the collie had sprinted off to catch its special owner.

He tensed the hand the dog had bitten earlier, and felt the blood begin to seep through his fingers. His leg hurt from his latest bite, but the woman wasn't moving.

Reaching over, he snapped the two-horn necklace from around her neck. She groaned in a feeble attempt to stop him.

He turned over the horns and clicked the two pieces together, to form a single crescent moon.

"You forgot to give her this," he said and a malevolent grin spread across his face as he watched the dogs run around the corner to catch the Time Child. "So much for the Temporatii".

He reached for his own Tumble Thunder and flicked it open. A golden light emanated from the middle, shining against the cold steel. Molten threads began to run through his palm, and the feeling of cold spread through his body.

Up ahead, he saw an amazing, golden glow from where the girls had disappeared seconds earlier.

Still smiling he allowed the energy to envelope him.

"And now, young lady," he said holding the moon on the necklace, "you'll need to face me if you're ever going to realise your full powers. I have something you cannot do without. The moon."

With that, he left 1830, never to return.

* * *

Slumped against a wall of Admiralty Arch, facing Buckingham Palace, Madam Lehzen was in pain. Drina had rushed to tend to her, quizzing her about the man. Telling her that Izzy had just vanished, like in a magic trick.

"It's not magic, my dear," said the woman who had waited her whole life just for the last half an hour, only to mess it up. She held her shoulder and looked toward where the Time Child had disappeared just seconds earlier. Her neck was scratched and she felt her bare chest where she'd kept the crucial piece to the Tumble Thunder for all these years.

"What have I done?" she cried out, pulling Drina close. "What have I done?"

Chapter 30

Izzy stared at her reflection in the bathroom mirror. She couldn't believe it had happened.

After running off from the Time Shadow she'd hidden behind a wall and watched him leave Madam Lehzen in a heap on the floor. He'd snapped something from around her neck and put it together. He had smiled in a way that scared Izzy.

Whatever was in his hands was too small to see from so far away, but she saw him say the word as clear as day just before the Tumble Thunder brought her home.

"Moon."

She had been so pleased with herself at saving Drina, she had failed to find it in time.

Brushing her teeth as she looked at the open Tumble Thunder on the bathroom shelf, she was convinced that the indented moon had faded slightly.

The small face that had pointed to three before she first ended up in Scotland, now pointed to one.

However, the Tumble Thunder did what it did, she wasn't stupid. It was a countdown. And there was only one left. How could she possibly do everything with only one turn left?

She might have found the star, but now the Time Shadow had the moon. She was never going to find her dad. However much she had changed. However much she could control the *fuzziness*. No matter how much stronger she felt. She had failed.

What was worse, was that the Time Shadow knew about the clock shop. Somehow, he'd found her there in 1830. It was only a matter of time before he came back.

She had put everyone in danger.

Tears ran down her cheeks and she splashed cold water on her face to hide them. Mum mustn't find out. She wouldn't even know that she'd been anywhere.

When she returned she'd been exhausted. Without even looking at her watch, she had taken a quick nap before heading to the bathroom to freshen up. In her own time, it had been a little over four hours since she'd returned from Stonehenge and headed to her room for some sleep, albeit without her favourite teddy; *like things couldn't get worse*, she thought.

In reality, Izzy's body clock thought it was thirty hours ahead in time. It was like she was suffering from the craziest kind of jetlag. Her body didn't know if it was morning, afternoon, or night. She felt dazed. It was as if the time slips were making her older.

In some fresh clothes she headed wearily downstairs to allow Greysock out of the front door for a few seconds for a wee. Foubert's Place was strangely empty.

In the kitchen her mum was reading. Next to her, steam slowly rose from a mug of coffee.

"There you are sleepy head," said her mum, slowly turning around, pushing down the creases on her top. She smiled, but it looked like her own face didn't believe her. Only her mouth moved. There were dark circles under her eyes like she hadn't slept. Her eyes were red.

"I wondered when you'd appear," she added, before Izzy could say anything.

"I know. I really needed that. Did you get any sleep, Mum?" Izzy's voice was tentative. Her mum didn't look right.

"I got some sleep yesterday," said her mum. "After we got back. Do you even know what day it is? It's 7am - on Sunday. I figured Stonehenge took it out of you."

"What?" asked Izzy, slumping down in a chair at the table.

"Izzy, darling, it's Sunday morning." She repeated. Her face lifted, the dark circles temporarily banished. "You've slept for almost a day. I couldn't even find Greysock."

"Oh," said Izzy, as her mum petted the collie.

Izzy took a second to take it in. When she'd left her mum and the professor in the kitchen after their huge breakfast, it was Saturday morning. She'd almost nodded off and then the Tumble Thunder called her. She'd spent an evening, a night and a full day in 1830s London, come back at the same time she'd left on Saturday morning in the here and now, and then nodded off... for virtually a full day.

It was confusing, Izzy could barely keep up.

She opened her mouth to finally tell her mum everything. She felt an urge to burst out with it all. From the Tumble Thunder, to the notes, to Scotland and Aleck, to London and Drina and how she'd tried to do it all herself but failed.

But just as she opened her mouth to speak, something inside grabbed her tongue, and held it tight.

Dad's voice. Calm and soothing.

'Where two worlds meet. Find me.'

"Mum, I need to speak to you about Dad. Something terrible has happened."

The smile that had attempted to hide her mum's fatigue dropped from her face. The dark circles under her eyes returned and Izzy realised something. Her mum was wearing the same clothes she had on when they had travelled back from her nan's in Great Chardan.

Which was yesterday, don't forget, Izzy told herself. That was yesterday.

While Izzy had slept for a day and a half, her mum looked as if she'd been awake the entire time.

"Izzy, darling, there's nothing else for you to know. He's just not here," said her mum. She gave a huge sigh. Her chest and her shoulders dropped.

"Mum, I know he's alive," she said, talking more quickly as she went. "You said he went missing, but you won't say if you think he's dead or not. He never came back that day at Stonehenge. And I know why."

Though her face still betrayed how tired she was, Jane sat up and looked Izzy in the eye.

"Go on," said Jane. She took Izzy's hands and patted them gently.

"He is alive Mum," Izzy broke in. "He is. I know it. He needs me to find him, but I don't think I can. I think I've messed it all up and I don't think any of us are safe."

Jane rocked back a fraction and raised her eyebrows slightly. Izzy saw a momentary glint in her mum's tired eyes.

Izzy was desperate to tell her more. To talk her through everything that had happened. And if the Time Shadow knew about the clock shop, then Mum needed to know everything. They were all in danger.

Except she couldn't. It wasn't the words in the note that came back to her this time, but Nan's. She remembered how she'd whispered to her in the attic when she'd given her the desk.

'She's not special like you,' Nan had said.

Whatever was still to happen. It was up to her put it right. She couldn't expect her mum to save them. Izzy had to. She had to find the final pieces of the Tumble Thunder, steal the moon back from the Time Shadow and find her dad.

"Izzy," said her mum sympathetically. "You don't understand what you're talking about. You're still not old enough to understand it all. Not yet"

"I am, Mum," said Izzy. "I am."

Jane stared at her daughter through tears. She wiped the corner of her eyes with the palms of her hand. She stood, wiped her damp hands down the front of her crumpled clothes, and looked directly at Izzy.

"Don't do anything silly," she said. "I can't lose anyone else."

With that she stood up and walked out of the kitchen. Izzy was shocked. Her mum had never walked out on her before. She heard her bedroom door clunk loudly closed.

* * *

Jane sat on the side of her bed and reached for the bottom drawer on her cabinet. She was tired. She hadn't slept since they had returned from the summer solstice with Izzy's nan, Robert's mum. Jane had never seen Betty react in the way she had at Stonehenge. When the commotion had happened near the stones, Betty had known instantly what to do. The smell from the crushed lavender that had obscured Izzy's aura had given them just enough time to escape.

Izzy was special. Jane had protected her as much as she could. As much as Robert had asked her to. Soon the time would come when Izzy would have to realise her own destiny as a Time Child. Until then, Jane knew that she had to keep the truth from her for as long as possible. It was clear Izzy sensed something was different about herself recently.

When she had been forced to move Izzy from school to school because of the unexplained things caused by her temper, Jane had been able to brush it off. Not a single headteacher had ever forced Izzy to leave. Jane had always insisted on it. It was the only way to keep her identity hidden until she was old enough to understand; old enough to be ready for the challenges that must lay ahead if she was to complete her training. As far as Izzy was concerned, she had been expelled. It was easier to keep her powers secret that way.

But it wasn't now. Things were changing. Izzy was developing, almost evolving. She was becoming aware of her true self. Jane had seen it.

Pushing away thoughts of Izzy's abilities, Jane reached down for the bottom drawer of her bedside cabinet. It slid all the way out easily and gave a gentle clunk as it came free of its housing. Jane placed it on the bed beside her and reached inside the cabinet. She pushed down on a small section of floorboard and pushed it aside. A small chest lay underneath, around half the size of a shoebox. She pulled it out, placed it on her lap, and gently opened the lid.

Inside, an old, rusty pocket watch sat on top of a photograph. The front cover clicked open easily and an ornate watch-face stared back. Inside the main numbers were three more dials. The watch counted only up to three, and now pointed at two. None of the hands on the old watch were moving.

Jane's Tumble Thunder was dormant. Waiting for its final call.

It had been lifeless since Izzy's dad had given it to her the day before he left. Both Robert and Jane had known he had to go. That for him to continue to live with Izzy while he carried out his work would inevitably draw the Time Shadow to them all before she was ready to face him. He had to protect Izzy. The only way he could do that, to protect her hiding place, was to leave.

Jane put the dusty Tumble Thunder down and picked up the picture.

A single tear rolled down her cheek as she gazed at her younger self.

In her arms was a small girl, no older than six months. Unlike Izzy, her hair was jet black. She seemed to be mid-giggle. Her head was thrown back and a wide smiled dominated her cute, round face. She wore a red band in her hair and red, buckled shoes. The picture had been taken outside of the clock shop.

"This isn't fair," she said quietly to the picture, and gently sobbed. She stroked her finger lightly down the girl's black hair one more time. "I love Izzy, Robert. I love her like my own. But I can't protect her. Just like I couldn't protect Eliza."

Chapter 31

The argument had left Izzy feeling bad all night. Her mum hadn't reappeared. She had never shut herself in her bedroom like that. Ever. It was weird. Izzy just figured it was to do with her dad. Her mum hardly ever talked about it. Izzy didn't think it helped.

She'd spent hours virtually filling a book of *Scramblings* and trying to piece together everything. She woke early the next morning to try and finish.

From the note and the Tumble Thunder, to Aleck, to controlling the *fuzziness* and how she'd felt when she added the star from Greysock's collar to the pocket watch.

As she'd written about Stonehenge, she'd realised that the Time Shadow must have been there too. It was the only explanation for why Nan had reacted so strangely. She was afraid.

But while she had saved Drina's life, she had failed to bring back the moon for the Tumble Thunder. He had it and she needed it back. It was the only way she could complete the Tumble Thunder.

Just the sun remained on the inside casing of the watch. The horizontal number eight sat just beneath it, but she had the feeling that however she used the Tumble Thunder next, bringing back the sun would be absolutely key.

'Complete it, to complete you.'

Then, and only then, would she be able to find her dad where two worlds meet.

She didn't have a clue what that meant, and she could only use the Tumble Thunder once more.

Thinking it all through should have terrified her. Instead, her decision to put things right had galvanised her. The spinning molten *fuzziness* felt like it was on standby.

Though she'd woken early, Greysock wasn't anywhere to be seen. Her bedroom door was ajar. She called softly down the stairs. He didn't appear.

Pausing to listen, she shrugged and settled at her desk with her *Scramblings* to complete what she could remember from 1830. She wrote down everything she could remember, right down to the stench and the heat. Her nose still hadn't recovered from the pungent smell. What had the newspaper seller called it? 'The Big Stink'. The more she concentrated, the more vivid her memory became. The huge house where Drina lived hung in her memory. But however much she focused, she couldn't picture where she'd seen it before. It was like something from a book.

As she wrote everything down, everything seemed to point back to the clock shop. The same desk in the same attic room. The cellar and the secret passage through London. Twelve Foubert's Place seemed connected to everything.

She looked at the clock in the corner of her room and jumped up. It was 7:50 am.

Despite being up so early she was almost late leaving for school.

She belted down the stairs and into the kitchen at top speed. Greysock was nowhere to be seen. Neither was her mum. The kitchen was eerily silent and cold. On the table, propped up against the fruit bowl, was a white envelope with 'Izzy' on the front. Her mum's writing. The hairs on Izzy's neck stood up.

The enveloped was crisp and opened rigidly.

> 'I'm sorry about last night. I've had to go away for a couple of days on some business with the shop. The professor is around. Make sure you make time to make time. Mum.'

"Hmmm," said Izzy. The note dropped to the table. Mum going away was nothing new. But her timing wasn't great. She grabbed an apple from the fruit bowl and headed down the stairs. The professor was in the shop, humming.

"Morning, Professor," she said to the head bobbing behind the counter. "Looking for something?"

"Morning Izzy," came the reply. He was slightly out of breath. "Nothing that I won't find in a minute. Did you see the note from your mum? She'll only be a couple of days she said. Not sure entirely where she's off to, but nothing to worry about. I'm around. You going to school? Have a lovely day. Bye."

With that, he scurried off behind the curtain and into the storage room behind the main shop.

"Weird," said Izzy. "You're all being weird."

"Sorry?" said the professor, sticking his head around the corner of the curtain. "What?"

"Oh, nothing, Professor. I'll see you later."

The bell on the top of the door jangled loudly as she left. Porter was leaning on the wall opposite, waiting. Waiting and eating. His rucksack was over one shoulder. Its fraying straps hung loosely down where he'd wrapped them around his hand so he could hold a huge bag of crisps.

"Hey," he said, with a mouthful of crisps. "We're going to be late. Crisp? They're ready salted. How was your trip to Stonehenge?"

"Porter, I'm so pleased to see you," she said,

and wrapped her arms around his neck before she realised what she was doing.

"Hey," he said, pushing her defensively off his crisps. "I'm pleased to see you too."

"You wouldn't believe my weekend. But there's something we've got to do today. I need to go to the school library at lunchtime."

Porter dropped in behind her as she marched off. They rounded the corner of Foubert's Place to be greeted by George, sitting on a stone step with Greysock. The old man was feeding the dog what looked like pieces of croissant.

"Hey little miss," said George. "My new friend just won't leave me be."

"Greysock!" said Izzy. "There you are. How did you get out?"

The dog dropped his snack and looked straight at Izzy. Then at Porter. Then at George. He gave a little bark-whine and went back to his breakfast.

"Your mum left him with me," said George. "Said she was going away and he needed looking after while you were at school."

"Oh, okay," said Izzy, with a frown. "I didn't know you knew her that well."

"Izzy. Little miss. Like I told you before, I know everybody around here. I've been here a looooong time. Have a nice day. And have a good day."

"Okay," she said to him, before turning to the dog "Greysock. Be a good boy for George. We'll see you later."

* * *

At lunchtime, Izzy met Porter by the grand entrance to the school library. The teachers said it was one of the best libraries in London. Western Grange was one of the oldest schools in the capital and felt like the tenth Izzy had been to in the past few years.

The huge oak doors were weathered by generations of grubby hands. Their marks, kicks and scrapes were left in the wood like an indignant calling card. An imperious dragon looked down on them from a stained-glass window above.

Having only been at the school for a few weeks, Izzy hadn't actually been in before. It was as big as the hall where she was made to do PE every Tuesday.

The three-metre-high doors gave a creak as they swung back into place. Several students, and the librarian behind the counter, all looked up. Mrs Johnstone, a thin woman with big glasses, was cradling a mug with two hands. Without breaking their gaze she put it down, slowly, and raised a single hand to the sign above her head which read, simply: Silence.

"Sorry," mouthed Izzy, and tugged Porter away to the nearest section of books.

"Good job we didn't want to sneak in," whispered Porter, wiping biscuit crumbs from his face. "Now, why the heck are we here, again?"

"Long story," said Izzy. "But I want to find out

more about the clock shop. We need the section on local history. Any ideas?"

"This way," said Porter, keeping his voice forcibly low. "Before you turned up at the school, I used to come here a lot. There are three sections on local history. It's tucked away around the back where no-one goes."

"So how do you know where it is then?" asked Izzy in hushed tones as they passed a huge row of books on geography and geology.

"I've never had many friends, so I make my friends in books," said Porter, turning down some stairs. He took out a pack of biscuits from his bag. "Plus, no-one bothers you down here. And you don't have to whisper."

He dropped his bag onto the floor with a clunk, sat down in the nearest chair and leaned back. He tore open his packet of digestives and put a whole one in his mouth.

Izzy looked at him disapprovingly.

"Fast metabolism," he said, through a mouthful of crumbs, and gesturing at his tall, slender frame. "And I walk everywhere."

He devoured his biscuit, swallowed hard and pointed in front of them. "Local history is there. There's loads on the centre of London. What are we looking for?"

"I want to see if there are any old maps and anything about the clock shop back in the 1800s. Also, if there are any books with pictures of famous houses in London. Ones with huge gardens that are three floors high."

"Erm, Izzy, this is London. There are hundreds."

An hour later and having decided to skip their first lesson back after lunch, they had found nothing.

On the table next to Porter was a huge pile of picture books and local maps, but Izzy couldn't find anything to do with the clock shop.

She had worked her way through the history of Carnaby Street, the next street along to Foubert's Place. But it didn't go back far enough. She'd read all about the famous Liberty department store, just around the corner from the clock shop. But that opened in 1875, almost 45 years after she'd met Drina and her dog, Dash.

She had almost given up when, at the back of the section on Carnaby Street in a black, leather-bound book, she recognised something. It was the Shakespeare's Head, the pub right next to where she lived.

The picture was dated 1825. In it, two men stood outside, smiling broadly. Behind them, down Foubert's Place, Izzy could just make out the front of the clock shop.

She skimmed the words, and slowly turned the page. Then stopped.

The shop where she had grown up looked much like it always had. The door that led into the clock shop had barely changed in almost 200 years. The gold letters embossed across the window in an arc shone in the sunlight despite the aged sepia picture. But it wasn't the gold lettering that made her nearly bite through her tongue in shock.

There, standing side by side, were Professor Wigglesworth and her dad. She checked the date on the picture: September, 1825.

They looked exactly the same age as they did now, in 2013.

It couldn't be. Could it? She blinked hard, to clear her eyes and her thoughts, and looked again. She read the full caption.

'Wigglesworth and Son Clock Shoppe. Opened 1825. Pictured are Charles Wigglesworth and son Robert on the opening of the shop in the earliest known photograph in history.'

She looked again and re-read the caption.

'...Charles Wigglesworth and son Robert...'

Her dad, Robert. His dad was the professor?

'Opened 1825'.

She felt sick and confused.

Then it hit her. If her dad was the professor's son, then the professor was her granddad.

"What?" she slumped down into the chair. "Dad? I don't get it."

Porter looked across at her. "What are you on abou..."

"Aww, did I hear you calling for your daddy again?" It was Ellie. Her voice was more of a hiss as she appeared from behind a bookshelf with a malevolent smile. Her sidekicks, Harriet and Georgia, were there too. Harriet was holding her phone in front of her face. She was recording a video.

Ellie looked around at the camera like a TV reporter, and gestured toward Izzy with her thumb: "What's the matter with the freak? Let's find out."

Izzy sat up and slammed the book shut on her desk.

"What do you and your Phoneys want, Ellie?" said Izzy. "I don't have time for your nonsense right now. We're busy."

"Yeah, shove off you lot," said Porter, getting to his feet. He stood beside his friend, towering over everyone.

"Shush, Tree Trunk," said Ellie, pointing at Izzy. "I'm here for her."

"What?" gasped Izzy. "What?"

"Quiet around there." It was Mrs Johnstone from behind her desk. Though she was keen everyone else was silent, she didn't mind hollering through the bookshelves.

Undeterred, Harriet and Georgia stifled a laugh.

"You really are a freak, aren't you?"

And with that, she raised her arm to throw a previously hidden bag of flour all over Izzy and Porter in an attempt to cover her from head to toe.

Except, it didn't quite happen like that.

Just as Ellie called Izzy a 'freak', she had

summoned the *fuzziness* like never before. She called it. Without the need to concentrate on a second hand. She reached for it instinctively because she needed to protect her friend.

She held it and, just as Ellie's arm began to raise to throw the flour over her, Izzy let go of the molten *fuzziness*. She didn't know how. She just did.

Everything froze. The Phoneys were standing, watching. A devilish laugh was stuck across all of their faces. Izzy turned and looked at Porter. He was looking down and locked in a frozen frown at Ellie. Her arm was halfway towards Izzy. The flour hung peeping from the open bag, suspended in mid-air. She turned to her friend and stepped right in front of him.

"Porter?" she said, looking directly into his eyes. He didn't move. She snapped her fingers in front of his face. Nothing. She reached up and prodded his cheek. He didn't flinch.

"Porter!" she shouted in his face. Not even a blink.

Everyone was still. She glanced up at the old-fashioned clock on the wall. The second hand had paused.

Nothing was moving.

She had made time stand still.

Even more, she could feel it. The *fuzziness* hung invisibly in the air. She could sense it.

Quickly turning the bag of flour around in

Ellie's hand, she pointed the open end toward the head Phoney.

She stood next to Porter, focusing on the *fuzziness*, and breathed it back in.

The clock sprung back into life, everyone moved, and the flour billowed all over Ellie. From head to toe.

"Hey!" screamed Ellie. "Eeewww."

"What the?" said Georgia, as Harriet turned the phone in the direction of Ellie. "That wasn't supposed to happen! You were supposed to get her."

"You," said Harriet, pointing straight at Izzy.

"I didn't do anything," said Izzy, with a smile.

"Yes, you did," said Harriet. "You did it! You must have done."

Ellie sneezed and a cloud of flour erupted from her hair as her head jerked forward.

"I really didn't do anything," protested Izzy, still smiling. "Maybe you should blame yourself."

The group looked at each other for what seemed like an age.

Ellie, covered in flour. Izzy, smiling in front of her. Porter's eyes were wide. He stood behind them as flour settled through the air like a fine snowstorm.

"You!" Ellie hissed. "It was you! How did you do that, you weirdo?"

Each word sent a small puff of flour into the air and Porter was stifling a laugh.

Mrs Johnstone clumped around the corner. She was still holding her mug of tea, and her face was a beetroot red.

"I've told you lot before. Quiet in my library and.." she stopped, and her jaw dropped. "What on earth?"

"It was Izzy, Mrs Johnstone," said Ellie without blinking.

Porter seized the moment.

"Time to go, Izzy," he said, his hands on her shoulders. He ushered her towards the exit, carrying both of their bags.

"You've done it this time!" Ellie shouted behind them.

The huge library doors had just closed behind them when they heard Mrs Johnstone.

"Isabella!"

For such a tiny woman, her voice boomed.

Well, that's breaking your own rules, thought Izzy, as Porter shoved her in the back.

"Run," he said. They darted down the corridor and around the corner.

Slowing to a quick walk they passed the staff room. Izzy could feel the sweat running down her back. Porter was breathing heavily.

They turned left toward the science block, when the school announcement system ding-donged above them. They paused and slinked into a recess next to an old fire hose.

There was a throat-clearing cough, and a familiar voice boomed out.

"Would Isabella Latimer report to my office

immediately? Without a moment's delay," said Mr Tompkins in his military tone. He ended with a 'harrumph' and the speaker above crackled as it was turned off.

For a brief moment, Izzy imagined him straightening his tie and his waistcoat, his red face blooming.

"Uh-oh," she looked at Porter. "I'm in for it now."

Porter looked straight at her and took a deep breath.

"Listen, Izzy. I don't know what it is that you do," he paused, searching her face. "But you do something. It was like in the school canteen. You know you do. Whenever you get angry, something happens."

"But I didn't get angry," protested Izzy. "I made it happen."

She thought of the *fuzziness*. How she had controlled it. How she had summoned it, and how Ellie had been covered in flour as a result. She could do something. She just didn't understand fully what it was, but she knew now that the *fuzziness* wasn't a tool for anger. It was something to help protect what she cared about the most – who she cared about – like her friends.

She looked up into the face of her best friend. His cheeks were still red, and a tiny trickle of sweat was running down his temple. But his eyes were honest. Trusting.

"Porter, there's so much I need to tell you. There's someone chasing me. He can't find me. I don't know what will happen if he does."

"Okaaay?" said Porter slowly, his eyes widening.

"We've got to get out of here. Get back to the shop. I need the Tumble Thunder. It's in my desk."

"The tumble whatnow?" asked Porter.

She pulled out the picture she had quietly torn from the history book in the library.

"Look. My dad is called Robert. Professor Wigglesworth. That's them. But it's in 1825... and it said my dad is the professor's son. I don't get it."

"Okaaaaay?" repeated Porter, more dramatically.

"We need to get out of here and get back to the clock shop without Tompkins seeing us. I need my Tumble Thunder and I know I need Greysock," she said. "

"Okaaaaaaaayyy?" he said before lowly repeating: "Your. Tumble. Thunder?"

Chapter 32

The door to the clock shop was wide open. The closed sign hung feebly against a cracked pane. Lopsided, it knocked gently on the frame. Foubert's Place was almost deserted. The street and the shop almost silent but for the hum of the West End traffic around the corner. A tramp, huddled up in the shop doorway opposite, snored just loud enough for them to hear.

They'd taken all of the back streets and alleys to get here, desperate to avoid as many people as possible. She didn't even stop by to get Greysock from George.

The sight of the clock shop scared her. The *fuzziness* hanging in her chest like a caged tiger.

Izzy stepped slowly inside. Porter followed and snuffled loudly. Izzy shot him a glance and they both stopped.

It was a mess. Shards from the glass cabinets were strewn across the floor. The old Winston Churchill picture that Professor Wigglesworth so lovingly polished was smashed. Its glass broken in the middle as if it had been hit with something.

Dust hung, illuminated in the afternoon sunshine. The few antique clocks that the professor kept on the shelves remained in their places behind the till. Untouched. The pocket watches were gone. All of them.

Mum was nowhere to be seen. Neither was the professor, no, not the professor - her grandad. What had happened to them?

It was like being hit in the stomach with a spade. She felt empty. The clock shop was more than just her home, it felt like the centre of her world. Finding the Tumble Thunder had made it something more. Like she was meant to be here. Like it made her feel stronger.

But it had made her easier to find too. It was as if using the Tumble Thunder and the *fuzziness* had sent a beacon into the sky to show where she was.

"The Time Shadow," Izzy said out loud. "He's been here."

"What?" whispered Porter, raising both eyebrows.

She didn't reply to the question on his face.

Instead, the *fuzziness* fluttered as the hairs on her arms had stood up. A shiver ran down her spine. Holding it, she took a breath. Stopping time wouldn't help her now.

The Tumble Thunder! It was upstairs. How could she be so stupid as to leave it?

Glass crunched loudly under her feet. She paused. And listened. Nothing.

She picked her way through the broken remnants of the shop she'd known all her life. Porter followed in her steps, avoiding the dagger-like shards.

In the hallway, it was clear the whole shop was empty. Every few steps they stopped to listen. There was nothing.

At the first floor the door to the professor's flat was also open. They peeked inside, but it seemed untouched.

"Mum?" Izzy whispered as loudly as she dared. "Professor?"

She'd only actually seen inside the professor's blue door once before. He had an office area, with doors leading off to a small bathroom and a bedroom.

Despite the ransacked mess downstairs, the office was fine. But the Time Shadow hadn't come for the professor. Or her mum. She knew neither of them were here.

The professor's battered leather office chair and his desk were sitting neatly together. A fountain pen sat in the inkwell on top of the desk. A pile of white envelopes stacked neatly to the left. Underneath the window that overlooked Foubert's Place, a low bookcase with old, leather-bound novels were in perfect order.

In the bathroom and the bedroom, she found nothing.

Light footsteps above made them freeze.

Their eyes locked.

Izzy motioned upstairs and whispered: "We need to get the Tumble Thunder."

She went to move ahead but Porter stepped in. He shook his head and led the way himself. His huge, teenage bulk took up most of the gap. Izzy could see sweat running down the back of his neck.

At the foot of the stairs, he stopped. He turned and she urged him upward. With a deep breath, he took the first step and slowly crept up the staircase. As they approached the flat she shared with her mum, he stopped and held his arms out behind him to shield her from whatever was waiting.

The kitchen door was open. Nothing looked amiss from the landing.

Like the professor, her mum was nowhere to be seen. Izzy figured - actually felt - she was still wherever she had gone before breakfast. Whoever they'd heard seemed to be hiding.

Scanning the landing, Izzy nodded toward her attic bedroom and they continued slowly up the stairs. Three steps from the top there was a loud scratching noise from inside Izzy's bedroom.

They held their breath and stopped. And waited.

A second later, they shifted onto a single step at the top of the landing and the tired floorboards gave a tell-tale creak. Izzy closed her eyes and winced.

From the other side of the open door, there was a scrambling of feet.

Porter pushed Izzy behind him. The pair shrunk back against the wall as the scratchy, scrambling grew louder.

He thumped into them at top speed. It was followed by an assault of saliva, whining and a wagging tail.

"Greysock!" shouted Izzy, wiping her face clean of the dog's gooey drool.

Wagging his tail, he bark-whined twice and sat to attention. His tail swept the floor behind him and his ears pricked up.

"Hey stupid dog. You scared Izzy," said Porter, deflecting his own panic and taking a relieved breath. He rolled his hand over the dog's head. He stood up, brushing dust from his tatty trousers. Sweat was running down his temple.

Izzy got to her feet and crossed the landing with Greysock leading the way. He left a trail of bloody pawprints.

"Hey boy, what have you done to yourself?" Izzy asked, as she walked into her bedroom.

He was sitting in front of her desk. There were deep, red scratches at the closed entrance to the secret drawer. His blood had dried on the wood, and his grey paw was matted red. He looked back at her, whined, and lay down.

Inspecting his paws, she saw three of his claws had bent back from where he'd scratched at the desk. He didn't seem overly bothered, despite the blood.

Her room was a mess. It was worse than the shop. Here, everything had been turned upside down and broken. Her bed was on its side. The mattress thrown against the wall.

Her heavy desk was still upright but each drawer had been pulled out and emptied.

Three books of *Scramblings* were open on the floor. The picture of her dad as a kid at Greenwich Observatory had fallen from one of them. It was ripped at the corner. She wondered if Nan would be mad that it was damaged. Scooping it up she stuffed it in her pocket.

The rest of her *Scramblings* were nowhere to be seen. There were four or five books missing. She flicked through those that remained. But all of the ones which detailed everything since she got the Tumble Thunder were gone. The dreams of her dad. The *Seeings* she'd experienced. Meeting Aleck and Drina.

She knew exactly who had ransacked her room, and what he was looking for.

The Time Shadow.

Frantically she reached inside the desk to find the hidden button to her secret drawer.

It clunked into place, and the Tumble Thunder slid out. She clutched it close to her chest and let out a deep breath of relief.

She held it tight and looked at the dog.

"At least he never got this," she told them both, as she felt the slightest warmth of comfort from the old pocket watch.

"At least who didn't get what? Izzy, what's going on?" said Porter looking around at the wreckage of her room. "Where is your mum? You've been burgled. We should call the police. And what were you saying at the library about your dad and the professor?"

The reality of her situation washed over her like a tsunami of mixed emotions.

She still had to find her dad, but now her mum and the professor were missing and the Time Shadow had found her. And he might still be here.

He had seen her inner most thoughts and memories of her *Seeings* with her dad. It could only have been him. Whoever he was, he knew everything now. Writing it all down hadn't been such a good idea after all.

It didn't make any sense. None of it did.

Drained, she slumped to the floor, frustrated and lost.

"Hey, don't be like that," said Porter, awkwardly

putting one arm around her shoulder, and looking around as if to check no-one was looking. "We'll sort it all out. Somehow. Maybe crisps would help."

Greysock nuzzled into her and Porter put his other arm around the dog. The trio sat together amid the wreckage of the room in a huddled group. Greysock rested his head on Izzy's shoulder.

"Where two worlds meet," Izzy said angrily to Porter, lifting her head. His eyes were blank. Confused. "I have no idea what I'm supposed to do. But I know I'm supposed to do something."

"I'm sure it'll come to you, probably when you least expect it."

The Tumble Thunder was still cold but the case clicked open easily. The hands on the face pointed resolutely to the X at the top. The eight-digit counter in the middle read like a row of bubbles: 00000000. The golden hand on the left, where another face went from 0-24, pointed straight up. The smaller, internal face, where the hand had pointed at three when she first found the mysterious old watch, now pointed at two. She had one more attempt left.

She willed it to happen. It didn't respond. Fiddling with the three dials on the side didn't make any difference either. The first time, when she pushed the biggest one in with a click, the Tumble Thunder had come to life. This time, there was nothing. There was no golden glow. No all-consuming warmth.

"I don't understand, Porter," she said into his

shoulder. “I feel like I can’t trust anyone. And why won’t this just work?”

“You can trust me, Izzy. That’s why I’m here. We’re in this together.”

She smiled at him. All the time she’d ever known him he’d been nothing but nice.

Sitting bolt upright she focused. She reached deep inside searching for the molten *fuzziness* that had come so easily in the library. She hadn’t realised at first, but her *Seeings* and the Tumble Thunder were intrinsically linked by the *fuzziness*.

She squeezed her hand around the Tumble Thunder and summoned it. Knowing she had to find a way to make it work for the sake of everyone she loved.

Porter held them all together. Greysock’s wet nose not far from his own. He gripped the dog’s collar and pulled Izzy closer.

And then it happened.

Chapter 33

"Urgh! I don't like it!" shouted Porter, pushing Izzy away and looking around in a panic. "What did you do?"

He couldn't see Izzy properly for the golden haze. He rubbed his eyes and opened them in an exaggerated way to check. He repeated it twice more until the hue faded.

"Okay, I'm not blind. Izzy, that was not fun," he said. "Now I'm starving. What are you trying to do to me?"

"Sorry," said Izzy. "I didn't know you'd come too. Or you, you daft dog."

She patted Greysock on the head. He was sitting in front of them like he didn't have a care in the world.

"Come where? What just happened?" asked Porter, rolling his shoulders and looking around at the room which looked exactly like the one they'd been sitting in moments earlier. "We haven't gone anywhere. Oh. Wait."

"It's not that easy to explain," said Izzy, cutting in and checking out her surroundings too. "This looks like my bedroom. But it isn't. We just time travelled, I wanted it to happen, and it did. I've never been able to do that before."

Porter looked at her, astonished, and began to giggle.

"You're having me on," he said and continued to laugh for a while longer until he saw her stern face. "Oh. You're not."

They were still in her attic bedroom. Except it wasn't. The carnage they had found when they got back from school, was gone. Where Izzy's bed normally stood there was a broken stack of wooden crates labelled fragile, as if they'd just been thrown at the wall.

A thick cloud of dust was slowly falling to the floor. But that wasn't the only smell. There was smoke too, is if someone had tried to start a fire.

The wooden floor was bare. Izzy's carpet had gone. Around her feet, the wood was blackened. A faint stream of smoke whispered past her ankles. Her trainers, like before, were fine.

The windows were covered with what looked like grey curtains that had been taped to the frames.

"I think this is my room," said Izzy, slowly. "It's just that I don't live here yet."

"I don't get it," said Porter. "I need biscuits."

Neither he, nor Greysock, seemed affected by the time slip. While the room was broken and the floor slightly burnt, both of them were fine.

The Tumble Thunder was cold again, but it had changed. The golden lustre had faded. The ivory white face looked a milky grey. The gold leaf hands pointed to 7:30pm, but they seemed less shiny than before. The numbers had turned to 09051940.

"May, 1940," she mouthed. Porter was still looking around with wide eyes, oblivious.

The hand that counted the hours to 24 was the only one that had moved. It had begun the day-long countdown. The dial that showed 0-3 had ticked over to three. The second hand glided effortlessly as always, oblivious to the drama.

But her eyes were drawn to the indented symbols. If the Time Shadow had the moon, then she still had to find the sun. Maybe it would be with the horizontal number eight. That bit still didn't seem to make total sense.

'Complete it, to complete you.'

"There's still more we need to do," she said to the boy and the dog. "Porter, there are some things I need to tell you. We just time slipped."

"We did what?" Like his eyebrows, his voice went higher. "We, what now?"

"Shush," she said, listening for any noise downstairs. "Don't ask questions. We might not have enough time. Someone might have heard us."

"If they did, they'd be up here already."

Izzy listened again. Convinced there was no immediate danger, she gave Porter a quick account of everything that had happened. She paused occasionally to listen and tried to keep it simple.

"I still don't get it," he said, when she had finished. "And I still need something to eat. I think I might starve to death."

She didn't quite believe it herself. An antique-looking, time-travelling device had mysteriously appeared in her bedroom out of nowhere! In an unfathomable way, it came from the dad she hadn't seen for three years, who she now had to find. The device had so far, seemingly come to life twice, helping her time slip to two different years for 24 hours. One where she'd found a weird boy and inherited a dog in Scotland, then escaped across a stinking, 19th century London with a rich girl while being chased by the man called the Time Shadow who wanted to kill her. Oh yes, she could stop time when she really needed to.

"We're in the year 1940," she repeated, holding up the Tumble Thunder in front of Porter's bemused face. "This is the Tumble Thunder. I got it for my birthday. It was in the desk with a note from my dad. It makes things happen. It feels like it's been changing me. I've been..."

An overbearing, wailing sound stopped her mid-sentence. It whirred loudly through the walls, becoming high-pitched before seemingly turning down into a deeper hum and back again. It continued up and down, up and down, like a monotonous wave of sound.

Izzy and Porter looked at each other. Greysock whined. They heard shouts from outside. The noise droned on. Up and down.

"An air raid siren!" said Izzy. "It's 1940. World War Two. It's an air raid! We've got to get somewhere safe."

"What?"

Porter, having missed out on whatever Izzy had previously wanted to tell him, was now a healthy shade of bemused pink. He pushed himself up and pulled Izzy to her feet.

"This is mad. Come on, this way," he said, and made toward the stairs that led to the kitchen.

"No," said Izzy, pulling him back. "We don't know who's down there." She looked around the room that wasn't her room in the time that wasn't her time, and her eyes fell on a familiar escape route.

"There," she pointed. "The basement."

They crept quietly down the back stairs that led from the attic room to the basement of the clock shop. In 2013, Izzy wasn't allowed to open the wooden door that led to the cellar. In 1830, she'd hurled herself through it in a blind panic with Drina to escape whoever was chasing them.

But now, in 1940, she was unsure as to what she'd find beyond the door. Or who else might be in the clock shop. She placed her hands on the cast iron doorknob and paused. The air raid siren continued, drowning out any noises from the shop above.

"Porter," she whispered to her friend. "I don't know what's beyond this door."

Porter looked back up the gloomy staircase. After a few seconds he shrugged. Turning back, he slowly put his ear against the heavy wooden door. Greysock gave a little whine as the air raid siren stopped.

Still listening amid an eerie silence, Porter shoved the wooden door. It didn't move.

"Stop," hissed Izzy, and he did. The pair looked at each other, holding their heads deep into their shoulders for fear of being heard.

They waited. Nothing.

As Porter lent into the door, a huge explosion made the whole stairway shake. They jumped and Izzy gave a little shriek.

"A bomb!" Porter said as dust fell from the ceiling above. "A bloody bomb! Where have you brought us?"

The door, freed by the vibrations of the explosion, opened easily.

"That felt close," Izzy said, as the door swung open. "It must have shifted the whole clock shop."

The cellar stood before her for only the second time. It was like a different room.

When she had found herself here with Drina, the walls and the air had been cold and damp.

But now, in 1940 and at the height of the Second World War, the room was warm and dry. Two gas lamps on the wall were still burning. The small windows that led to Foubert's Place above were blacked out with paint. The room would be unseen from the street.

Dust was still slowly falling from the ceiling. Outside, she could hear fire engines and shouting.

At the far end, the cast iron fireplace was where she remembered it. Except, this time, it was pushed ajar revealing the entrance to the hidden tunnel that had taken her and Drina underneath Carnaby Street and to safety. She had absolutely no intention of going back down that tunnel. She'd hated it last time. There was a slight draught that caused the nearest gas lamp to flicker gently. Its yellow light spread across the floor like waves of marmalade.

Next to the fireplace there was an old bed, *like the kind you'd see in prison*, she thought. There was a rolled-up blanket and a pillow.

The wooden workbench from her first visit was still there, along with the old stool. Yet above it, instead of a bare brick wall, there was a zigzag of brown string that criss-crossed a wooden board.

She stepped closer. There were four photographs attached to numbers and writing. There were more spaces. They were all blank.

At the very top of the maze of string was her picture. Next to it the words: 'Izzy Latimer.'

Several strings were joined to her picture. So were the blank spaces.

She traced her fingers along it to the next picture. It was of a grumpy-looking old woman in a black dress. The woman looked sad. Next to it, a young girl with a dog. She recognised both.

"Drina," she whispered to the wall.

She scanned the words next to the pictures and read them out loud.

"Drina. 1830. Later, Queen Victoria. Saves her life." she said slowly, her eyebrows raising with her voice. "What?"

Puzzled, she scanned across to the next picture on the string matrix.

It was of a young boy in tweed clothes with a flat cap. Next to that a white-haired man with a bushy beard.

"Aleck. 1860. Later, Alexander Graham Bell. Helps invent the telephone," read Porter over her shoulder. "Those two are dead famous, Izzy. We did about them in history."

"What?"

"Those two. That bloke invented the telephone like it says. Queen Victoria was, well, she was queen for ages. But why is your picture up there? Who did all of this?"

In the middle of the wall, was a black and white picture of a building. It looked like a grand house with a dome at each end. Just to the left of one, there was what looked like an iron weathervane. On the top of the pole, there was a ball.

Izzy chewed her lip.

Outside, the fire engines seemed to be closer. The shouting was louder.

"It's Greenwich Observatory," she said to Porter, whispering in the new-found silence.

"I've been there too on a school trip," he said. "It's cool. It's the place where they set Greenwich Mean Time. You know, so they work out the time difference whether you're in New York or Moscow. That ball helps them set the time."

"Dad did this," she said, pointing to the wall and then the bed. "It's been him all along. He's been here. He's been sleeping here. I think this is where he's been all this time. He sent me to meet Drina and Aleck. Helping them was what I had to do."

"There you go again," said Porter. He rolled his eyes and took a deep breath. "If your dad did all of this, then why isn't he here now?"

It hit Izzy like a thunderbolt.

She grabbed Porter by the shoulders and looked straight at him. Greysock jumped up at them both in a triumphant, canine hug.

"The observatory at Greenwich. The line that sets time for both parts of the world. Where east meets west. It's like he said in the note he left me: Where two worlds meet!"

She thrust her hand into her pocket and pulled out the old picture of her and her dad standing in front of the same iron gates.

"Nan gave me this. Look at it," her voice was trembling with excitement. "That's where he wants me to go. That's what Dad has been trying to tell me. He used to take me there all the time when I was little. He knew it would be important."

"Eh?" Porter was blank.

She waved it in front of Porter's face, pointing to the wall.

The pictures of Drina and Aleck, linked by interwoven string stared at him.

"Where two worlds meet. That's where we need to go."

"What?"

"Greenwich. Don't you see?"

Greysock had jumped up against Porter. The boy pushed him down and rubbed both hands down the outside of his thighs.

He looked at his friend. He looked down at the dog. He looked at the wall. He eyes slowly tracked the pictures and the note. He looked around the cellar with its gas lamp and blacked-out windows. Then back at Izzy.

"Nope," he said and shrugged to emphasise his point. "Nope. Nope. Nope."

He leaned onto the workbench beneath the pictures. Greysock leapt up to copy him, standing against the boy on his hind legs. He nuzzled

Porter's arm and jumped up onto the workbench.

"I know," said Porter, cupping the dog's ears and rubbing them. "I don't understand it either."

He turned to Izzy just as Greysock jumped between them, knocking a small wooden box to the floor. Its contents scattered.

They clanked and clunked across the floor. A round piece of glass bounced once and rolled away. Its helter skelter bid for freedom halted by the bare, brick wall opposite.

It was an odd assortment. There were small pieces of circular glass. Brass cogs smaller than peas. A handful of golden, round casings. Tiny springs and even smaller cogs. Small, blunt pins. Some needle-like arrows. Among them, a small magnifying glass, with a single brass arrow, enlarged beneath its lens.

It reminded Izzy of the tests her mum would set her before breakfast.

"They're watch pieces," said Izzy. She rolled one of the small arrows between her thumb and forefinger. "Dad has been building pocket watches down here."

"This one looks finished," said Porter, passing Izzy a small pocket watch on a chain. "It's beautiful too."

It felt familiar and smooth in the palm of her hand. The hands were still. Within the main face were two smaller dials. Below them a row of numbers, all set to zero.

"No. It's not finished. They're not watches. These pieces aren't right. Look at the three dials on this one," said Izzy, her own face lighting up as it dawned on her. "They're not watches. They're Tumble Thunders. My dad has been down here trying to build Tumble Thunders. We've got to get to Greenwich. That's where Dad is."

"Izzy, you've either got to give me food, or you've got to explain what the heck you're going on about. I'm lost."

Porter slumped to the floor. His shoulders sagged. His jumper rode up his back as if he'd been suspended on a giant hook.

Rolling the part-built Tumble Thunder over and over in her hand, Izzy felt a huge surge of guilt for her confused and tired friend.

She showed Porter the face of her Tumble Thunder and explained how it worked.

"You see the small dial there," she pointed, inside the main watch face. "It's counting down hours from 24. I have a day every time it works. The row with the numbers is the date."

She described how the *fuzziness* had grown stronger the whole time. Then she told him how time had actually stood still in the library when she covered Ellie in the flour. Porter listened. He sighed. A lot.

"I didn't realise at first, but I can't use the *fuzziness* or the Tumble Thunder when I'm angry or because I want to. It's like I can only use it when I'm doing something good. Or," she paused, "protecting my friends."

"Oh," said Porter.

"I think my dad needs me to get to the Greenwich Observatory. I don't know why. And I don't know who the Time Shadow is either. But I know he's been following us. I don't know what will happen if I actually find him but I know I have to face him. I need the moon. It's the only way to complete this."

She held her Tumble Thunder in front of them both.

"Izzy," said Porter. "That's a lot of don't knows. And it's a lot to take in. But I think I'm following you."

"Good," she said, holding up the half-built Tumble Thunder she'd found, "because I think I need to try and fix this one. I need a horology set. I bet there's one upstairs."

"A what? Forget it," said Porter, before adding: "So, upstairs, fix that thing, avoid the Shadow bloke and then get to Greenwich without being killed by a bomb? Seems fairly easy. Shall we get going?"

"Are you trying to be funny?" asked Izzy. "Because I don't appreciate it."

"Sorry," said Porter, standing up. "But this is all mental. And I'm starving. Come on."

He shrugged his shoulders as Greysock obediently padded past him.

Porter opened the door and they looked up the stairs.

At the landing they paused, listening. Greysock whined quietly. Izzy thrust out a hand to shush him. He stopped at once.

The drone of the air raid siren had long since gone and neither of them really knew what to expect.

Izzy stared into space, straining her ears. For a second, she was convinced she heard someone. She waited. Nothing. Greysock cocked his head.

Porter motioned them forward. They had to go up three flights before they reached the level of the kitchen, hop out onto the landing, and then back down the main stairs to the shop.

"It's weird how that basement is so hidden," whispered Porter. Izzy nodded in agreement.

The door to the flat on the first floor was closed and they tiptoed past to the final set of stairs.

When they reached the clock shop, it was empty.

"Wow," said Izzy, loud enough to earn a sideways glance and a shush from Porter.

The Wigglesworth and Son Clock Shop looked exactly like it always did - just about. She glanced around. The glass cabinets were dustier than normal. Their red velvet coverings lay across them. It was as if the shop had been abandoned for weeks. Except the door was slightly ajar, just like Professor Wigglesworth would leave it on hot days.

The professor though, was nowhere to be seen - presuming of course, he was around at all. On the counter nearest the back room, there was a till. It was made of dark wood, with a wide draw at the bottom. The numbers were made of metal. There was a criss-cross of white tape across the huge front window. Just like the shop opposite where a man lay sleeping, propped up against the doorway.

Had she thought about it properly, she'd have wondered why he was there at all. In the middle of an air raid.

This whole shop in 1940, seemed pretty much like the one she walked through every day more than 70 years in the future. She had always figured Professor was the 'son' in the Wigglesworth and Son partnership. She didn't know how old he was, but she figured it was about 70 or 80. He never talked about the old days like most old people. He only talked about his adventures.

But then she'd found the picture in the library.

'Charles Wigglesworth and his son, Robert,' the caption had said. The professor. Dad's dad. Her granddad. They looked just like she knew them, except the picture was supposedly almost 200 years old. The oldest picture ever recorded.

Just thinking about it, made her head hurt. Somehow, the professor - her grandad - had been running the shop for almost 200 years, but he hadn't aged. There was so much she didn't understand. There was so much she couldn't even work out...

She shook her head to clear the confusion.

"Forget all that," she whispered to herself. "Just find Dad."

"Eh?" said Porter, his voice low. "How are we going to get to Greenwich? There's no way I'm walking all that way. It's miles."

Izzy paused, biting her lip.

"I don't know. Let me try and fix this first," she said, holding out the newly found, but not quite finished, Tumble Thunder.

She placed it on the red velvet counter and began opening the drawers underneath. There was a selection of older pocket watches, and she placed three on the counter as she looked.

It took two more drawers for her to find what she was looking for. The old leather wallet was held together with a hefty brass buckle. Inside there was a combination of what looked like tiny pliers, spanners and a tiny hammer. The tools gleamed.

"Perfect," said Izzy. "Every clock shop worth its salt has one of these handy. At least, that's what the professor says." She picked up a tiny screwdriver in her right hand. Holding the new Tumble Thunder in her left, she deftly made a couple of alterations. Quickly she wound it up. "There, it's ticking. At least it works as a watch."

The second hand had begun sweeping around the face. But the other hands remained dormant. Unlike hers, there were no symbols on the left. It looked like a fairly basic version. Something wasn't quite right with it. But it could tell the time, if nothing else.

A thump from upstairs interrupted Izzy's ponderings. She held her breath, Porter and Greysock did the same. All three looked at the ceiling and waited. There was another thump.

"Hello," came a voice from upstairs. "Is someone down there?" Footsteps followed.

"Isn't that the professor?" said Porter, confirming what she already knew.

"He can't find us," said Izzy, making a snap decision. "I think it would be bad."

"What? Why?" whispered Porter.

"I don't know. Just a feeling. Like it isn't supposed to happen."

She dragged Porter into an old storage cupboard next to the counter. It was no more than a metre wide. There were footsteps on the stairs.

She had pulled the door closed before she realised Greysock hadn't followed. She peeked out. He was sitting looking toward the door that led upstairs to the kitchen, wagging his tail.

"Greysock," she whispered. "Come here!"

The collie glanced up at the doorway to the stairs. He looked straight at Izzy, confused. Then he shot out of the open front door and into Foubert's Place.

Porter pulled the cupboard door shut on them both, just as the professor emerged.

"Hello?" called Professor Wigglesworth into the empty shop, inspecting the empty corners. "Hello?"

There was a tiny gap in the wooden slats on the cupboard, and Izzy peaked out. Porter peeked out from below her.

The professor, right down to his perfectly oiled moustache, was exactly as she knew him, more than 70 years from now.

"What?" mouthed Izzy, recalling how he looked exactly the same in the picture in the library.

The professor limped slowly into the room.

"How very odd," he said, slowly, noticing the tools on the counter. "I can't remember leaving all of that out."

He began placing them back into the wallet. Twice he stopped and looked around, as if he suspected the room. Slowly he began to roll up the velvet parcel.

The front door's familiar bell broke the silence as two men entered, both wearing navy suits.

"So, as I told you, Smith, I know we shouldn't be out and about. But I needed some time to think," said an older-looking man with a bald head. He had a huge cigar in his mouth and wore a dickie bow with a white shirt. Izzy knew who it was instantly. She had seen him before on the TV and in pictures. In fact, in a picture that hung on the very wall behind where he now stood; it just wasn't there, yet.

"Yes, sir," said the second man. He stepped back and looked up and down Foubert's Place through the huge, taped-up window. "We really shouldn't be too long, sir. It's best for you not to stay around in the city like this."

"Nonsense," said the first man. He looked at Professor Wigglesworth. "Now, my good man why aren't you in a shelter? There's an air raid on you know."

"True, true," said the professor. "But I always like to be around to keep an eye on things."

"Whatever," dismissed the man. "Now, I've heard fine things about this shop. I need your help."

"And good day to you, gentlemen," said Professor Wigglesworth with the merest hint of a smile. He put both hands flat on the counter, and leaned in. "What can I do for you?"

The first man slipped his hand into his waistcoat pocket and produced a small pocket watch. Uncoupling it from the chain, he tapped it on the counter.

"It's dead," he said. "Can't do a thing with it. Old Smith here said he'd happily come along and get me another. But I can't abide cheap rubbish when it comes to a pocket watch and I know a fine timepiece when I see one. Time is important to me. Because time is money, you know, my good fellow."

"Agreed," said the professor. "Now, how may I help you Mr.. erm."

He waited for the other man to fill the silence.

The old man with the cigar looked slightly unimpressed at not being recognised.

The professor, raised his eyebrows and motioned his head forward slightly. He had a look of bemused mischief on his face.

The man with a cigar broke first with a distinct "harrumph".

"It's Churchill," said the man, almost spitting the words from the front of his mouth. "Winston Churchill. Now, come along. What can you offer me by way of a new pocket watch? I'm not too fussed about the price. But it needs to be good quality and it needs to tell me when it's time for breakfast and supper and, most importantly, when it's time for a whisky."

In the cupboard, Porter jabbed Izzy in the ribs and silently mouthed, "Churchill!"

"Of course, sir," said the professor. "And, may I say, what a pleasure it is to serve a member of His Majesty's government."

He took out a small tray of pocket watches from under the counter. The man called Churchill peered at them all.

"Hmmm. Not really what I'm looking for," he said, picking up a gold one, with a fine chain.

"These are some of my best pieces," said the professor. "I collect watches from the best makers from every corner of the world. This particular one, is from a famous maker in Switzerland. I bought it personally. I'm not even sure if they're still in production, given the war."

He didn't have the chance to go any further.

"What about that one?" said Mr Churchill, oblivious to everything the professor had just said.

"We really should go, sir," said Smith. "We have to get back for the vote."

"Quiet Smith. They can wait for me. I've waited long enough for them," said Mr Churchill, and pointed to a single pocket watch, next to the tray. "That one, there," he said to the professor.

Confused for a moment, Professor Wigglesworth picked up the watch Izzy had just fixed and looked at it.

"I'm not sure where this one is from," said the professor, before recovering... "but, it's clearly a piece of the highest quality."

In the cupboard, Izzy's mouth fell open. It was the watch she'd been fixing. The watch she was convinced was a Tumble Thunder. If only she could have fixed it properly.

Mr Churchill took it from the professor, and held it in his hand, feeling its weight. He turned it over in his fingers.

"Hmm, I like it. I like how it feels. There's an inscription on the back," he said. "Smith, read this can you? My eyes are too old."

He foisted the pocket watch into his companion's hand. Smith held it up, and then turned it to face the light coming in through the window in the clock shop.

"For the many, go the few," he read slowly.

"For the many, hey? That feels quite apt for the

little pickle we find ourselves in," Churchill said with a laugh and slapped Smith on the back. He turned to the professor, "We'll take it."

"If you're sure?" said the professor, cautiously.

"I'm certain," Churchill replied. "Now, Smith, what are we to do?"

In the cupboard, Izzy tapped Porter's shoulder. She pointed behind them and put her finger to her lips.

They turned. The cupboard was actually a small storage room, which offered a way into the shop from the street for deliveries. Izzy didn't think it had ever been used in her time, yet she'd always known it was there. She squeezed past Porter and put her hands on the iron latch. Slowly, as the men continued to chat behind her, she lifted it. The door opened and they squeezed through. The fresh air of Foubert's Place was a welcome release from the tension of their temporary hiding place.

"Izzy. Was that really Winston Churchill?" whispered Porter, rolling his shoulders and looking up. Though darkness was a long way off, the shadows were long in the part of the small street that was home to the clock shop. The man she'd seen through the window in the doorway opposite, looked awake now. He pulled his hat down over his face and raised his coat collar around his neck against the cool evening air.

"Yes, it was Churchill," she said. Behind them there was a flash from inside the shop window. "That reminds me. There's a picture of him with the watch and the professor on the shop wall. The professor gave it pride of place and was always polishing it."

"But is it a Tumble Thunder thingy?"

"I don't know. The second hand started working. The rest of it looked like one, but it didn't feel right. I think Dad has been building them. He must use them to travel through time. I'm sure that's where he's been staying. He wants me to get to the observatory at Greenwich. That holds the secret to the final part of my Tumble Thunder."

"I think you're right," said Porter. "I think that's exactly where we need to go. And where is Greysock?"

"I don't know," she said, and called his name both ways down the street.

They headed toward Carnaby Street, passed the homeless man, and away from the shop. Outside of the Shakespeare's Head pub, two men in heavy coats were leaning against a black car. The falling sun made long shadows stretch beyond the bonnet like creeping oil.

The men had stern faces and were smoking. They stopped talking as the children approached. The heaviest of them stood up and looked at Porter.

"What have you two been up to in an air raid?" he asked Porter in a gruff voice, almost ignoring Izzy despite the empty street. "You should be down in the shelters with everyone else. Probably go on all night again."

"Nothing mister," said Porter, doing his best to appear as young and innocent as possible, despite his height. "You haven't seen a dog, have you? A collie? It got scared by the siren and legged it."

The second man flicked his cigarette onto the floor and trod on it with a hefty boot. He wiped his face with his other hand and motioned with his thumb.

"Little blighter went that way," he said, pointing down Carnaby Street. "Pretty thing. One white foot. Quick as a flash he was."

"Okay, thanks," said Porter, and grabbed Izzy's hand. "Come on, sis. Let's see if we can find him."

"Erm, okay," said Izzy, understanding Porter's attempt to get away from the surly looking men. "Let's see if we can catch up with your silly dog."

They turned to follow the imaginary path of the man's thumb, when there was a bark-whine from behind them. Trotting down Foubert's Place from the direction of the clock shop, seemingly without a care in the world, came Greysock.

Izzy put her hands on her hips. "And where have you been?" she asked the dog directly, as if scalding a naughty child.

Greysock looked at her. He bark-whined again and began turning in circles.

"What are you doing?" It was Porter's turn to ask the question.

The dog ignored them both. Instead, he stopped turning and looked back down toward the clock shop, wagging his tail.

A second later Winston Churchill and the man called Smith appeared.

The collie ran to them as if he were greeting old friends. Smith stooped to tickle the dog behind his ear.

"Come along now, Smith," said Churchill, as a line of dark silhouettes passed overhead. "We've chanced our luck enough in this air raid and we need to think over what we're going to do."

"Sorry, sir," said Smith, a boyish grin on his face. "We had collies when I was little on my father's land."

"Smith, I neither need to know that, nor care. A dog is a dog is a dog. Now come along. Jenkins, let's go."

The two men who had been leaning on the black car without a care in the world, were now standing up, ramrod straight. As Churchill approached the smaller of the two saluted and opened the back door.

As he did a huge explosion at the other end of Carnaby Street shook the air. The sound was so loud Greysock whined and scuttled behind Porter. Izzy covered her ears to the noise as a huge cloud of dust and smoke rose over the bottom of the street.

Jenkins and the other man rushed to Churchill's side as a string of overhead whistles began to descend from the silhouettes far above.

Smith reacted first as another bomb exploded nearby.

"There's more of 'em," shouted Jenkins, looking around for somewhere to shelter and spotting the Shakespeare's Head. Pointing at Izzy and Porter, he bellowed, "you lot! In here!"

Chapter 34

They'd been in the pub cellar for a good couple of hours and the bombing above had been incessant. Three times the walls had been shaken so violently by nearby blasts that they'd heard bottles being rattled and smashed in the bar above.

Izzy didn't think it was the safest place to be, but it had seemed like the best option at the time.

Jenkins had almost lifted Churchill off his feet as he manhandled him into the old pub when the first bomb had dropped.

The whistling as the bombs fell had been terrifying as they all piled into the pub. Izzy's ears, already more sensitive than they used to be, were still ringing.

Hiding in a pub cellar wasn't top of Izzy's list when it came to making their way to Greenwich. But neither was being killed in an air raid.

They were an odd group in the damp cellar. Five adults, two children and a border collie. There had been three other people in the bar. A man with grey, slicked-back hair, was already halfway down the ladder into the basement when they barged through the door in a panic. The other two had passed Izzy and the group on the way out and ran off down Carnaby Street at top speed.

Izzy was now sitting with Porter on one of the temporary bunk beds. The cellar was murky. It smelled like wet socks and stale beer. It was cold too.

Twelve wooden barrels were lined up along the far wall. There was one more bunk and a collection of sandbags made into a makeshift bench.

One of the men lit some candle lamps. The room brightened, but not by much. Jenkins and the other man, Churchill's other security guard, Izzy guessed, had taken two chairs near the ladder back to the bar.

Using the flickering light, Izzy took out her Tumble Thunder. She strained her eyes at it. The shadows from the candle danced across the face.

"What?" she elbowed Porter and shook the Tumble Thunder. "Look. It says there's only 18 hours left. We haven't been here that long."

Porter took it from her and stared at the moving

watch hands through the candlelight.

"Izzy," he said nervously. "It's going faster..."

She counted to 10 as the second hand turned. As she mouthed nine, the second hand swept past 20.

"No. That's not fair!" said Izzy, shaking the old timepiece. She looked again. The second hand continued its jog around the numbers at almost twice its normal speed.

"Is it broken?" asked Porter. "Can you fix it?"

She looked at Porter and shrugged.

Above them there was another huge rumble, as if thunder was coming through the ground. The cellar walls shook slightly. Izzy grabbed her friend, her nails digging into his arm. The adults might have been used to air raids, but Izzy and Porter weren't. A trickle of sweat ran down her back.

"That wasn't far away," said Smith. "We stay here for now. We need to wait for the all-clear."

* * *

Hours passed. Izzy and Porter barely talked. They tried to sleep but a combination of fear and the occasional explosion, kept their eyes wide. Sleep would not be their friend tonight. Instead, she stared at the sweeping hand of the Tumble Thunder. The time was literally slipping away and she had to get to Greenwich. She couldn't risk messing up like she had with Drina. There was so much at stake.

Churchill and Smith sat in the corner, whispering

to each other, away from the others. Every now and again they paused to look up at the roof of the cellar as another bomb dropped on London. Some close, some distant. They continued their hushed chat.

On the bunk nearest the children, sat the landlord from the pub.

As he poured Jenkins a beer from a dusty bottle, the pub landlord, Tom, told how he had run the Shakespeare's Head for 15 years. He'd been excused having to join the army because of an injury he suffered while working on the London Dockyards, almost 20 years before.

Somehow, Izzy and Porter managed to avoid any conversation at all. When she saw Jenkins finally realise how oddly they were dressed - at least by 1940s standards - the pair pretended to be asleep.

The ploy worked a little too well.

When she woke up some time later, Jenkins and his pal were asleep.

She instinctively checked the Tumble Thunder in the flickering light.

10 hours to go. She shook her head.

At the end of the bunk and propped up with a rolled-up blanket, Porter was snoring. Even Greysock, curled up next to her, was fast off.

Churchill and Smith, wide awake and convinced that everyone was asleep, had raised their voices a little. Even then it was little more than a conspiratorial whisper in hushed tones.

Izzy closed her eyes again, pretending to sleep

and straining to hear.

"I simply don't know, Smith," said Churchill. "I feel it is my duty to do so, for King and Country, but I simply don't know."

"Don't know what, sir?" said Smith.

Izzy listened, intrigued. She needed to speed up the conversation. She needed to get out.

"I just don't know," said Churchill, answering a question, with a question, and not giving either of them an answer. "I didn't get where I am today by ducking a fight. But neither did I get where I am today by being stupid in the face of overwhelming odds. Maybe I'm not the right man."

"But the House has voted on it, sir. They expect you to take up the position of Prime Minister tomorrow. What would happen were you not to be in office?"

"I'm not entirely sure," said Churchill. "But I think someone else should do it."

He put his hand in his pocket and ran his fingers over the watch he had bought from Professor Wigglesworth a few hours earlier. He placed it on the small table in front of them, the clock face reflecting the dim candlelight.

"But sir!"

"Nonsense. Be quiet, man. I'm perfectly entitled to turn down the office of Prime Minister if I wish. I don't want to be the man who lost the war. What would that say about me? I'm not even sure I want the job, after all. I don't want to be a failure."

"But sir," Smith was pleading now.

"I say it before, and I say it again. I don't want to be Prime Minister. We shall turn them down in the morning. Someone else can do it."

Izzy's intrigue had turned to astonishment.

Winston Churchill was Britain's most famous prime minister. He led the allied forces to victory over Adolf Hitler and Germany in World War Two. She'd learned about that one day in primary school.

She'd talked to her dad about it for ages when she got home. Her dad had described him as one of the greatest Britons to have ever lived. When she talked to Nan about it, she'd almost been in tears about how much Churchill had done.

"He's a bloody hero," she'd told Izzy.

But here he was, in the cellar of a pub in the middle of an air raid, deciding to turn down the job. Because he didn't want to lose. How could that be? How dare he? The country needed him.

He was one of the most famous people she'd ever heard of. His speeches were legendary. She'd learned all about it at school. She considered herself a virtual expert.

So, she decided to do something about it, and she thought she knew just how to convince him.

Concentrating, she kickstarted the *fuzziness* and forced it out to meet her. Like a controlled burst of energy, she felt it rise at being beckoned in defence of others.

Just like in the library, she steadied it and then let it sweep over the room.

Churchill and Smith seemed to pause. Porter stopped snoring.

Time stood still.

She moved over to where Churchill sat, and turned over the pocket watch, so the inscription faced upward. Smith's face was frozen in a worried frown. Without thinking, she tapped Winston Churchill's cigar on the makeshift ashtray next to him. The ash fell off.

As she sat back down on her bunk, she looked at the sleeping Porter and Greysock and smiled.

Turning back to the two men she breathed the *fuzziness* back in and it retreated. As it settled back into her chest, Churchill looked down at her. Porter started snoring again. Time was moving once more.

"How long have you been awake young lady?" he asked Izzy.

"Long enough, Mr Churchill," she said, feeling the warmth of the *fuzziness* hanging behind her heart.

"And what have you overheard?" asked Smith.

"Nothing much," said Izzy. "But Mr Churchill, I think you'd do a good job. You shouldn't worry."

Churchill looked at her and, for the first time since she'd seen him in the clock shop, he smiled. But though his mouth said one thing, his face said another. Izzy thought he looked scared.

"Really, young lady. Now I think you seem to be getting ideas above your station," he said. He picked up the pocket watch that he'd only bought because Izzy had fixed it just hours earlier and fiddled with it. "A man like me doesn't get into this position without being ready for a good, old fight, you know."

He looked down at the watch and the inscription caught his eye. He paused, and took a deep breath, blowing out his cheeks.

"Sir?" said Smith.

"*For the many, go the few,*" he read slowly, squinting at the text, and smiled again. This time he wasn't hiding anything. His face flushed and he took a deep breath. "*Never have so many, owed so much, to so few.* You know Smith, the girl's right. She's right. I have to become Prime Minister."

Smith looked over at Izzy and winked.

Chapter 35

Finally, he had found them.

He had searched through the centuries, weakened to the point of death by the continued time slips.

With each one he became a little weaker. Recently, when his Tumble Thunder had mirrored hers, he had felt a slightest glimmer of strength. It hadn't been enough. It was taking longer and longer to recover, as if moving through time was a body blow to his very soul.

But now, he had them. And he had them right where he wanted them.

He had tracked down the clock shop address and the year 2013, from the slip of paper that fell from Izzy's pocket before she met the Drina girl. He'd almost got her then. His calf was still sore from the way that blasted collie had bitten his leg and held on.

But the dog bite in 1830 was worth it. He had snatched the moon from the Temporatii woman. One of the crucial pieces that would complete the girl's Tumble Thunder and help her ascend to her true standing as the Time Child. By now she would realise that she needed to face him. That was just how he wanted it.

In 2013, he'd arrived at the shop while the girl was out. There was no sign of her dog either. He presumed she was at school. He had chuckled at the thought of how they'd been hiding her in normality. Like she was just another girl who needed geography and woodwork classes.

She didn't. She was special beyond her comprehension. But she was learning. He feared she was learning too fast. Her strength was building.

It hadn't taken him long to ransack the flat. He'd been determined to make it look like a burglary.

The professor hadn't been around either. The whole shop was strangely empty.

Scanning through the books of notes on her desk, he'd learned something about Izzy's dreams of her dad. They were like a diary of how she was learning her powers. He smiled and tucked them into his coat. Robert had warned her he was coming. Now she knew she had to face him. It was all coming together.

His own Tumble Thunder, sat cold in his pocket.

The real one, held power over all time. Over the very future of the sun, the stars, the moon and everything on it. But it could only be used by a Time Child. It was nowhere to be seen. He presumed she had it with her.

The girl with the long curly hair didn't realise it, but she was as much a part of the Tumble Thunder as everything else. It was all useless without a Time Child.

He had tried so many times to make one like it. But the contraptions he made just landed him in random times and places. It was like a train without a track, randomly shooting off in whatever directions in time they seemed to want to go. He had finally mastered the art to visit specific times in his search, but he had paid a heavy price. This was the closest he had been. His current Tumble Thunder had imitated the girl's time slips almost by accident. He hadn't expected it to happen.

From the first moment she had unknowingly activated hers, his had responded. Every time she time slipped, he was transferred to the exact same timeline, and more or less the same location.

If it wasn't for the years of weakness brought on by the constant movement through time, he would have had her by now. He would have the real Tumble Thunder too.

Yet every time his body underwent the strain of time travel, he needed a short spell to recover;

it was as if his body was taking longer and longer to reset.

He'd felt refreshed by the trip to Stonehenge. Like the Temporatii, his life force was boosted just being near the stones on midsummer's day. It hadn't lasted long.

Yet being in the clock shop had given him the same feeling. Like the building itself possessed some strange healing power. He didn't quite understand it, but the strange little shop in the middle of west London, seemed to be some kind of fountain of energy.

Feeling briefly refreshed he headed out into Foubert's Place and looked for a place to wait.

He didn't see the old man in the fingerless gloves until it was too late. A heavy walking stick hit him square in the temple and the lights went out.

"I've waited a long time for you," growled George. Making sure the man in the black trench coat was unconscious, he dragged him to the doorway opposite the shop. It would be hours before he woke. He hoped it would buy Isabella enough time. He was lucky. The small alley was briefly deserted. Besides, no-one would care about two homeless men having a fight. Straightening his jacket, he headed back to his favourite spot in Kingly Street, doffing his hat and saying a hearty "hello" to an old woman as he went.

* * *

When the Time Shadow woke, the floor was cold. His bad leg ached. His head throbbed.

Blinking against the pain in his temple and the stars dancing in his vision, he came round.

Wigglesworth and Son was in front of him. Whoever had hit him had dragged him to the shop front opposite. He wondered if he'd missed the girl.

The sound of feet on broken glass opposite answered his question.

He'd watched her and the tall boy go inside the shop. He gave them a few minutes after they disappeared upstairs before he pulled himself to his feet to follow. He almost fell back down. The Temporatus who had hit him, he presumed that's who it was, had hit him harder than he realised.

But it wasn't enough. Finally, in 2013, it was time.

He wiped the concrete dust from his hands with his trousers. Looking left and right down Foubert's Place for the man with the fingerless gloves and the stick, he took a deep breath.

The air had barely reached his lungs when he felt the warmth of the Tumble Thunder in his pocket. It spread quickly and he instinctively reached down for it.

"No. Not now," he said, closing his hands around it. "Not now."

He landed in 1940 in the exact same doorway across from the clock shop.

The warmth of the time slip left his body as quickly as it had come. The Tumble Thunder was cold in his pocket. He bit his lip and tasted blood.

He looked down at his hands. They were grey. He made a fist, but a rush of dizziness swept over him and he fell to the floor. His bad hip took the fall on the shop pavement, sending a sharp pain up his back. His head throbbed too, as if he'd been hit all over again.

He was used to being weak after moving through time. But now he felt empty. His throat was dry. He tried to get up but couldn't. His legs wobbled at the strain of trying to stand. He gazed at the clock shop opposite and wondered if he could make it - if it still held the same power of rejuvenation as in 2013. It was no use. He was too weak.

Facing up to the inevitable wait, he pulled his long coat around him. Fidgeting from one side to the other, he made himself as comfortable as he could as the air raid siren wailed and people rushed past on their way to shelters.

He had been in exactly that spot when the girl and the boy had emerged from the shop.

He had tried to get up but failed. Worried she would recognise him he pulled his hat down over his face. A few minutes later the pesky collie scampered out of the shop as none other than Winston Churchill entered, followed by a second man.

Almost immediately, the girl with the long curly hair had appeared and looked directly at him.

Had she paid more attention, she would have seen him properly. Had she been more careful, she wouldn't have talked quite so loudly about going to Greenwich to find her dad.

Under the hat he'd pulled low over his face, the Time Shadow smiled as the pair walked past. His yellow teeth flashed behind his thin lips. A few moments later, Winston Churchill passed too. He watched them all rush into the pub at the end of the narrow road as bombs fell nearby. He'd been in the Second World War before. Air raids were dangerous, but they were nothing new to him. Once it was dark, he would set off.

He knew it would be hours before the all-clear sounded.

It was all the head start he needed.

Chapter 36

In the end, it had taken little persuasion.

After the all-clear, the man named Smith had been keen to get everyone out.

"You just helped Winston Churchill make a very important decision," Smith told Izzy as they climbed out of the cellar of the Shakespeare's Head. "What can I do for you in return?"

"We could do with a lift," said Porter, yawning and stretching simultaneously.

"I thought you might say that." Smith replied.

They were helped into some of the seats in the back, and they had headed toward the Thames.

She didn't notice the tramp further down Foubert's Place had gone.

A few minutes later, the car pulled up at the Houses of Parliament. Mr Smith jumped out first and checked left and right before directing Mr Churchill to an unassuming, small door near the bottom of Big Ben.

But before he disappeared, Smith leaned back into the car window.

"Here," he said, pulling something out of his pocket and thrust it into Izzy's hand, holding it closed to cover it up. "I've waited a long time to give you this. You've earned it. Good luck. Jenkins! Off you go."

Smith stepped back toward Churchill and waved as the car pulled off. Izzy opened her hand. A small key on a chain. She frowned and turned it over in her hands. At the end of the key was a decorative emblem.

"The sun," said Porter, "like the one you…"

"I know," said Izzy, frantically reaching for the Tumble Thunder and flicking open the casing.

It was the perfect match.

As their chauffeur-driven, government car pulled out and set off over a deserted Westminster Bridge Izzy picked at the sun on the end of the key. She scraped at it with her nails and then remembered how the star had almost floated out.

She held the sun emblem close to the Tumble Thunder and the old pocket watch began to glow. The molten gold that was now so familiar, surrounded the indented sun symbol on the case.

As it made its way fully around, it rose toward the key until a vacuum of golden dust was gently pulling it from Izzy's hand. Gold fleck by gold fleck the sun transferred from the key to the casing, like sand caught in the wind. It filled the shape and settled into the Tumble Thunder. As it did, Izzy felt a rush of adrenaline wash across her body as the spinning molten *fuzziness* reached out and was engulfed. But instead of changing itself, the purple glow of Izzy's aura covered her in a magical haze.

"Oi!" said Jenkins. "What the ruddy hell are you doing?"

Izzy was vaguely aware of the car screeching to a halt as her aura changed from purple to gold and glowed so brightly it shone out of the car windows, firing like lasers across the city and into the London sky.

"Out!" A distant shout. The car door opening. The smell of the leather stinging her sinuses. Her heart was beating SO loud. The blood rushed through her veins like a flooded river. For a second, she could sense her muscles moving in every part of her body.

As the sensory overload faded and the lasers dissipated, she heard a car screeching away. A dog was barking strangely.

"Izzy! Izzy!" It was Porter. "You okay? They chucked us out."

"I'm okay. I'm okay," she said, shaking herself back to reality. "Don't worry. I'm fine. It's the Tumble

Thunder. It's what it's meant to do. Something is changing in me, Porter. I can feel it. I can feel it all."

The Tumble Thunder had stopped glowing. The sun had fully transferred into the casing from the key.

But there was one problem. It felt like the rules had changed too.

They had been in the shelter all night and the small hand on the clock face showed only seven hours left. Yet it didn't feel right. Whatever was happening to her, she felt helpless to stop it. Somehow, the Tumble Thunder had reacted too. It had sped up.

She had no idea how much faster time was flying by, but she knew it was running out.

She grabbed for Porter's arm as she tried to stand on wobbly legs. Greysock gave a final bark-whine at the vanishing car and the three friends stood propped against each other, alone at the edge of Tower Bridge.

"What do we do now?" said Porter. "Greenwich is ages away."

"I think," said Izzy, with a deep breath. "That we start walking. Walking quickly."

Below them the Thames was empty as they crossed the bridge. The skies were filled with barrage balloons that hung like swollen double decker buses. She counted 12, before the looming buildings stole the skies on the narrower streets.

She'd learned about the balloons in history at one of her schools. They were to make it hard for the German bombers.

"Izzy," said Porter. "How long do we have left?"

Izzy looked. Her forehead furrowed.

"That's not fair!" she shouted at the pocket watch and then looked at Porter. "Six hours. When we were at the bridge it was seven. It's going faster! So now I'm guessing, maybe three."

"That way," he said pointing and setting off with Greysock at his heels. "Come on."

"Right, let's go," said Izzy, and they increased their stomping speed in the direction of Greenwich Observatory.

In the direction of her dad.

"I could murder some chips," said Porter without breaking a step.

"You'll turn into a chip you will," said Izzy and they both laughed.

Izzy's sides hurt and she snorted in lungs full of dirty London air as they paced.

Despite the dust and the smell, it felt good after the night in the musty cellar. Time was spinning by, but she was convinced her dad was close.

Still giggling they headed in the direction of the rising sun.

But Porter had a point. Izzy was hungry. And thirsty. Her stomach ached. She was almost envious when Greysock stopped to take a drink from a suspicious-looking puddle.

"It must be another five miles," said Porter, watching the dog drink his fill. "That's going to take us an hour and a half. More if we get lost."

"I think we'll be okay," said Izzy. She felt strangely confident. She'd been desperate to find her dad, but as time went on, completing the Tumble Thunder felt like it had a bigger purpose. Like it was the most important reason she was on this quest. "Greenwich is on the south bank of the Thames. So, if we walk and keep the river on our left, then we'll get there in the end."

They walked for a good 15 minutes in silence. Greysock padded alongside them. Neither Porter nor Izzy wanted to bring it up again. But the clock was ticking. And it was ticking faster than they were walking. Instinctively she pulled the Tumble Thunder from her pocket. As she raised it, Porter grabbed her arm.

"Why don't you try that thing again?" he said. "You know, stop time and then we can get ahead of ourselves. Make a bit of time up. Maybe even get there in the same minute. Maybe even get there before we actually get there."

"It doesn't work like that," she said confidently. "It only works when there's some kind of greater purpose or danger. Otherwise, I could do it all of the time and never be late for school." So they kept walking. They walked as quickly as they could.

Porter had been wrong. It wasn't five miles to Greenwich. It was closer to six. But Izzy had forced him into a near jog for half an hour. His long legs meant he was faster, and he kept looking around to make sure they were still together. He hated running as much as she did.

They arrived at the long lawn leading up to the observatory, out of breath, sweating and with their legs burning from the effort.

Greysock, for his part, looked positively delighted by the whole thing.

Izzy bent over with her hands on her knees and pulled in great gulps of air. Her chest hurt and the sweat was running down her back. Despite the early morning, the sun was warm for spring.

"Now you can look," said Porter, pulling himself back vertical. He gestured to Izzy's pocket. "How much time don't we have left?"

The Tumble Thunder opened easily. The second hand was still swooshing around at an abnormal pace. The hand sped past 12, around the face, and back to 12 before she was able to count to 30.

"It's definitely going twice as fast as it should," she said. "It says we've got an hour. It might not even be half that."

Walking up the steep hill, Izzy turned to take in the view. The Observatory sat on top of a hill that looked down on the Greenwich Naval College. It was a magnificent old building. Unlike when she'd visited with her dad, there were now anti-aircraft guns on the roof. There were dozens and dozens of sandbags. Down the hill, London sprawled into the distance. Blimps hung in the sky. Overhead she heard the drone of a plane. Looking up, she couldn't make it out. Being used to the daily aircraft traffic from Heathrow in her normal time, she was used to ignoring planes overhead.

"I wonder if they're German or British?" said Porter, following her gaze skyward.

Izzy didn't answer. She was already at the gate that led to the observatory.

The Greenwich Meridian Line was an imaginary line that stretched from the North Pole to the South. It had traditionally been used to set the time zones for different countries and was a standard measure used around the world.

"Greenwich Mean Time," said Izzy, as she walked up and down the steel rail embedded into the ground that signified the line. "What's so mean about it?"

"Ah, I was hoping you'd work that out, given you've dragged us here already," said Porter, his voice short. Greysock bark-whined.

"Ssshhh you two," said Izzy. She continued to pace up and down the line.

"Soz."

"That way," she pointed toward the sun, "is Europe - east. That way," she swivelled around, "is America - west. Where East meets West. So, where's my dad?"

The buildings and the park were deserted. Even the observatory itself looked closed.

Greysock nuzzled her side, his wet nose wiping across her hand.

Pulling her hand out of her pocket, the picture she'd brought with her fell to the floor.

She scooped it up. She was probably five or six years old. Her dad had one arm around her shoulder, and the other lazily placed just underneath the clock at the gate. His blue eyes shone.

The picture was years before Dad had disappeared. She was wearing some hideous blue dungarees, and her hair was tied tight in pigtails. Her two front teeth were missing. One of her hands was on the gate, her last three digits tucked in, her index finger and thumb forming a handgun pose. Dad had always stood like that, and she'd copied him for as long as she could remember. He'd said it would make her stand out.

Greysock bark-whined again and nuzzled her free hand.

"Stop it boy," she said. "I'm trying to concentrate."

Wiping his nose dew on her side she leaned on the wall. Her hand naturally copied the picture. Three fingers tucked in. Index finger and thumb splayed apart.

Just like Dad. Just like Dad had told her to.

In the picture Dad was leaning on the wall. His handgun fingers pointing at an imaginary target. "That's it," she said out loud, making Porter snap his head back in her direction after he'd been craning his neck at the sky. "He's pointing!"

She scurried around the observatory gate, her feet sliding in the gravel. Holding up the picture she looked at the wall, and then back at the picture.

Measuring brick by brick from under the number six, she put her hand on exactly the spot her dad was pointing to. The brick wobbled. The cement either side was loose, she pulled at it to open a small gap between the bricks.

She attempted to prise the central brick out with her fingers, but it wouldn't budge. Picking up a small stone she scraped furiously at the cement either side. In less than 10 seconds, it was wobbling. After thirty seconds, it was almost free. But it held fast.

"Here," said Porter, who had been watching with a mixture of puzzlement and intrigue. "Let me do it."

He wrapped his fingers either side of the brick and tugged.

It fell out with a thump and his momentum made him fall back on his bum. The dust that jumped up from the floor made Greysock sneeze.

Izzy looked at Porter. Greysock looked at them both.

Beneath the clock was a hole. Izzy bent down and peered in. It was empty.

Taking a deep breath, she slowly put her hand into the dark space the brick had left.

Her arm was almost elbow deep when her fingers bumped into a small metal box, hidden deep in the wall.

Chapter 37

"I can't come with you, Robert. I can't leave him!" the woman shouts from beneath the hood of her cloak. She is as tall as Robert and looks directly at him.

Like black slugs, the rain continues to creep down the shiny bricks of the pyramid.

The silver slit in the world through which the cloaked figures had disappeared shimmers in the darkness.

Robert, Izzy's dad, pulls his hands back from the edges. His face is solemn and tired.

"He's gone. You can't save him. Izzy is all we have left. The only thing we can do now, is try and prevent the eschaton," he says.

He gestures around at the black, lifeless square and up at the torrents of rain.

"It's what we must do. To help save her. To save all of us. There's no time."

The woman glances down at a swaddle of blankets she's hugging closely to her chest. She leans forward and pulls the blankets away from her body slightly.

A flash of lightning reveals a baby's face. The rain bounces off its tiny forehead, leaving a grimy footprint stain.

"You can't think that. You're wrong. You're all wrong. I can't come with you. I have to find him," says the woman, taking down her hood in the rain.

"He's gone. He's stolen. We'll never see him again, Ava. Please. Please come."

Izzy floats. Watching. A visitor to a memory she knows but can't recall.

The couple stare at each other. Izzy wills herself to move. She floats effortlessly into the scene and stands - no, floats - next to Robert and the woman.

Ava?

Izzy looks into the woman's face. She sees her long, blonde curled hair underneath the hood of her cloak despite the rain. Her pronounced cheek-bones and her piercing blue eyes.

They're just like mine, she thinks. We look the same.

Robert reaches out. Ava backs away. Out of reach.

"I can't. I must know. We can save them both. Robert, we can. If we wait, we can save him too. And then prevent all of this."

"No, Ava. He's gone. Taken. He's dead." The words as cold as the rain.

"No, Robert!" she screams over the storm. "This is a mistake. He's alive! Our son is alive! And I will find him!"

Instantly, the storm drops to a whisper.

"Ava," says Robert in a softer tone, reaching out for her. "He's dead. We've got to hide Izzy where they can't find her. After what happened to Eliza, she's the last of them now. Betty will never recover her strength. If we can keep Izzy alive until she comes of age, then she can save us all. The Temporatii have taken their pieces back separately. He won't find her that way. I'll help her realise her true strength. She can build the Tumble Thunder as she goes. But only when she's old enough."

Izzy hangs, stunned. She tries to mouth a word, but her lips won't move. She looks at the woman. Back at her dad. Back at the woman.

"What?" she asks, forcing her confused mouth to make words. "You're not my mum. I don't have a brother. You're lying. You're both lying!"

She shouts at the pair of them. They can't hear. Izzy feels the fuzziness rising like a crescendo in her chest. It rides a wave of tears pushed on by a surge of astonishment and almost consumes her vision.

With a crash, the storm resumes. The rain gets heavier, angrier. The woman in the dream, the memory, whatever this is, ignores her. Not hearing. Unable to hear.

Robert shakes his head slowly and his shoulders drop.

"Ava. Our son isn't alive. Pass me Izzy. We've got to go."

Ava bends her neck and kisses the infant Izzy lightly on the forehead.

"Make time to make time," she whispers and holds her tiny daughter out for Robert to take. He glances down and pulls her close to his own chest.

"Come on. We don't have much time left. The storm is getting worse," he says, and takes his wife's hand. Ava steps forward slowly and kisses him lightly on the shoulder. They turn toward the silver streak of light still hanging in the sky.

With his other hand, he pulls at the side of the portal. The world around them bends and distorts.

"The Tumble Thunder helped me open the portal before I removed the emblems," he said, opening his hand. "I have to hide it all for her. The Portal will make them forget all but who they are. They won't even remember where they were when they went through it. We must be quick. It's beginning to fade."

He shifts on his feet to open the portal more widely for Ava, and places one leg inside.

"Robert!" she shouts. "Tell her to 'make time to

make time.' She must remember that. 'Make time to make time.'"

"What?" he says, turning, briefly off balance. As he tries to right himself with Izzy in his arms, Ava lunges forward and shoves him and baby Izzy into the portal.

They are gone. Immediately, like a zip on a coat, the bright portal seals itself from bottom to top. With a pop, and a crash of thunder from above, it is closed.

Ava is alone.

"I love you both," she shouts. "I love you. But you're all wrong. I have to find him."

"Dad!" screams the dreaming, 13-year-old Izzy. But there is no noise. Dad is gone.

Izzy turns to Ava. To the woman who is her mum but isn't. She looks in her eyes, and she believes. And she understands.

"Make time to make time," Izzy whispers to herself.

Ava is wearing a garland of lavender. It is old and dried, but it is unmistakable. The same kind of flowered garland Nan makes every year for the summer solstice.

She knows that Ava, this woman she has never met, is her mum. Her real mum. And it stings like a betrayal to the mum she's known all her life.

A shadow passes over her and she looks up. The rain has stopped. Ava is staring into a broiling black cloud.

"I'll come back for you, Robert. One day."

She turns and makes her way slowly down the huge steps and into the night. Izzy watches her every step. Her mum's every step.

Chapter 38

"Izzy! Izzy!"

Her name came to her like distant shouts on a deserted beach. Her eyes were sticky from a long sleep she hadn't had – they were open before her brain was awake.

"Are you okay?" Porter said. "Jeez, will you stop doing that?"

Porter's nose was almost touching hers. His hands were on her shoulders. His face red, his eyes wet. Behind him the sun glared brightly.

Finally, Izzy's brain found first gear. The *Seeing* lingered like a terrible cloud. She shook her head to clear the mist. It worked. A little. Haziness remained. Second gear still some way off.

"I think she's coming round," said Porter to someone she couldn't see. The alarm had left his voice. His tone had softened. Izzy slowly opened her bleary eyes.

A figure blocked out the blaring sun.

"Hey, kiddo."

The words were like a bucket of cold water to the face. Her brain jerked into the fast lane. The *fuzziness* cowered into her chest like a naughty puppy. Suddenly alert. Fiercely awake. She stared past Porter, shielding her face from the glare of the sun.

Straight into the familiar, steely blue eyes she'd missed for so long.

"Dad!" she shrieked as she jumped up and threw her arms around him.

"You've grown," he laughed as he pulled her tight and smelled her hair.

Hugging him for the first time in three years the tears overflowed down her cheeks.

She buried her head in his shoulder as she clung onto him in a wave of relief and joy. Finally, finally, she had found him. The relief rushed through her as the *fuzziness* rose and dipped in her throat. "Dad," she sobbed again, into his shoulder.

Robert held her tight. A hug for a daughter he had purposefully abandoned for the greatest of causes.

Porter blushed not knowing where to put himself. Mentally and physically exhausted he turned to avoid Izzy seeing the tears running down his dirty cheeks. He'd never felt happier or prouder. His work was done, but Izzy didn't need to know any of that.

And so he just waited as the emotional reunion ran its course. He looked down at Greysock, who nuzzled into his leg. Even dogs could feel awkward sometimes.

"I'm sorry," Robert told Izzy, pulling her to eye level. "I'm so sorry. I had no choice. I couldn't risk him finding you before you were ready."

"I think I know," said Izzy, feeling strangely calm, as tears rolled down her face.

"And you forgot someone," said her dad, producing her favourite teddy from inside his jacket. "How did you manage without him?"

"You found him!" she shrieked and threw her arms around him once more. "Where? I thought I left him at Stonehenge."

"There's no time Izzy. I know it's hard, but there's no time."

"Dad, I know. I've seen it. I understand why you went away. I know about Ava, about my mum. About my brother."

Her Dad looked her up and down, with a half-sad smile. He hugged her again and then looked into her eyes.

"You've grown," he said. "You're taller. And you're ready. I'm sorry I had to go. I missed you so much. I saw you sometimes, but I couldn't let you know."

"But where have you been?" pleaded Izzy, as planes droned overhead.

Her dad looked up, ignoring the question. Porter followed his gaze as six black shadows passed high overhead.

"Heinkels on their way home," said Izzy's Dad, looking at Porter. "The air raid went on for hours."

"This was under the clock," he said. "It's what you needed to find. But you had to be ready. If you had found it too soon, the power of the completed Tumble Thunder, mixed with your own, might have killed you. I couldn't bring it to you, or he'd have found it too. It was written that the discovery had to be yours. Our people have guarded it and hidden it for centuries."

He dropped a small metal box into her hand.

It was no bigger than a jewellery box. She pushed it open and there, on a protective bed of velvet, was a number eight.

She opened her Tumble Thunder and placed the number eight onto the indented casing.

Nothing.

"You need the final piece," said her dad. "Nothing will happen without that. They need to be added in order. It's been waiting for you for a long time. I had to keep the symbols hidden until you were ready. If you'd found it before you'd learned to master your powers, it would all have been over."

She wanted to understand but knew she didn't. The hairs on the back of her neck prickled.

"The Time Shadow has it. He has the moon," she said, looking at the piece in her hand. "I need to find him, Dad. I need it back."

"You do. I always guessed it would come to that. Once he grew strong, I knew you'd have to face him."

"But, Dad?" she paused, rolling the final piece between finger and thumb. "Why a figure eight? I understand the star, the sun and the moon. I kind of get them. But why a figure eight?"

Robert smiled and rolled his eyes.

"Not a figure eight, you dummy," he said, taking it over and turning it on its side. "It's the symbol for infinity. Whoever can bring the pieces together will have the power over all of time."

"Oh. Course," she said, blushing, confused, and suddenly realising she hadn't introduced her friends. "This is Porter. He's pretty good at looking after me. And this is Greysock."

"It's good to see you again Porter," said her dad, and Izzy frowned. "And I know who this is. He was my dog for a long time when you were small. Your mum, Ava, developed an allergy to dog hair when she was pregnant with you. I made sure Mary found him when the time was right. I knew he'd look after you."

"Dad, I've changed things in the past," she said. "Won't that change things in the future? I need to know it all. I need to know about Ava. From the beginning."

"That's not really the beginning, Izzy," he said, scanning the park. "It's not even the opening chapter. But you haven't changed anything. You kept time on its truthful path. It was your first test."

"I feel it, Dad," said Izzy. "I feel almost all of it. Like the Tumble Thunder helps me see. But I think he's coming here too. I need the moon. It's the only way I can do what I'm supposed to do. I'm the Time Child, aren't I?

"The prophecy says," Robert went on, "that you're special, Izzy. You're the only remaining Time Child. Born every 1,000 years, a Time Child has the power to ensure everything happens as it should in the future, and the past. You were born in the year 3,000. By then, we've ruined this world. The Earth was dying Izzy. We knew you were special, and that you could change it all. But we had to hide you. I belong to a special group of scientists. Down the generations we've been called many things. Some knew our kind as knights of the round table. Others as the Knights Templar. But our real name is the Temporatii. We have guarded the secret of the Time Children for more than a thousand years. The Tumble Thunder had been passed down through the generations of our families. It held the key to time travel, but only for someone powerful enough to master it."

"Me." said Izzy, already one step ahead of him. "Ava is my mum. I have a brother. I saw her push you through the portal you made with the complete

Tumble Thunder. It was dark and raining. She said I had a brother and that she had to find him."

"You did," said Robert. "A twin brother. But the Vindicta took him when you were very young. We had to hide you."

"The Vindicta?" Izzy asked, raising her eyebrows and wiping her cheeks.

"Our sworn enemies. They're faithful to their one, true leader – and they want the Tumble Thunder to rule over the world, Izzy. We can't allow them to have it."

"Ava is still alive," said Izzy, distracted. "So is my brother. He's out there, somewhere in the future. But he's scared."

Robert smiled again: "Maybe, Izzy. You will know more than me."

"I've met the Temporatii. I know them," said Izzy. "Madame Lehzen when I saved Drina's life. And last night I convinced Winston Churchill to become Prime Minister. Smith gave me one of the emblems. Hang on! I helped Aleck invent the telephone and Mary looked after me. They all gave me an emblem!"

Porter shook his head and looked at his friend. "You've been busy," he said.

"But they're not all," said Robert. "We surrounded you with our friends."

"George," said Izzy, without thinking. "Even Mr Tompkins. Nan and the professor – he's my grandad. You brought them back too."

"There to keep an eye on you," said Robert. "They're part of us, Izzy. We hid you in plain sight so he couldn't find you. We didn't think he'd be able to go back to that timeline. We had to protect you."

He paused and beckoned to someone out of sight.

Jane, the mum Izzy had always known, appeared from behind some small buildings slightly further down the hill. "We all had to protect you," she said as Izzy's face lit up.

"Mum!" Izzy jumped up and ran to greet her, wrapping her arms around her tightly.

"Hello darling," said Jane. Her flowery summer dress was dishevelled. Her face was drawn and tired.

"How did you get here? How did you get to 1940?" asked Izzy, though she knew. "He found you too?"

"Yes," said Jane. "I had to lead him away from you. I couldn't lose another daughter."

"What?" said Izzy, temporarily confused.

"My daughter, Eliza, was a Time Child too. Born in the year 2000. Your Dad found me after Eliza was killed."

"By the Time Shadow," completed Izzy, remembering her *Seeing*.

"Yes," Jane said, her face falling. "I promised I'd help you, for Eliza."

"So, you hid me in the clock shop. You took me in. Even when Dad had to go."

"Yes. Eliza had always been special, even from the day she was born. She was killed when she was very young. That was when your dad found me and I knew I had to give my life to help."

Izzy pulled her mum close and looked up at her.

"I know. I think I've always known," she said, and hugged her mum once more.

None of them reacted quickly enough when the bomb fell.

* * *

The German Heinkel HE 111 was returning from a mission to the naval base of Portsmouth. The young crew, all in their 20s, were all on the first flight of their Luftwaffe careers. They'd agreed on the flight over from Dortmund that they'd save one of their bombs to drop over the famous city of London on the way back.

They had cheered when they had released it over the London Docklands. Flying high enough to avoid the anti-aircraft guns, they watched it drop toward the city below, before disappearing from view as they headed for home.

* * *

On the ground, just outside the gates of the Greenwich Observatory, Izzy stood with Jane and their small group. Greysock was at Porter's heels.

It was Robert who looked up first when the whistling began.

The bomb landed directly on the courtyard gates, just metres from where they'd been standing moments earlier.

Izzy opened her eyes and stared at a cloudless, blue sky. The world around her was spinning. Her ears silently screaming after the blast.

To her left, Greysock lay whimpering in the dust, licking a bloody wound on his leg. Porter was already standing, holding his side. He was coughing but seemingly unhurt. His clothes, hair and face were covered in dust. Izzy could taste it. The courtyard gates were crumpled and the tree next to them was burning. Smoke hung in the air.

Robert was next to her, standing at an odd angle with his weight on his left leg. His right trouser leg was shredded. Blood matted his hair and dust covered his face.

"Is everyone okay?" asked Robert.

"Aren't you supposed to see these things coming?" asked Porter, looking at Izzy with a smile. "Could've done that stopping time thing. Thought you were the Time Child? Wish you could take me back to breakfast."

They allowed themselves a painful laugh.

"Wait," said Izzy as the dust began to settle and the tree continued to burn. "Where's Mum?"

Behind them there was a deep, gurgling breath.

"She's here," a voice hissed.

Robert, Izzy and Porter spun around.

There, with his arm around Jane and a knife

to her throat was the man who had tried to grab Izzy when she was with Drina. The tramp she had seen and ignored outside of the clock shop. His right hand, the one around Jane's throat, was bandaged... *'from when Greysock bit you in the cellar,'* she remembered.

"You..." growled Robert. "Let her go."

"Oh no," said the man with the grey, thin skin and the long black coat. He was calm. "I've got everything I need right here."

Izzy saw his yellow teeth. He looked old before his time, and he stood uncomfortably with his weight on one hip.

"Give me the Tumble Thunder," he demanded. "That's all I want. Give it to me, or she dies."

His cackle came from low in his chest. Wheezing, but enjoying his own joke. A trickle of blood ran down Jane's neck and onto his hand. Her breathing was short and raspy.

"No," said Izzy, defiantly. "No."

"I have the moon. Give me the Tumble Thunder," he hissed. "I've never been chasing you, you stupid girl. I want the Tumble Thunder. The true power the Temporatii have kept hidden. The legend of the Time Child is a fairy tale. I know where the true power lies."

He opened his free hand to reveal the tiny moon he had taken from Madam Lehzen's necklace.

Her dad took a step forward.

Keeping low, to the Time Shadow's right and

hidden by Jane, Greysock crept closer.

"Don't you dare," croaked the Time Shadow at Robert, but missed the advance of the dog. "You stay there."

Jane opened her eyes, blood still trickling from her mouth and nose.

"I'm not going to make it, Izzy," her voice bubbling with a raspy breath in her throat. "I love you. I always did. Remember what I've always said. It was what your real mum wanted you to remember. 'Make time to make time.'"

"I can't, Mum," said Izzy, her eyes filling with tears. "I can't. We can all make it."

"You know that's not true," her mum said. "You must."

Tears streamed down Izzy's face, but she knew. She understood exactly what she had to do. Now was the moment.

"Shut it you lot!" roared the Time Shadow, pressing the knife into Jane's throat and addressed Izzy directly. "Don't you try anything."

"She's right, Izzy," said Robert, ignoring him. "Make time to make time. It's the only way."

"It's okay, Izzy," rasped Jane, her breathing shallow as tears rolled down her cheeks.

Encouraged by her dad and the woman she knew as Mum, Izzy reluctantly and slowly nodded. She took a deep breath.

Needing it more than ever, she summoned the *fuzziness*. Needing to use powers she didn't fully comprehend. Needing it to protect more than just those she loved.

As she willed it, a calm washed over her. Her eyes sparkled and she smiled at Jane.

"You'll always be my mum," Izzy promised her. "Always. I love you."

With that, the last remaining Time Child, the only hope for the future of humankind, brought the world she needed to save to a standstill.

The *fuzziness* hung in the air as if her purple aura was holding everyone in place.

She walked slowly to the Time Shadow and clicked her fingers in front of his unblinking eyes. Without taking her eyes from him she took the tiny moon from his open hand. She pulled at Jane, but quickly recognised she was unable to separate her mum and the Time Shadow. Focussing on her mum, and careful not to touch the Time Shadow further; Izzy gave her a gentle goodbye kiss on the cheek. She pulled the photograph of her dad and her from her pocket, and tucked it into her mum's hand, carefully closing her fingers around it.

Overhead a plane hung in the sky, frozen in flight. The flames of the burning tree stood still, their fiery dance locked in place. The odd collection of people and the solitary dog were motionless, and the purple haze of the *fuzziness* surrounded them all like a light mist.

Giving herself room in the observatory garden, she brought the moon close to the Tumble Thunder alongside the sun, star and infinity symbol. What had happened slowly before with the other pieces, happened in an instant with the final piece of the magical puzzle.

Her mind felt like it had been hit so hard, it actually left her own body.

She fought for air as the world swirled around. She was flying. Zooming. Her vision was a spinning mess of black nothingness and coloured everything. There was a huge explosion in the middle of a dark abyss; a dinosaur roared; a sabre-toothed tiger brought down a mammoth; faster and faster her mind spun. A cave man making fire; a Roman emperor, commanding legions; battles she didn't recognise; London on fire; Aleck, Drina and then, more slowly, bombs falling on London and, slower, and slower, Churchill and then...

It spat her out and she landed, like a cat, crouched, panting and ready.

The internal time-glimpse tsunami calmed, and she took a deep, slow breath.

Her hands seemed to glow. Around her, everything was brighter.

It was as if someone had dialled her up. In every way imaginable.

Everything was now possible.

Quickly, she went to work with the completed magic that only the Time Child could bring to the Tumble Thunder.

All everyone else saw, was a tiny, almost

imperceptible shimmer. Like a blink, she brought everything back.

The Time Shadow was suddenly leaning at an awkward angle.

Greysock pounced forward and snapped at him on the calf. It was enough to unbalance him further. With one dying effort, Jane dug her feet into the ground and pushed back with the last of her strength.

The pair fell backwards, and Jane smiled at Izzy as she tumbled out of sight into a silver line that had appeared in the air behind them. The Time Shadow's scream was cut short as they fell. The universe shimmered and rippled as if it was bent out of shape. As the pair of them were lost into the nothingness, the time portal Izzy had created closed like a zip and disappeared with a pop.

"Goodbye, Mum," whispered Izzy as tears trickled down her cheeks.

"Jane..." said her dad forlornly, releasing Izzy and looking directly into her eyes. "But you did it."

She opened the palm of her hand and there, shining in the sunlight, was the open Tumble Thunder. On the case a moon had joined the star and the sun, enclosed in a horizontal figure of eight.

"I made time to make time," she said, the tears falling onto her clothes. "Just like Mum taught me. And none of you even realised. I'll never forget her, Dad."

Robert pulled her closer into his chest. A daughter and her dad, hugging in the morning sunshine on a hill near Greenwich Observatory.

"Like in the library," said Porter, and ruffled Greysock's head next to them. The collie replied with a triumphant bark-whine.

Izzy looked at her dad. She studied his face. He was happy and sad in the same smile.

"You still can't come back, can you?" she said, understanding. Ever since she'd seen those blue eyes glinting in the sunlight, she knew it wouldn't last long. Robert shook his head slowly. "You need to find Ava," she added.

"I'm sorry but I must know what happened, Izzy," he said, holding her. "It has consumed me since we came back from the future. But I had to protect you first. Now, it's my time. I need to find your mum. Your real mum. She loves you so much, Izzy. And I love her too - so much."

"Let me come with you," she pleaded. "I can help find her. I can use the Tumble Thunder and we can go to the right time and find her."

Robert looked at the three of them, and then back to Izzy.

"You can't Izzy. It doesn't work like that. You know it doesn't," his voice was low.

"But Dad, then we can be together. The Time Shadow will be back. He went through the portal but he won't forget who he is. I saw you tell Ava. He'll forget the clock shop and where he was, but he won't forget me. He'll be back. And I know he won't be alone. Let me come. I don't want to lose you again."

"He'll be back," said her dad. "And maybe others too. Someone sent him. With each time slip, your aura gets brighter. The Time Shadow and his followers can trace it. Use the lavender, Izzy and stay within thick walls."

"The lavender, like at Nan's?" said Izzy, remembering the cottage. "She's special too, isn't she? She's a Time Child and that's why she hides?"

"You're perceptive, Izzy," said Robert. "The Temporatii, led by the professor, rescued your nan from the past. She was born in the year 1,000, but she wasn't strong enough to bring the Tumble Thunder together. She almost died. You've seen her scar. The professor nursed her back to health and they fell in love, then she gave birth to me."

"The Time Shadow thinks she's dead," said Izzy, understanding.

"Yes. When I grew up, I was able to build my own Tumble Thunder so I could time slip. But no-one could harness the power of the real one. We knew we had to put our faith in you. Your grandfather refused to hide because he doesn't glow like you and Nan. He wanted to be front and centre and the guardian of the shop. The clock shop was his idea too - you make it strong. You, Izzy. It's why your nan visits regularly. Everyone draws strength from you. We thickened its walls so they couldn't see you. The professor - my dad, your grandad - thought it was funny to hide the Time Child in a clock shop. Find him. Go to your Nan's house. Check the cellar of the clock shop before you go. You'll know what to do."

Crying again, she kissed him on the cheek and hugged him close. Her fingers dug into his shoulders.

"I can't lose you again, Dad. This isn't fair," sobs wracked her body as she clung to him. "I want Mum."

"I'm so sorry, Izzy. But our destinies are different. Your adventure starts now. You're ready. The world is depending on you. You're not finished."

Izzy released her dad and stepped back to look at him.

"I love you," she said wiping at her eyes. "And I will see you again soon. I promise you that."

She pulled Porter and Greysock close as the Tumble Thunder began to glow. The warmth spread through her and she smiled at her dad. He smiled back, and the world was briefly overtaken by a golden hue.

When she opened her eyes, she was standing on the landing outside her bedroom in the flat above the clock shop. World War Two London was gone. So was her dad... and her mum, Jane. The grief hit her again and was overwhelming, but she understood. For the first time ever, despite the separation, she felt whole.

Greysock scuttled down the stairs. Porter looked at her and his stomach rumbled loudly.

"Let me guess, breakfast?" she said, and the pair of them laughed as she wiped the tears from her cheeks. They headed down the stairs and walked into the front of the clock shop.

There was still broken glass everywhere from where the Time Shadow had ransacked it, searching for the Tumble Thunder.

She picked up the Winston Churchill picture from the floor and looked at Porter.

"He did all right in the end, didn't he?" she said, smiling.

"Must be something to do with a watch we sold him," said a familiar voice. "Now, I think we need to go and see your nan."

Izzy turned. There in the doorway was the professor, his thumb hitched in his waistcoat pocket as he twisted the corner of his perfectly oiled moustache. Alongside him, stood George with a huge smile from ear-to-ear. Izzy looked at her homeless friend, her protector, and then back at the professor.

"Hello, Grandad," she said, for the first time ever.

THE END

Milton Keynes UK
Ingram Content Group UK Ltd.
UKHW011914030923
427983UK00002B/5

9 781739 172602